Tampa on My Mind is made possible through the kind support of a proud, caring community. Bay Press is especially grateful to the following individuals and organizations:

The Honorable Mayor Pam Iorio and the City of Tampa
Ms. Liana Lopez and the Public Art Program
Professor Gary Mormino
Busch Gardens
Adventure Island
MacDill Air Force Base
Hillsborough Community College
The Florida Aquarium
Tampa Theatre
The Florida Orchestra
Tampa Downtown Partnership
Seminole Hard Rock Hotel & Casino
The Ybor City Museum Society
Big Red Balloon Company
The American Victory Mariners Memorial & Museum Ship
Tre Amici @ The Bunker
Hyde Park Village
Florida Museum of Photographic Arts
Museum of Science and Industry
The Home Association
Cigar City Magazine
Swope, Rodante PA
The Tampa Bay Performing Arts Center
Mr. Marcos Ceruto
University of South Florida
The Hillsborough Public Library System

Contents

Foreword

In 1824, three years after Florida became a United States possession, a remote military outpost to be called Fort Brooke was cleared from a dense jungle. This outpost marked the beginning of a frontier village—a village named Tampa. This village endured Federal occupation and blockades during the Civil War, and through it all a young, spirited city began to take shape.

Tampa's expansion began when developer and railroad builder Henry B. Plant extended rail lines to the Hillsborough River in 1884, attracting visitors to stay in his extravagant hotel and expanding Tampa's business opportunities. With greater access to new areas for development and trade, Vicente Martinez Ybor opened the city's first cigar factory in 1886, establishing the hand-rolled cigar industry in our city, in an area that would become known as Ybor City. Progress in Tampa continued throughout the 1890s as the cigar industry, mining, and shipping created a bustling economy. Tampa began to transform into a city with a thriving harbor, and in 1898 it became a critical embarkation point for Theodore Roosevelt and his Rough Riders bound for the Spanish-American War.

By the early 1900s Tampa had endured and was beginning to boom. In 1914, when American pilot Tony Jannus conducted the world's first scheduled commercial airline flight from St. Petersburg to Tampa, the city made aviation history. As the Model T increased in popularity, Americans migrated south, where new

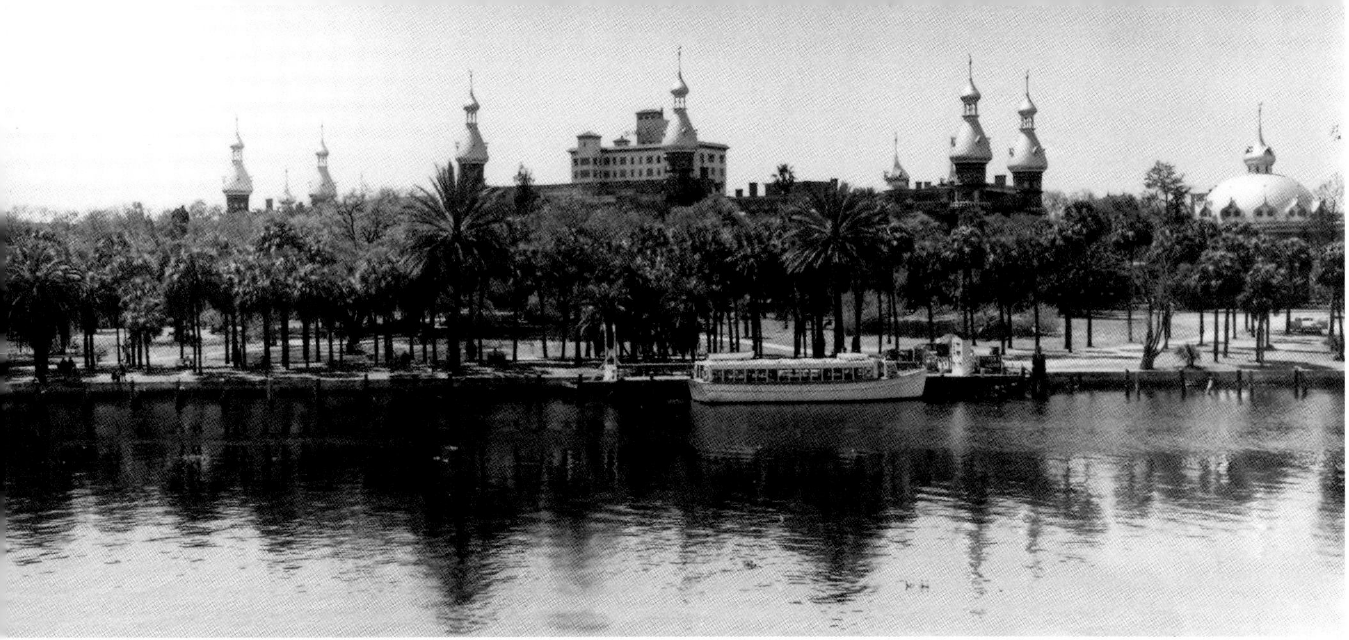

A view of the Tampa Bay Hotel from the Hillsborough River.
Courtesy of Hillsborough County Public Library.

residents settled into new developments like Davis Islands. Throughout the 1950s and '60s, historic Central Avenue hosted legendary performers such as Duke Ellington and Ella Fitzgerald, drawing crowds to the energetic entertainment and business district. Tampa was evolving.

If the history of a city speaks to its future, Tampa has long been destined for greatness. Henry B. Plant's luxurious hotel is now a historical landmark and home to the University of Tampa. Visitors once traveled by railcar to the Hillsborough River, but today Tampa is a destination with one of the highest-rated airports in the world. Tampa's port is now the seventh-largest in the nation, serving several premiere cruise lines and connecting the city with locations around the world. Where Americans once prepared to depart Tampa for war in Cuba, now Central Command orchestrates our nation's military campaign in the Middle East from MacDill Air Force Base, located at the southern tip of our city. Where innovative

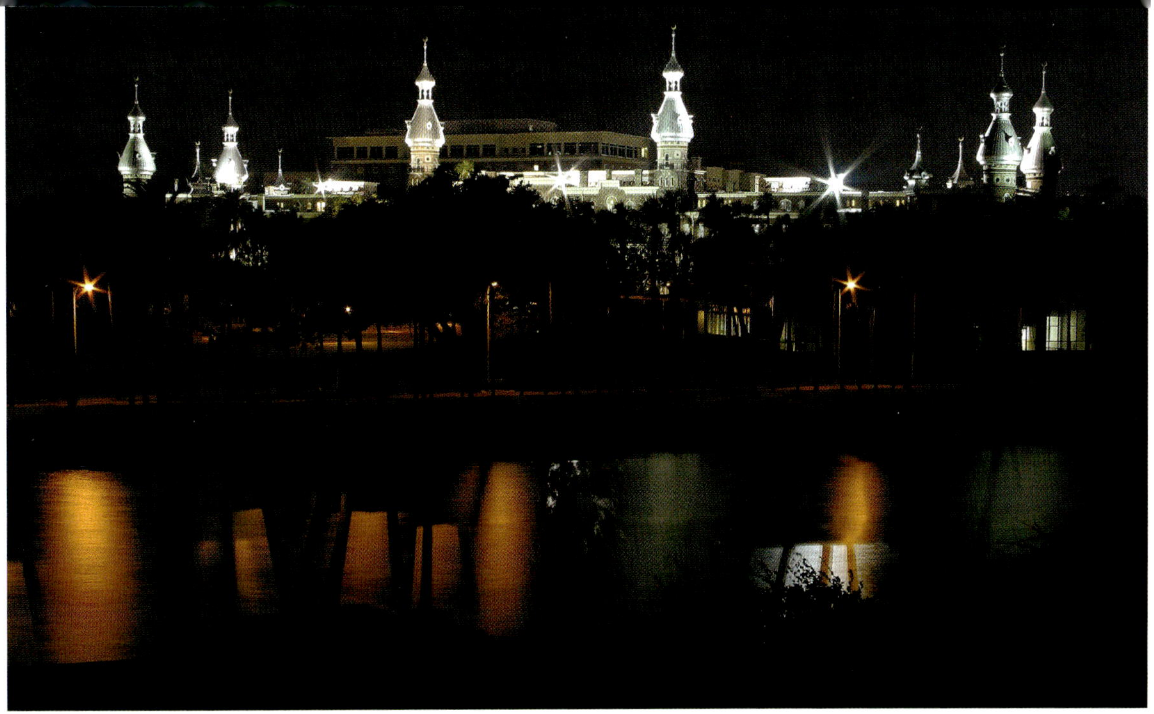

University of Tampa reflected in the Hillsborough River.
Photo by Ron Williams.

risk-takers once ventured alone to forge new industries, major corporations have invested in our ever-expanding skyline, and our convention center hosts visitors from around the world.

We have come a long way from Jannus's historic flight and waves of new residents arriving in their Model Ts. Yet one thing is certain, Tampa has always been a culturally diverse, progressive city, home to residents who take pride in their community. We have been recognized as one of the best places to live and work in the United States, and we enjoy a downtown with great economic and cultural potential. Our neighborhoods are quality communities rich in their own distinct character and identity. Our universities and colleges are institutions of excellence. Our cultural institutions enjoy widespread support, and our natural environment is simply beautiful.

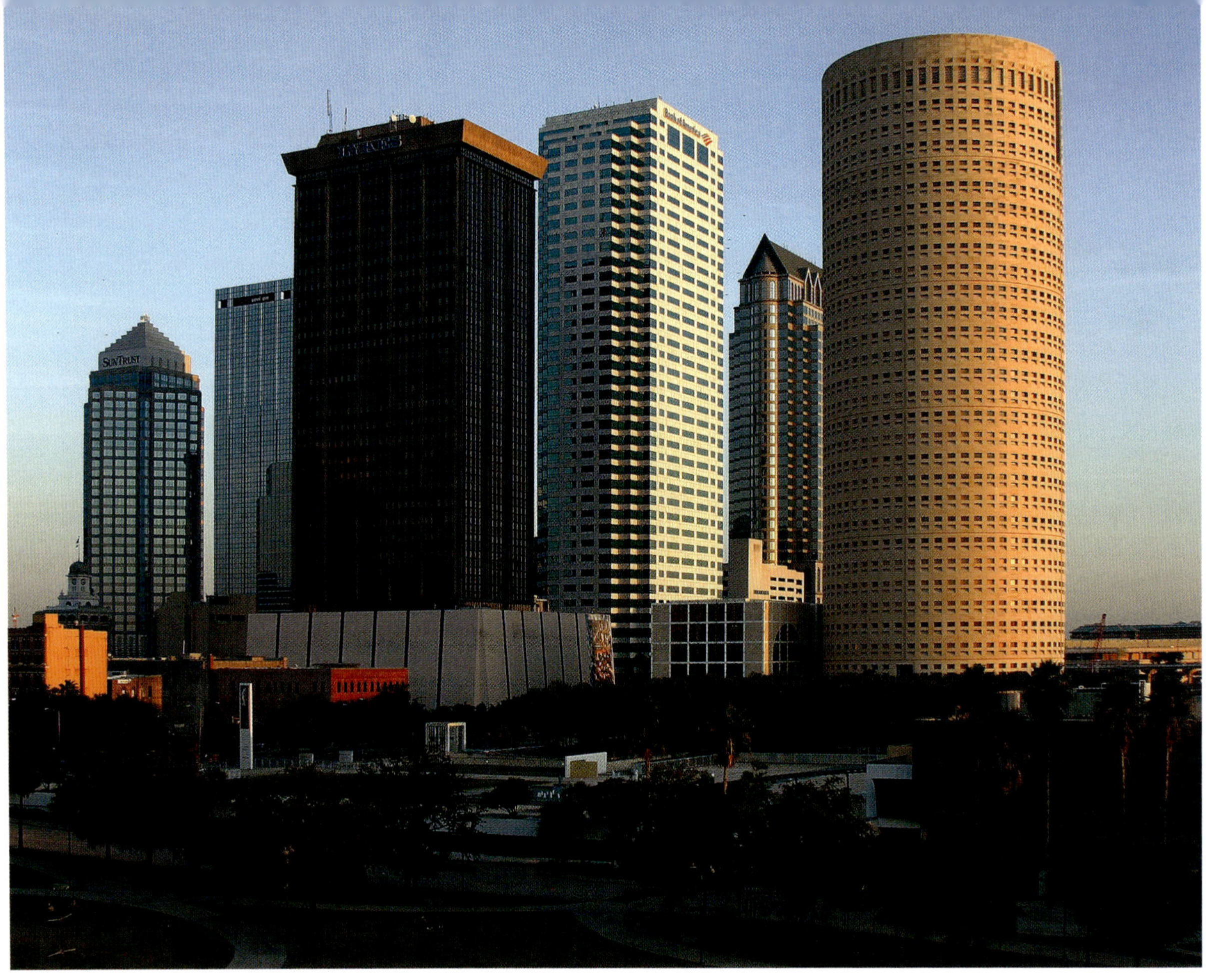

A dazzling view of the city at sunset. Park Tower (*left of center*) still bears the insignia of its former owner, LYKES. The 36-floor building was the first substantial skyscraper in downtown Tampa. Completed in 1973, it was the tallest skyscraper in Tampa until the completion of One Tampa City Center in 1981. The Sykes Building (*right*) is affectionately known as the "beer can building" and was featured in the movie *The Punisher*.

Photo by Ron Williams.

Tampa is a treasure for sports fans. We have hosted the Super Bowl on several occasions. We are home to the Super Bowl Champion Tampa Bay Buccaneers, Stanley Cup Champion Tampa Bay Lightning, and Arena Bowl Champion Tampa Bay Storm. Major League Baseball's storied New York Yankees call us home during spring training, and right across the bay baseball fans cheer on the Tampa Bay Rays. We are home to world-class golf courses, runners travel from afar to participate in our city marathons, and many professional tennis players train on our courts.

Tourists enjoy discovering our city and the many adventures we have to offer. Anheuser-Busch opened a brewery just east of downtown Tampa in 1959, and it was known for its lush landscapes and colorful bird exhibits. Today, Busch Gardens is one of the most popular tourist destinations in Florida and is home to some of the most exciting roller coasters in the world. Lowry Park Zoo is the "Number 1 Zoo in the United States for kids," according to *Child* magazine. This enjoyable attraction also educates little ones through exposure to animals from around the world. For those who enjoy challenging their imaginations and minds, the Museum of Science and Industry is the largest museum of its kind in the South.

Tampa is a city based in strong traditions. For over a century, residents and visitors have enjoyed the Ye Mystic Krewe of Gasparilla's annual invasion, where hundreds of colorfully costumed pirates "sail" into downtown Tampa on their pirate ship—the *José Gasparilla*—kicking off one of the largest celebrations in the South.

Hidden amidst tourist attractions and beautiful waterfronts are treasures that support Tampa's artistic side and provide a glimpse into Tampa's rich history and vibrant future. For more than twenty years, the City of Tampa has supported a Public Art Program, which has enhanced our parks, community centers, streets, and buildings. Public art projects celebrate Tampa's culture, diverse population, and history. Not only have they provided a vehicle for individuals and groups to express their identities, but the arts have also become part of our community.

A crowd gathers outside the Tampa Theatre.

Courtesy of Hillsborough County Public Library.

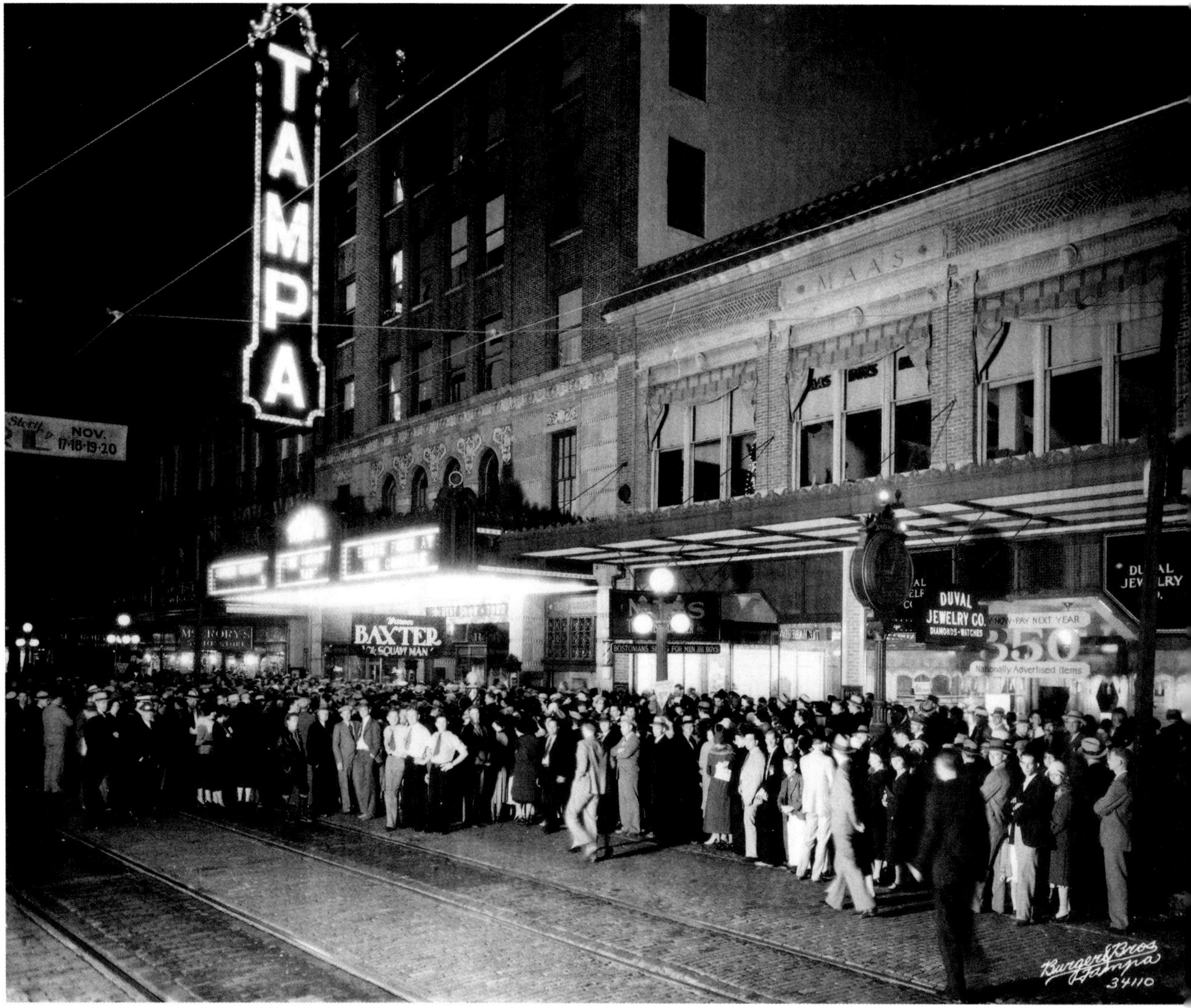

Tampa has become a place where creativity can flourish. The expansive Tampa Bay Performing Arts Center, the largest in the Southeast, hosts touring Broadway productions and nationally known performers, as well as local community theater presentations. The Patel Conservatory provides training for young performing artists as does H. B. Blake High School, located just across the Hillsborough River. Art programs have created partnerships with the private sector, nonprofit organizations, and community groups that connect our projects to the life of our city.

Tampa is well on its way to being recognized as a city that celebrates the works of artists, writers, performers, filmmakers, and all forms of fine and commercial

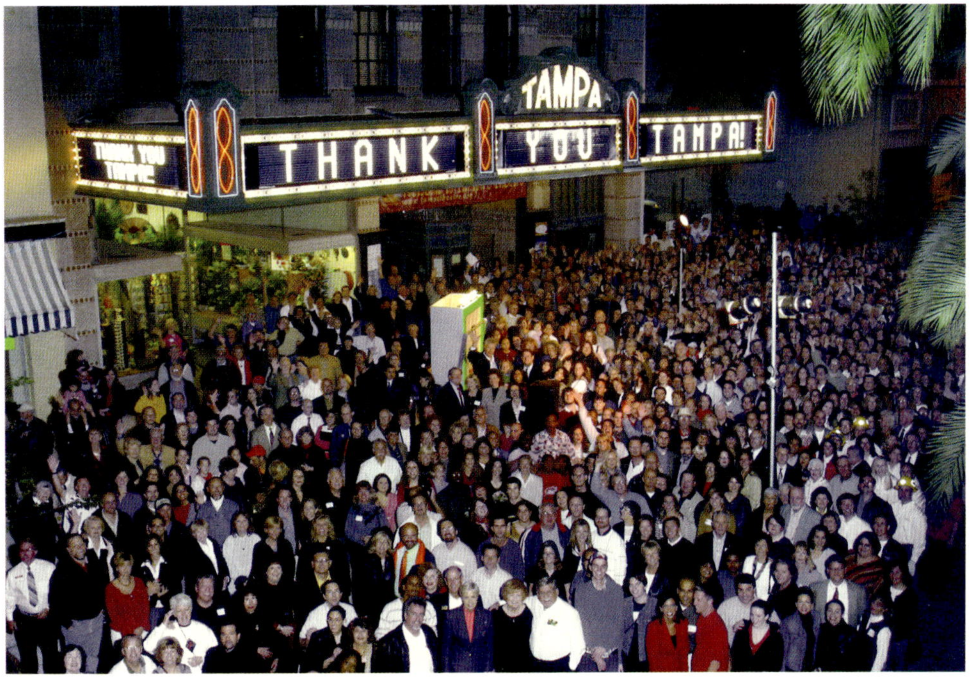

The new Tampa Theatre sign lights up before an enthusiastic crowd.
Courtesy of Tampa Theatre.

arts professionals, providing opportunities for residents and visitors of all ages to enjoy and be enriched by a variety of creative pursuits while encouraging the growth of creative businesses.

Tampa is a great tourist destination, but more than that, it has long walks on Bayshore Boulevard, quiet neighborhoods, and hand-rolled cigars. Historic districts like Hyde Park and Ybor City add remarkable charm and character, and a vibrant waterfront is also perfect for family outings, movies, and first-class dining.

With a lively urban center on the horizon, our downtown is transitioning to a residential community that will serve as everybody's neighborhood—a dynamic area that will draw people for a number of activities. Here along downtown's waterfront, the Tampa Riverwalk will extend along the east side of the river, incorporating pedestrian accommodations, art, retail shops, restaurants, parks and open space, and other urban amenities. The 2.4-mile Riverwalk will open the waterfront to residents and visitors by providing a wonderful environment for enjoying events along the water's edge. It will link various destinations along the river and will be a catalyst for economic development and tourism, creating an enjoyable place using one of the city's most valuable resources—the waterfront.

Our progress signals a transformative time for Tampa—a time when we recognize the importance of providing a high quality of life for our residents and a high-quality destination for our visitors. Rich in history, beauty, and culture, our city offers something for everyone. Tampa is indeed a city of possibilities—a city focused on a positive future.

The Honorable Pam Iorio, Mayor, City of Tampa

Introduction

Gary R. Mormino

From Paleoindian settlements along Tampa Bay to its emergence as one of America's leading metropolitan areas, Tampa has one of the longest and most interesting histories of any community in the United States. For three decades historians have studied and tried to comprehend events and personalities. The following narrative is not intended as definitive but merely as this writer's perspective.

Ice Age Migrations

Modern-day Cassandras concerned about the threat of global warming may take comfort in or feel angst with the knowledge that such radical shifts in climate have occurred before. The first human inhabitants on the peninsula now known as Florida arrived 12,000 years ago, during the Pleistocene Era. The Great Ice Age locked up so much water that sea levels sank as much as 350 feet along the Gulf Coast. As giant land mammals migrated across a land bridge connecting the continents of Asia and North America, humans followed.

Hunter-gathering tribes, called Paleoindians, eventually migrated southeastward to the warmer climates of Florida. They had been preceded by giant mammoths, mastodons, and saber-tooth tigers, whose bones have been excavated in Polk County's famed Bone Valley, Ruskin, and the Hillsborough River. Spear and arrow points fashioned from rock pits near present-day Thonotosassa made lethal killing implements. The efficient hunting skills of the Paleoindians may have led to the extinction of the lumbering beasts. Ironically, the horse was hunted to extinction only to return a millennium later with the arrival of Europeans.

Many of the Paleoindian camp sites were subsumed by water, owing to the warming period that began around 9000 B.C. As the ice caps and glaciers melted, sea levels began to rise, a process that lasted for thousands of years. Florida's climate changed dramatically. From a cool and dry climate, Florida perceptibly warmed and was accompanied by a much wetter environment. Indians adapted by establishing camps by springs, creeks, and wetlands. The coastal areas offered ample protein sources. Tampa Bay emerged from this radical climate shift, assuming its distinctive shape.

Archaic Period Cultures

Humans adapted to many changes in the land and environment. Settlements along the Gulf Coast and Tampa Bay expanded as the climate warmed and groups began to settle in semipermanent camps.

Shifts in food gathering and social contacts followed. Around 2000 B.C., new examples of pottery appeared. Fired-clay pottery, tempered with Spanish moss or palmetto fibers, allowed foodstuffs to be carried, cooked, traded, and stored. One distinctive stamped and fired type of pottery developed, called the Weeden Island period style, so named after excavations at the Pinellas site.

The adoption and adaptation of agriculture also brought profound changes. Fields of maize (corn), squash, and beans reflected a more hierarchical social and economic structure. The waters of the Gulf, bays, and rivers were so rich with seafood, shellfish, and fish that agriculture was not as vital here as elsewhere. The

Calusa Indians of the Charlotte Harbor area established sophisticated hierarchies without an agricultural base.

Burial mounds appeared around 250 A.D. Today, scores of burial and ceremonial mounds still dot the Tampa Bay area. The most famous temple mound, located near the confluence of the Hillsborough River and Hillsborough Bay, stood until the 1880s, when it was excavated for road fill. Other mounds exist at Safety Harbor, Terra Ceia, and Crystal River.

Spanish-Indian Encounters

Tampa Bay richly deserves its title "Gateway to North America." A succession of Spanish expeditions highlighted its importance to several generations of Spanish navigators and engineers.

Historians are now in consensus that Juan Ponce de León did *not* land at Tampa Bay; rather, it seems as if his second voyage of exploration sailed as far north as Charlotte Harbor. Many believe that Alonzo Alvarez de Piñeda first mapped Tampa Bay in 1519. He was succeeded by Panfilo de Narváez, who may have sailed to Tampa Bay in 1527 and anchored off the coast of modern Pinellas County.

Touching land on 16 April 1528, Narváez and his expeditionary force of 400 soldiers set out to find native gold and silver. A veteran of the successful Cortez expedition in Mexico, Narváez was intent upon conquest and fortune. He often subjected the natives to unusually cruel and inhumane treatment.

Two remarkable members of that expedition were Cabeza de Vaca and Esteban. Both men managed to survive the infamous trek northward, the disastrous effort to sail back to Mexico, and captivity by Gulf Coast Indians. The former wrote a famous account of the saga; the latter, an African slave, became the first black man to set foot on Florida soil. He later died at the hands of Southwest Indians while in the service of Coronado.

The Narváez episode did produce one Tampa battle saga that has survived for almost 500 years. A Spaniard, Juan Ortiz, was captured by natives, and, according to Ortiz, Chief Uzita sentenced the young captive to be burned to death. At a dramatic moment in the torture, the chief's daughter Ulela intervened to save his life. Ortiz survived and remained with the tribe until rescued by Hernando de Soto eleven years later. The tale was widely circulated in the Old World, and some historians believe that Captain John Smith's deliverance by Pocahontas was pure fiction, a literary device stolen by the Englishman from the Spaniard.

Another captivating narrative figured in the very naming of Tampa in 1545, when a ten-year-old Spaniard, d'Escalante Fontaneda, was shipwrecked off the Ten Thousand Islands in Southwest Florida. The Calusa raised the young man, who traveled freely throughout South Florida. In 1566, the founder of Spanish St. Augustine, Pedro Menéndez de Avilés, liberated Fontaneda. The former captive returned to Spain where he wrote one of the first descriptions of life in the New World. He regaled Europeans with tales of a giant lake "Mayaimi." In describing the villages surrounding Charlotte Harbor, he began, "First, a place called Tanpa, a large town." The mysterious village of "Tanpa" became "Tampa." Historians believe Tanpa was a settlement at the mouth of Charlotte Harbor, where, according to archaeologist Jerald Milanich, "the Calusa maintained a large mullet fishery." A fitting tribute to the noble mullet! How ironic that the City of Tampa misappropriated from Charlotte Harbor not only the name of Tampa but later the legend of José Gaspar!

Hernando de Soto, a celebrated hero of Pizarro's conquest of Peru, departed Spain with the greatest armada to sail to the Americas. His eight ships carrying 725 persons, including two women and hundreds of horses and pigs, arrived at La Bahía de Espiritu Santo (the Bay of the Holy Spirit—Tampa Bay) on 25 May 1539. The site was probably near the mouth of the Little Manatee River. The discovery of the captive Juan Ortiz was providential, in that he served as a translator. The de Soto party spent six weeks in the Tampa Bay area before departing on its epic journey.

The Columbian Exchange

The most momentous event in the history of Tampa Bay and Florida occurred in the early sixteenth century when a Spanish conquistador waded ashore. There, at an unmarked point, the worlds of Europe and the Americas came together. The consequences were enormous, global in scope.

Scholars call the encounter between Europeans and Native Americans "the Columbian Exchange." Most dramatically, the intermingling of pathogens and germs resulted in a succession of disastrous plagues and epidemics that scoured the defenseless natives. Lacking immunity to Old World diseases, Indians perished when inflicted with influenza, whooping cough, measles, smallpox, and diphtheria.

The consequences can be witnessed in the maps and log of a 1757 map of Tampa Bay. Don Francisco Maria Celi piloted the *San Francisco de Asis* into a familiar body of water they renamed La Bahía de San Fernando, today's Tampa Bay. The expedition spent a month charting the waters and hinterland, leaving a meticulous map of the area. A party rowed upstream and christened the body of water El Rio de San Julian y Arriaga (the Hillsborough River). The surviving map (in a Spanish archive) documents the eight turns of the river. In the vicinity of today's Hillsborough River State Park, the party halted and turned back. Their mapmakers' inscriptions endure. They called the piney peninsula along the Gulf Coast "Punta de Pinal," while signifying today's Hooker's Point "Punta Carrascon" (Oak Point). Juan Franco, a talented draftsman, wrote in the ship's log, "The natives give this bay the name Tampa," adding, "We could not find a more delightful and comfortable place."

Curiously, the surviving map and accounts make no mention of Indian settlements or Native Americans. The Native Americans who hunted, fished, and lived in the Tampa Bay area had perished or been taken captive.

The legacy of exploration, conquest, and settlement must not be interpreted solely as bleak and calamitous. The introduction of Old World plants and animals enriched the environment and economy of Tampa. Many familiar Tampa Bay vegetables and fruits—strawberries, sugarcane, citrus, peanuts, okra, sweet peppers, melons, and grapes—came from Europe, Asia, and Africa, adding spice and flavor to the local diet. In return, Indian corn, potatoes, tomatoes, pumpkins, and tobacco enriched the world's cuisine.

Perhaps even more dramatic was the introduction of animals. Horses, cattle, and pigs spread across the landscape, quickly becoming familiar icons. New traditions (rodeo, cowboys, and roast pig marinated in *mojo*) led to new relationships. Fittingly, the origins and the very name barbecue can be traced to Caribbean Indians who roasted meat on spits of wood they called "barbacoa."

British Rule

Spain, ruler of La Florida since the sixteenth century, ceded the colony to Britain in 1763, the result of Spanish misfortune during the Seven Years War. Essentially, Spain swapped Florida for the captured city of Havana with Britain. Thus, Florida was a colony of England during the British period, 1763–1783. The colony was immediately divided into two provinces, East Florida and West Florida, with provincial capitals at St. Augustine and Pensacola. Reality, however, ruled. No one lived in the Tampa Bay region to be governed. The original Native Indians were extinct; no American pioneers had penetrated the area; and pirates ignored the area because even brigands needed victims.

The imperial majesty of Great Britain meant little to the occasional Cuban or *mestizo* (the so-called Spanish Indians) who operated seasonal fishing *ranchos* along Tampa Bay in the late eighteenth century. Spanishtown Creek, a largely forgotten site in Hyde Park, was one such operation in which fish were smoked and salted and sold in Cuban markets.

The most significant name enduring from the British era is conferred upon a man who never visited Florida. Colonial officials chose to honor Wills Hill, the First Earl of Hillsborough and the British Secretary of State for the Colonies. A future county and a river carry his name today.

Fort Brooke and the Origins of Modern Tampa

When Spain reacquired Florida in 1783, the once-great European empire had been reduced to a second-rate power. It was only a question of when, not if, the United States would expand its boundaries southward. Seeds of nationalism, sown during the War of 1812, germinated during the conflict as war hawks exhorted the young republic to rid the continent of European empires. Brilliant military maneuvers by General Andrew Jackson and deft diplomacy by Secretary of State John Quincy Adams resulted in a treaty that ceded the Territory of Florida to the United States in 1821.

A problem confronted the U.S. government: What to do with the quarrelsome Seminole Indians residing in Florida? Officials decided to erect a military fort to check Seminole advances. On 11 June 1823, Indian Commissioner James Gadsden wrote Secretary of War John Calhoun, "I am inclined to think that the Bay of Tampa presents the most eligible site for a military fort."

Secretary Calhoun promptly ordered Colonel George Brooke to Tampa Bay to select a site and build a fort. Brooke and four companies of infantry sailed into Tampa Bay in January 1824. He chose a place on the east side of the Hillsborough River where the river flowed into Hillsborough Bay. The fact that an American family named Hackley had already cleared the land and erected a home influenced the decision.

Was this the most strategic site? Many historians have argued that Safety Harbor would have been a better choice than Fort Brooke. Modern Safety Harbor was earlier known as Tocobaga, the largest Indian settlement on Tampa Bay. The Native Americans had chosen their village site wisely, as it was the safest place on the Gulf Coast for withstanding hurricanes. The future residents of Tampa would learn this lesson when an 1848 hurricane—the worst in modern memory—washed away most of the buildings and structures.

From the beginning, Fort Brooke was more than a military fort. It stood on the edge of a vast frontier, serving as a social center for the pioneer settlements that formed on the fringes. The fort softened the edge of harsh frontier life. Soldiers erected a Japanese pagoda atop the imposing Indian mound. By 1829, Fort Brooke consisted of a guardhouse, barracks, storehouses, wharves, and stables. Everyone commented favorably upon the natural setting: ancient canopies of live oaks towering over the wooden buildings. The sense of mission and the pervasive sense of isolation engendered camaraderie among the soldiers and civilians.

Fort Brooke was also a refuge and beehive during war. Two bloody Seminole Wars (1835–1842 and 1855–1856) made Fort Brooke and the emerging community of Tampa Town an essential anchor in the southern frontier Indian wars. Overall, thousands of soldiers spent time in Tampa, some more impressed than others. "It is a paradise for those who love the open air," observed Lieutenant George A. McCall. The Second Seminole War (1835–1842) ended tragically for Florida's native peoples: more than 3,000 were killed or removed and forced westward.

The emerging community of Tampa that grew around the fort brought together an astonishing cast of characters: European immigrants who fled poverty and oppression in the Old World; West Indians attracted by the opportunities in a dynamic town; military veterans who returned to homestead land; and African slaves whose misfortune brought them to the Deep South. Early residents included descendants of Minorcans who left St. Augustine, Scottish sea captains, and the second sons of Old South families. The Florida legislature created Hillsborough County in 1834, and Tampa became its first and only county seat.

In 1858, Captain James McKay gambled that free-range cattle, rounded up in the Florida interior and driven onto barges at Ballast Point, would find an appreciative market in Cuba. His gamble succeeded wildly, and he in turn was followed by others seeking fortunes in the cattle business: Howell Lykes and William B. Hooker.

Population growth followed. In 1855, census takers counted 3,013 residents in Hillsborough County, which included 746 slaves and 6 free blacks. The City of Tampa numbered about 800 inhabitants, but census figures are misleading as to the importance of Tampa's role as a fluid, dynamic center of trade and commerce.

Civil War and Reconstruction

Twice weekly, residents of Tampa received the mail via the Gainesville stagecoach. The stagecoach carrying news of 13 January 1861 brought electrifying developments: Florida had seceded from the Union and had joined the Confederate States of America. The city was ablaze with the news, although rebel yells disguised the tensions and divisions within the population. The masthead of the city's newspaper, the *Florida Peninsula*, brandished the words "The South Should Rule the North."

An idle Fort Brooke suddenly bristled with energy and activity, although, as events showed, the fort was as obsolete as it was insignificant. Federal gunboats quickly sealed off Tampa Bay. An occasional blockade runner escaped, but the dawn of war brought hardships to the citizens of Tampa. Privation, sacrifice, and hope characterized the mood on the home front.

In October 1862, Federal troops conducted a daring raid, burning vessels owned by Captain James McKay and loaded with cotton. The Scottish-born McKay may or may not have been a double agent. Yankee raiders harassed coastal salt works. In a celebrated incident, Tampa resident Joseph Robles erected a salt works on Rocky Point, only to be raided by Federal troops. The five-foot Spaniard hid inside an iron kettle, sprang to his feet holding a shotgun, and ordered the raiders to surrender. Robles lived until the 1950s, celebrating his 107th birthday and enjoying the status of the oldest and last surviving Tampa Confederate veteran.

When the city and fort finally surrendered, on 6 May 1864, three Union gunboats landed at Palmetto Beach, unloading several hundred sailors and marines. The invasion force included a handful of African American soldiers, an ironic twist in the winds of war. Fort Brooke fell; its fortifications were destroyed, and its brass cannons dumped into the river. Troops liberated slaves and valuables. A Union officer's report read simply, "Tampa is desolate in the extreme."

The conquest of Tampa was brief. Invading troops left the next morning.

Within a year, the South had surrendered, and the once noble cause became the lost cause. Veterans returned to a world in chaos.

The Reconstruction era, 1865–1876, was a turbulent period for Tampa and Tampans. Most dramatically, hundreds of African American chattel slaves were now free. Freedom stirred, and it took many forms: new schools for children and freedmen, black churches, and African American leaders. Liberated slaves exercised their freedom to move, and a black neighborhood appeared on maps—"the Scrub," located northeast of Oaklawn Cemetery.

The *Florida Peninsula*, commenting after one of many "incidents" involving fracases between citizens and the occupying force, remarked that the "riot" at least relieved the monotony likened to "the Egyptian darkness." In 1875 a government agent predicted that Tampa would almost certainly "go backwards for years to come." Physical conditions deteriorated: the courthouse was on the verge of collapse; Oaklawn Cemetery lay overgrown with weeds and neglect; hogs rooted for garbage in the sandy streets. From a population of 885 in 1860, Tampa had declined to 720 residents by 1880.

Pressed by hard times, the citizens of Tampa elected John Lesley mayor in 1869. He ran for office on a platform pledged to dissolve the city if elected! The City of Tampa was so dissolved. The local newspaper decried in 1871, "We now have no Sheriff and are at the mercy of the lawless, the rowdy, and the drunkers. Firearms are freely used on the street and the lives of peaceable citizens are in danger daily."

Adding injury to insult, epidemics swept the city, inflicting death and pessimism. Yellow fever, spread by mosquitoes, scoured the city in 1867, 1871, and 1876, killing many residents. As no one knew the cause of the disease, citizens were defenseless. Sidney Lanier, the celebrated southern poet, visited Tampa during these lean years and described it as "the most forlorn collection of one-story houses imaginable." Lanier, dying of tuberculosis at the time, wrote "Tampa Robins," arguably the most famous poem about the city.

War and defeat lingered for decades. Throughout the nineteenth and into the twentieth centuries, residents fumed about Black Republicans and Radical Reconstruction.

The Coming of the Railroad and Henry B. Plant

For much of the nineteenth century, residents heard each evening a "sunset gun" fired at Fort Brooke. By the 1880s, locomotive and factory whistles imposed a new order. The story is told that when Samuel Morse flicked the switch that sped the first telegraph message across America, boosters gushed that now Maine could talk to Florida. When Ralph Waldo Emerson heard the news, he remarked, "Yes. But has Maine anything to *say* to Florida?"

Florida, indeed, had a lot to say to Maine and other distant states. Farmers and businesses needed reliable transportation to ship frostproof oranges, Ruskin strawberries, Bone Valley phosphate, Tarpon Springs sponges, Safety Harbor grapefruit, Keystone cypress, Odessa pine, Wauchula cucumbers, and Ybor City cigars.

The Gilded Age produced many pivotal figures, but few changed a city's destiny more than Henry Bradley Plant. The robber baron infused the city with a sense of energy and direction, altering its skyline and reorienting its economy. On 24 January 1884, Plant's South Florida Railroad arrived in Tampa. "Tampa never saw so many strange faces," observed the *Sunland Tribune*. The *Ocala Banner* put into perspective what the railroad meant for Tampa and its rural area: "Only a little while ago it took two days to go from Ocala to Tampa and four days to reach Jacksonville. Now we can speed over the route in a few hours in comfort. Because of the railroad, the whole country is being magically transformed."

Tampa's population surged from 720 in 1880 to 2,376 in 1885. In spite of a devastating yellow fever epidemic that raced through the city in 1887, a new confidence encouraged investment. Plant led the way, building wharves, warehouses, and rail lines at Port Tampa, essentially a company town. The elegant Port Tampa Inn dominated the cluttered waterfront.

Pioneer photograph of Tampa in its early years.
Courtesy of Hillsborough County Public Library.

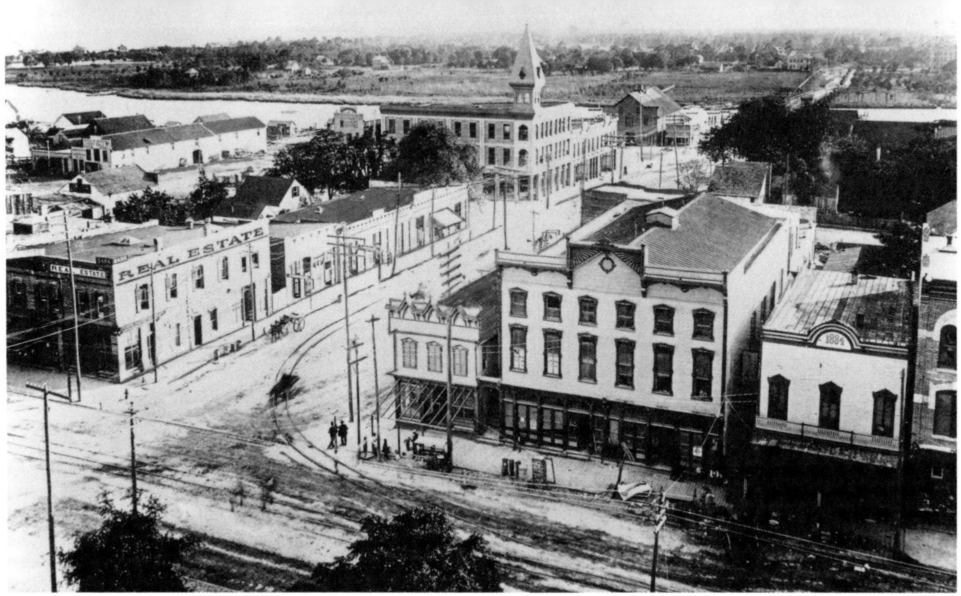

But nothing stamped Plant's signature upon Tampa as did his decision to erect the monumental Tampa Bay Hotel. On 26 July 1888, Mayor Herman Glowgowski declared a holiday to mark the laying of the cornerstone of the Tampa Bay Hotel. Residents marveled as the hotel began to take shape: 13 brick and tin minarets, 511 rooms, a wooden veranda that seemed to wind endlessly around the edifice. Plant and his wife imported eighty boxcars of furnishings from the Old World. Even the grounds of the hotel seemed worldly. The hotel opened 5 February 1891.

A new neighborhood grew up around the hotel. The west bank of the Hillsborough River had been sparsely populated, but Hyde Park promised the middle classes the comforts of the suburbs. A new streetcar system whisked bankers and accountants to downtown offices. In the late nineteenth century, Queen Anne and gingerbread Victorian structures predominated, soon to give way to the popular bungalow. To the north of downtown, another middle-class neighborhood, Tampa Heights, prospered.

Ybor City and the Coming of Cigars

The decision by Vicente Martinez Ybor to relocate his cigar factory to Tampa in 1885 dramatically changed the city; indeed, one could argue that no other event so altered the city's character and composition.

Ybor City attracted thousands of Cubans (white and black), Spaniards (Asturians and Galicians), and Italians (principally Sicilian). Ybor City almost immediately recast Tampa as an island in the Deep South. It was a Latin enclave in a region dominated by WASPs and African Americans. Its rhythms were industrial in a region characterized by agriculture and small town life; its immigrant mutual aid buildings radiated a sense of elegance and grandeur.

Ybor City, once the "Queen City of the Gulf," recast Tampa as "Cigar City," and for good reason. By 1900, Tampa and the new industrial satellite of West Tampa were producing an astounding 100 million cigars a year. An editor noted that cigars were to Tampa what iron was to Pittsburgh. Tampa was fast becoming the most important industrial city in Florida.

Ybor City was an extraordinary ethnic immigrant community of ideas and books. Cigar workers hired one of their own to read to them works of classic literature—and radical tracts. *Lectores* (readers) became lightning rods in a decades-long struggle for control of the workplace. Generations of Tampa officials clashed with radical cigar makers in a series of protracted strikes. D. B. McKay, a five-time mayor of Tampa, boasted to voters how he personally helped kidnap several Latin labor leaders during the strike of 1901.

Ybor City served as a cockpit of international intrigue and activities during the Cuban Wars of Independence in the late nineteenth century. José Martí rallied large crowds to the dream of *Cuba Libre*.

The sinking of the USS *Maine* in 1898 redefined the Cuban War of Independence. By the late spring of 1898, the vanguard of 25,000 American troops arrived in Tampa, a city of 15,000 nervous residents. In spite of all the national press

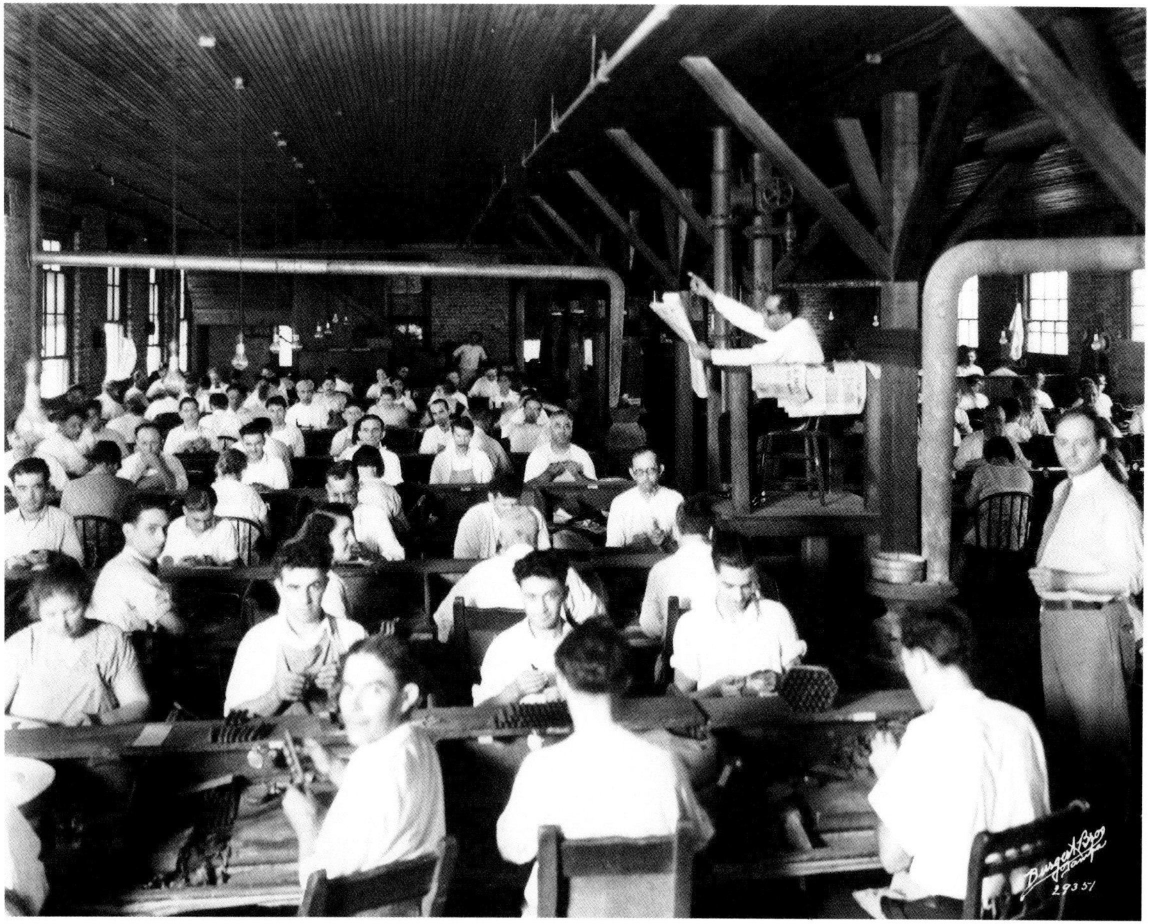

Cigar makers and *el lector* at the Corral Wodiska y Ca., Incorporated. *El lector* (the reader) entertained cigar workers in Ybor City factories before the days of radio. Many of them read from daily newspapers so Cuban immigrants could keep up with current affairs. Literature, particularly romance and adventure novels, were also great crowd pleasers. Courtesy of University of South Florida.

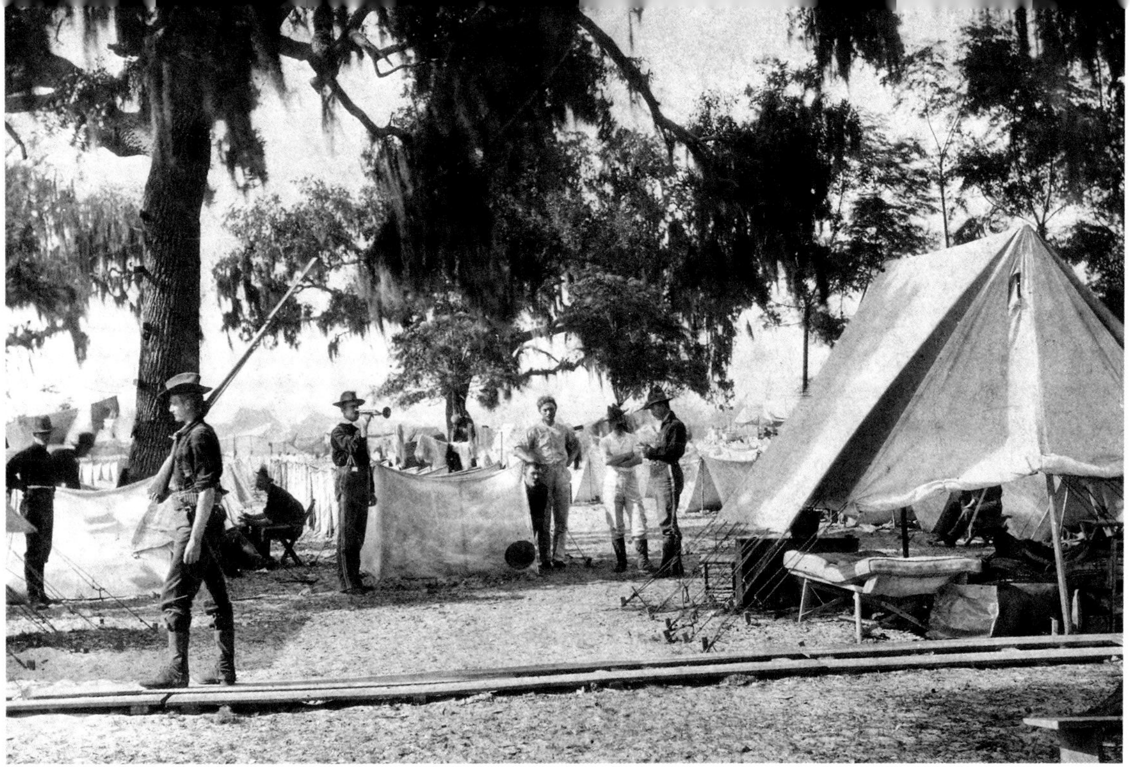

Photograph from 1898 of soldiers in Tampa preparing for the Spanish-American War.
Courtesy of Hillsborough County Public Library.

coverage, Tampa's port and rail facilities proved inadequate, and the Spanish-American War had little impact upon the future of Tampa.

A Modern City Emerges

The tumultuous events of 1898 reinforced a point many observers understood: more and more, Tampa's future depended upon decisions made not in Tampa but on Wall Street, in Havana, and in Washington, D.C.

The first decades of the twentieth century transformed the city. Paved brick streets, a modern trolley system, electrification, new suburbs, department stores, and the first skyscrapers marked a new coming of age.

The 1920s sparked a major transition in the history of the state. Florida became a state instilled with the values of leisure, romance, and dreams. The Florida Dream, the notion that sunshine and saltwater could rejuvenate tired bodies and restore youth, touched Tampa.

Out of Tampa Bay muck and mud, David P. Davis created his Florida Dream with the opening of Davis Islands in 1925. It was an overnight sensation. Architecturally, Davis Islands introduced the Mediterranean Revival style, with stucco, columns, terra cotta, mezzanines, and piazzas. Businesses, most notably the Tampa Theatre, also adopted the popular building style. Other neighborhoods also came of age or expanded, such as Sulphur Springs, Temple Terrace, and Tampa Beautiful.

The automobile redesigned Tampa in the 1920s. Tin-can tourists descended upon a city grateful for travelers. A tin-can tourist camp opened at De Soto Park in Palmetto Beach. The *Tampa Morning Tribune* and *Tampa Daily Times* devoted page upon page to the lure of the automobile.

Central Avenue, the major commercial and social center for Tampa's African American communities, thrived during the 1920s. Black-owned businesses and black voluntary associations catered to a large African American population. A black elite was emerging. The census identified 67 black clergymen, 18 teachers, 2 lawyers, and 4 dentists among the population.

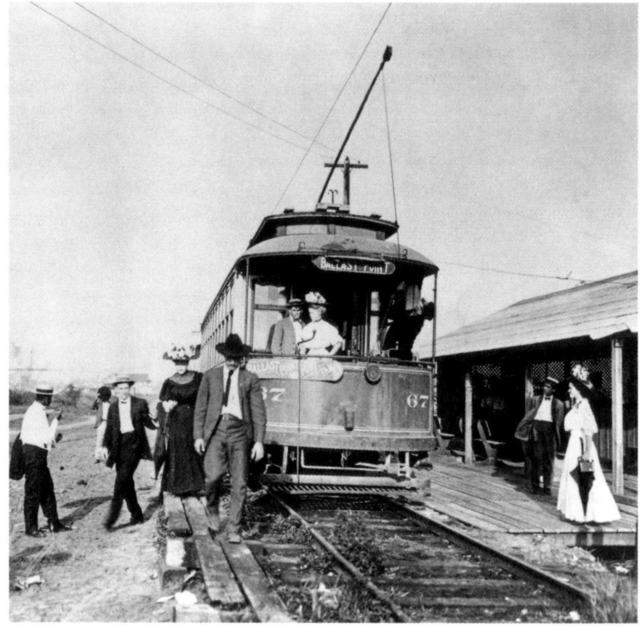

This 1911 photo shows passengers exiting and boarding a streetcar.
Courtesy of Hillsborough County Public Library.

The Lean Years: The 1930s

The boom decade of the 1920s ended on a gloomy note. First, Florida's land boom crashed in 1926, followed by a national depression in late 1929. The Great Depression hit Tampa especially hard, with the collapse of the once-vaunted cigar industry. In bad times, consumers make choices, and the popularity of cigarettes devastated the market for Tampa's fine hand-rolled cigars. The industry never recovered. The last great cigar strike occurred in 1931. City officials, looking for a scapegoat, demanded that the beloved readers be removed. Cigar workers lost their cherished voice, never to return. Radio largely replaced the readers, just as machines were beginning to replace the hand-rollers.

Tampa reeled when many home-owned banks collapsed during the first economic crisis. The citizens of Tampa searched for answers while one industry thrived: *bolita*. Imported from Cuba, bolita (an illegal game of chance) was a popular form of entertainment. Initially, Cuban immigrants bet pennies, hoping the weekly bolita-throw would enrich them. Quickly, bolita expanded its boundaries beyond Ybor City. As the game became an industry, it became inextricably intertwined with Tampa politics. The business needed police and legal protection, favors granted for a cut in the action. Bolita became so powerful that it corrupted the body politic.

James Clendinen arrived in Tampa in 1935, a young journalist shocked by what he found. "Tampa was one of the rottenest cities in the United States," he remembered. "The underworld pretty much controlled politics."

The year 1935 brought bolita and politics together in a celebrated display of corruption. In September 1935, Tampans went to the polls to elect a mayor. The election pitted two powerhouses against each other, Robert E. Lee Chancey and D. B. McKay. The governor, anticipating the worst, mobilized 300 National Guardsmen to preserve the peace. The chief of police recruited a thousand "enforcers," while the county sheriff deputized 600 men to guard the polls. A machine gun sat atop the Daily Times building. If the threat of violence was not enough, nature complied with a hurricane for punctuation. When the precincts closed, 3,000 more votes than voters stuffed the ballot boxes.

Out of desperation, the city looked to the federal government for help. President Franklin Roosevelt's New Deal may have prevented a social and economic catastrophe. He instilled a sense of confidence while Congress distributed funds

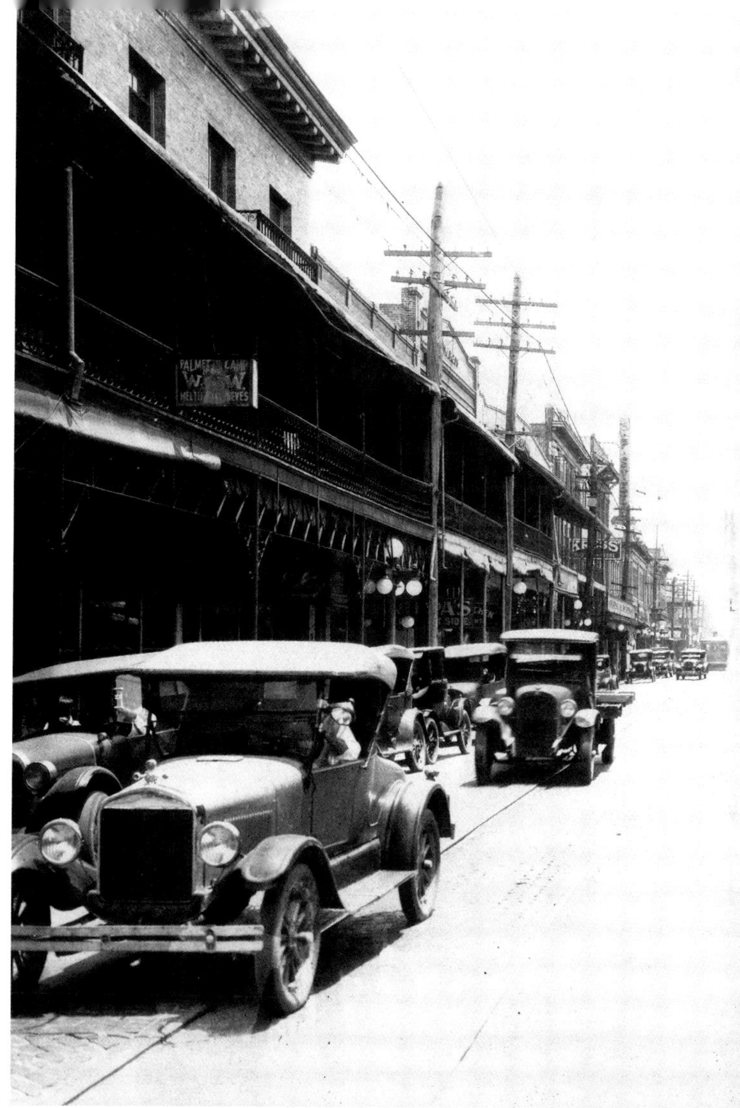

A view of 7th Avenue in Ybor City, 1927.
Courtesy of University of South Florida.

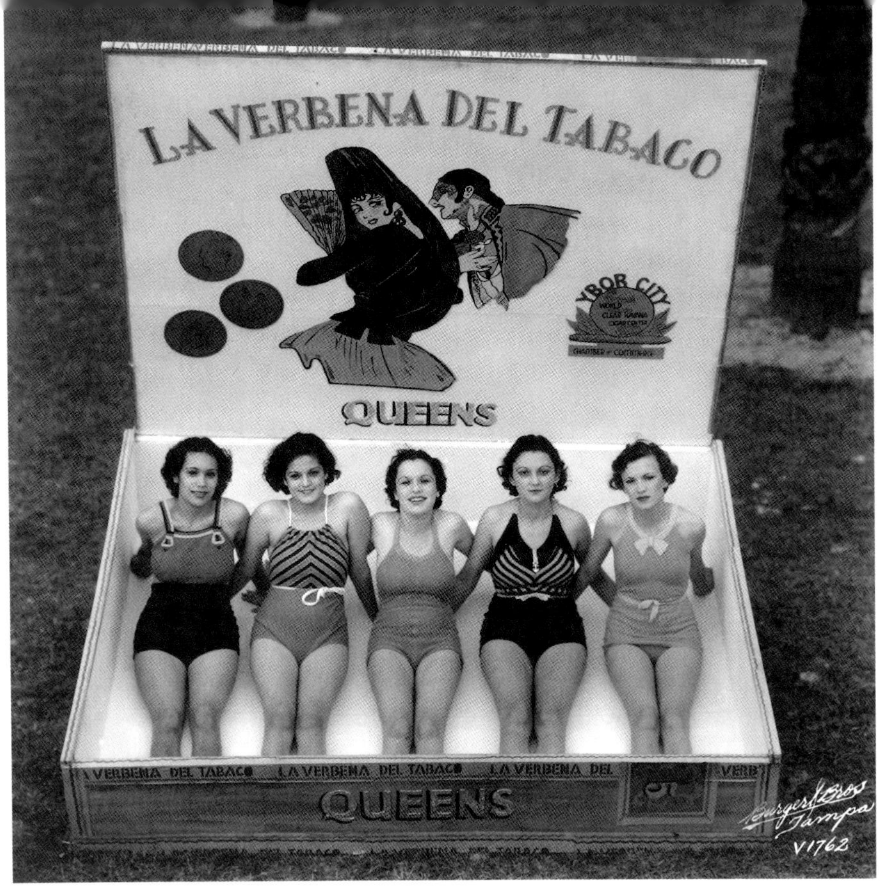

Women in swimsuits in a large cigar box for the La Verbena del Tabaco Festival; photograph taken in 1935. Courtesy of University of South Florida.

for the unemployed and needy. The New Deal did not simply distribute welfare checks; rather, Washington helped build and rebuild the city's infrastructure. The New Deal's legacies include a reconstructed Bayshore Boulevard (with new seawalls and balustrades), the refurbishing of the Tampa Bay Hotel (which in the mid-1930s became the new home for the University of Tampa), murals for the Peter O. Knight Airport on Davis Islands, and the construction of Fort Homer Hesterly Armory. Hundreds of young men were employed by the Civilian Con-

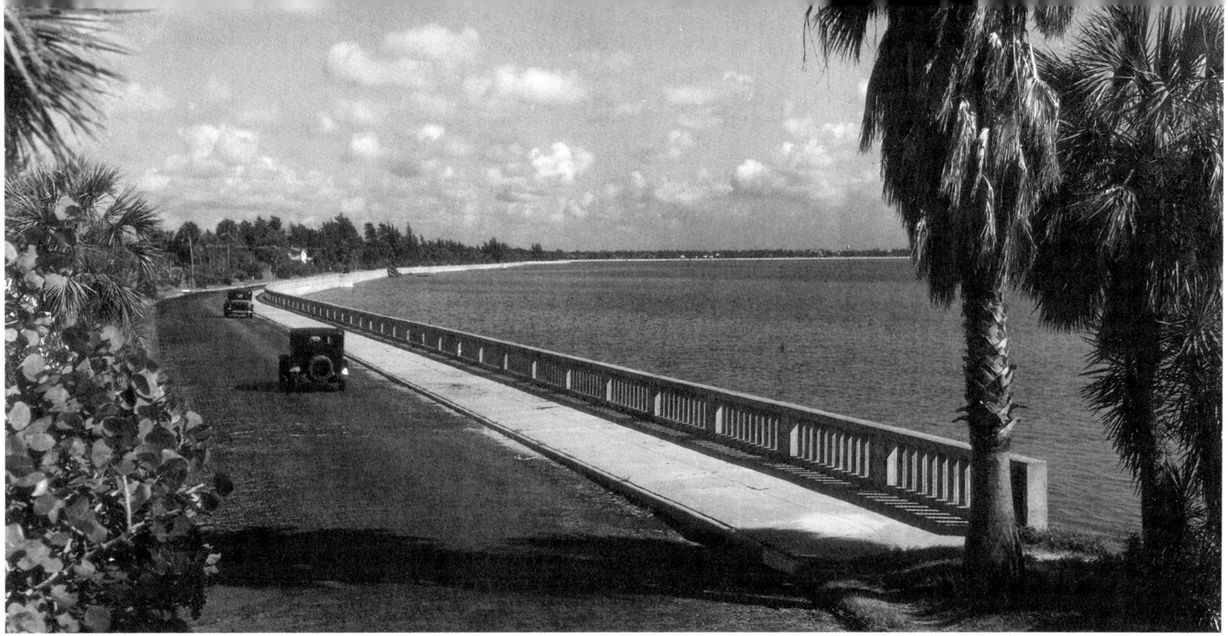

A 1936 photo of beautiful Bayshore Boulevard.
Courtesy of Hillsborough County Public Library.

servation Corps in building the Hillsborough River State Park. Works Progress Administration workers constructed a 7,000-foot runway for the new city-owned Drew Field.

On July 14, 1939, the *Tampa Tribune* headline read in banner letters "WE WILL GET AIR BASE." The news was most welcome. Located at the southern end of a largely uninhabited peninsula, MacDill Field boosted the city's morale. The county agreed to donate 3,500 acres and the government purchased another 3,000. Work crews began constructing a new road connecting Drew Field and MacDill Field. The road honored the memory of a gallant aviator, Dale Mabry.

The new air base encompassed Gadsden Point, named for James Gadsden, who helped guide Colonel Brooke to the area 120 years earlier. During the 1820s, a letter from Washington, D.C., reached Fort Brooke in twenty days; by the 1940s, news from Washington arrived via radio waves.

World War II

News of the Japanese attack on Pearl Harbor reached Tampa early Sunday afternoon, December 7, 1941. Fort Homer Hesterly officially opened that fateful day. Many young Latins learned the news when band leader Don Francisco addressed couples at the weekly Sunday Tea Dance at the Centro Español ballroom. Others listened to the radio or heard from friends at corner drugstores and movie theaters.

World War II, not the New Deal, ended Tampa's depression. Once again, war breathed life into Tampa. The Port of Tampa boomed, boasting three busy shipyards. The shipyards employed thousands at union wages, including hundreds of young women popularly known as "Joans of Arc." A young West Virginian arrived in Tampa eager to earn good wages as a welder. Robert Byrd then returned to West Virginia and became a U.S. senator.

Tampa's finest hour may have been the war years. War brought shared adversity and an extraordinary outpouring of volunteerism. Young and old, black and white, Latin and Anglo gave mightily to the war effort, contributing everything from old tires and scrap iron to kitchen grease and backyard scrap metal. Tampa youth enlisted in the Victory Corps and the Junior Commandos, while adults gave up their second cup of coffee and sugar bowls. In 1944, Tampa residents donated 210 tons of newsprint. The greatest civic lesson occurred not on the battlefield but rather in countless small gestures: having a victory garden, giving rides to hitchhikers in uniform, and buying a war bond. In 1943, every one of Tampa's 135 underpaid garbage workers purchased a war bond.

War brought unexpected benefits and changes to the area. U.S. Senator Claude Pepper, running for reelection, forced the Gandy family to sell the namesake bridge spanning Tampa Bay to the federal government. Motorists cheered when the last toll booth came down. Also in 1944, the Davis Causeway opened. Later renamed for local politician Courtney Campbell, the bridge allowed motorists a direct route from Tampa to Clearwater.

The Postwar Years, 1945–1950

The immediate postwar years helped transform Tampa. In 1947, the federal government decommissioned Drew Field, selling the modern air base to Hillsborough County for one dollar. Drew Field became Tampa International Airport. MacDill survived budget cuts and became a Cold War fortress. Henderson Field, located in northeast Hillsborough County, was also decommissioned. Hillsborough County obtained the land and pledged to use the site as an industrial park. The land would eventually house Schlitz and Busch breweries and parts of the University of South Florida.

Perhaps the most popular and successful measure Congress has ever implemented, the G.I. Bill affected Tampa in myriad ways. The bill rescued a foundering University of Tampa, a private institution strapped for cash and accreditation. In 1945, the university's enrollment had plunged to 210 students. By 1947, over a thousand students had flocked to the campus, many of them veterans. The University of Tampa was a lifeline for local students unable to travel to an out-of-town college. As hundreds of local youths took advantage of the university's proximity, observers began to complain that the closest four-year public university was the University of Florida in Gainesville. In 1955, local legislator, war hero, and G.I. Bill alumnus Sam Gibbons fought hard to secure a four-year university for Hillsborough County, the University of South Florida.

The G.I. Bill ignited a housing boom that began after the war. Few realized the implications at the time, but the G.I. Bill unwittingly undermined older neighborhoods such as Ybor City and Seminole Heights. In order to qualify for G.I. housing benefits, veterans had to purchase new homes. The ranch style soon replaced the bungalow. A front-porch society was being replaced by emerging trends made possible by television and air conditioning.

Jim Walter personified the pluck and creativity of returning veterans. In 1946, he began marketing "shell homes," inexpensive units that new homeowners could afford. The Jim Walter Corporation also introduced modular construction to the housing market.

New housing construction in 1945–1950 was occurring beyond the boundaries of the City of Tampa. In 1945, about 125,000 residents called Tampa home, a city restricted by its narrow geographical limits. Port Tampa, Palma Ceia, and Sulphur Springs were still outside the city limits. The city eventually annexed these areas between 1953 and 1960. The South Dale Mabry area was especially inviting to contractors. The era of the "suburbs" had begun.

Although few citizens noticed, downtown Tampa was reaching its zenith. Motorists from Arcadia to Zephyrhills still made the drive to shop and dine along Franklin Street. Maas Brothers was the most modern department store imaginable, and the majestic Tampa Theatre lured movie patrons with air conditioning.

Since the turn of the twentieth century, riding the streetcar downtown for a nickel was a popular means of transportation. But in 1946, the Tampa Electric Company announced its decision to pull the plug on the streetcar lines. In postwar America, the automobile was king. Few observers seemed to notice that future discussions of traffic gridlock and parking problems would be related to the loss of the city's trolley system.

African Americans still rode in the back of the new buses and were not allowed to vote in the Democratic primaries until 1946. A Supreme Court decision prohibited the city's White Municipal Party that forbade blacks from joining and voting in the city primaries. African Americans also successfully challenged the school system's discrimination against paying qualified black teachers the same as white teachers. Thurgood Marshall, representing the local NAACP, and local black teacher Hilda Turner successfully changed the law in the courts.

In 1947, the *Tampa Tribune* launched a new crusade aimed at reforming the city, especially the baleful influence of bolita. The paper had assigned investigative reporter "Jock" Murray to write a series of damning indictments. The locals shrugged their shoulders at another bolita story, but in 1950, the Kefauver Commission got people's attention. The national hearings aimed at exposing underworld corruption tarnished Tampa's image. Charlie Wall, once the most important figure in Tampa's underworld, appeared as the first witness. Wall's murder in 1955 was the story of the year.

Tampa's image took a hammering in the late 1940s. The influential *Holiday* magazine profiled Tampa in 1948, suggesting to readers and tourists that the city smelled bad, that its Gasparilla festivities smacked of a "slapstick comedy," and that its slums "beggared a Mexican peon village."

The Fifties

The decade of the 1950s brought Tampa to new heights but also exposed the city's problems. It was an era of dazzling new technologies, most notably the popularity of air-conditioning. Air-conditioning not only made hot cool; it also changed architectural styles, cultural habits, and economic patterns. Once restricted to the finest department stores and movie theaters, window air-conditioning units became available in the early 1950s. Still, as late as 1960, only about one in five households had adapted climate control to their homes. But the technology was irresistible. The miracle pesticide DDT also was adapted and adopted and used indiscriminately. The pesticide eradicated mosquitoes but brought terrible consequences to bird life and wildlife.

By the 1950s, WDAE FM could be heard on street corners and beaches in another new medium: transistor radios. Television came late to Tampa Bay, not introduced until 1953 when a UHF station opened atop St. Petersburg's million-dollar pier. On Gasparilla Day in 1955, Tampa's WFLA—an NBC affiliate—debuted, followed by WTVT two months later.

In 1956, Tampa's first shopping centers, Britton Plaza and Northgate, opened, symbolizing the new residential pattern and signaling the decline of downtown

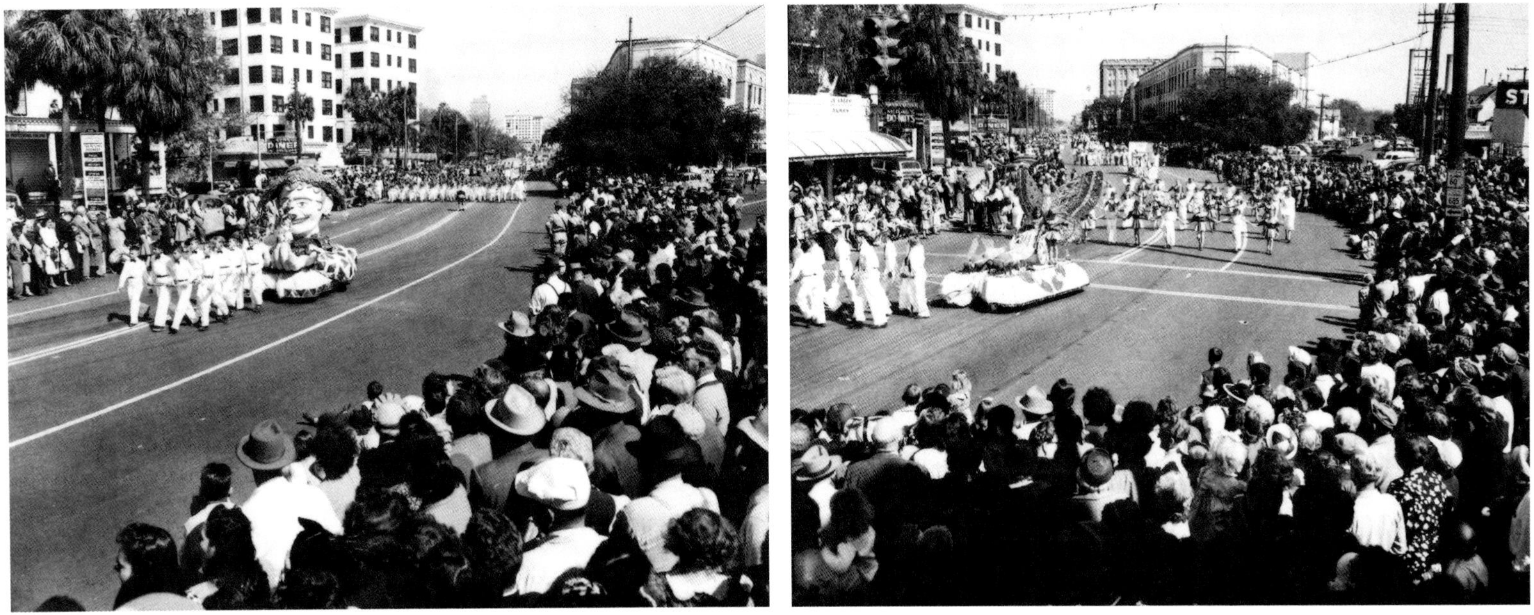

Historic images of the Gasparilla parade, 1951.
Courtesy of Tampa–Hillsborough County Public Library System.

Tampa. Local merchants and Tampa politicians would not and could not believe the facts, but each year for the next three decades, another venerable institution (Falk's, Newberry's, the Franklin Theatre, Wolf Brothers, even Maas Brothers) closed its downtown doors.

In 1950, the government was searching for new ways to classify urban growth. Officials designated the term *metropolitan* to describe the cities of Tampa and St. Petersburg. Tampa Bay, once a body of water, became a term for urban-metropolitan growth. Soon, the counties of Pasco and Hernando joined Hillsborough and Pinellas as a Standard Metropolitan Statistical Area. If the growth of Hillsborough County was impressive, the surge in the other counties was startling. Demographers had to create new terms to understand the growth: edge cities (describing the growth around TIA and Interstate 75), boomburbs (Wesley Chapel), and ex-urbs (Bloomingdale).

By the end of the decade, Tampans looked forward to the federal government's most dramatic construction project in history: the interstate highway system, a large endeavor planned with little thought for the consequences. By the late 1960s, the consequences were becoming apparent as I-4 and I-275 dissected historic neighborhoods (Ybor City and West Tampa), demolished historic centers (Central Avenue), and reconfigured residential patterns (suburbia). Few planners could have imagined that by the 1980s, commuters would be commuting to downtown Tampa and WestShore from Dade City, Brandon, and Ruskin.

The 1960s and Beyond

Each day after 1960, for every new resident who moved to the Tampa city limits, dozens relocated to the county periphery. New suburbs and housing developments appeared where dairies, orange groves, and cypress groves once stood. Businessmen reinvented the Florida dream, helping develop and create new communities. Some, such as Carrollwood, Town N' Country, and New Tampa, were wildly successful.

New residents migrated to Tampa in search of second chances and new opportunities. New communities catered to senior citizens. The opening of Sun City Center in the early 1960s dramatized the significance of senior citizens as a major new group. The Florida dream of happiness amid tropical splendor was reinvented in places such as Avila and Westchase.

By the 1960s and 1970s, the dangers of rampant, unchecked growth were becoming apparent. A lead story in a 1981 *Sports Illustrated* shocked many readers: "Tampa Bay, once the glory of the state, is now filth. An oyster will never grow in Tampa Bay again." A huge swatch of the bay's sea grasses, mangroves, and marshes had disappeared. The beautiful Hillsborough River, ignored for decades, was polluted. Water, which for centuries had irked settlers simply because there was too much of it, now became a precious commodity.

An environmental movement began to take shape in this era. Politicians and officials such as Betty Castor and Roger Stewart championed responsible growth and growth management. Planning in Tampa and Hillsborough County has been described as an exercise in controlled chaos. Optimists point out that Tampa Bay is cleaner today than it was in 1950, when many municipalities simply emptied raw sewage into the bay.

The trajectory of an obscure island in Hillsborough Bay exemplifies the change. Early in the twentieth century, the city of Tampa dredged the bay, creating Seddon Island from muck. The island was given to the phosphate companies to be used as a loading depot. Reinvented and unveiled in the early 1980s as Harbour Island, the island was declared a tourist and waterfront attraction. Tourism fizzled, but Harbour Island became a great success as a gated residential and commercial district.

The decline and rejuvenation of downtown Tampa represents one of the most significant themes of modern Tampa. In 1960, Mayor Nick Nuccio spearheaded the purchase of 21 acres of downtown riverfront land facing Ashley Street. Unfortunately, the downtown languished. The planning and construction of Tampa City Center (including the Hyatt Regency) in the late 1970s and early 1980s marked a major advance for the downtown. The 1980s quickened the pace as new skyscrapers appeared. By the 1990s, the Tampa skyline was almost unrecognizable to older residents.

New, gleaming structures attracted downtown workers but generated little public affection for the architecture or municipality. To many inhabitants, the buildings were sterile and indistinguishable from one another. Almost every Tampan knew the name of the Floridan Hotel or Citizens Building, but few residents knew the names or functions of the modern towers.

During most of the history of Tampa, Franklin Street served as the city's financial and commercial center. Through war and depression, Franklin Street was home to the city's most prestigious department stores, theaters, and banks. By the 1970s, Franklin Street had declined perceptibly; by the 1990s, it was desolate. By the 1980s and '90s, the WestShore district had more office space than downtown Tampa. For all of the thousands of downtown workers, few seemed to come out of their offices to patronize the local merchants. Parts of Franklin Street boomed, although it was South Franklin Street that was buoyed by the 1990 opening of the Tampa Convention Center.

Beginning in the 1990s, the focal point of downtown Tampa began to shift from Franklin Street to Channelside. For decades, the channel district had slumbered, a forlorn collection of warehouses and terminals. Investors recognized the opportunities, and Tampa rediscovered its waterfront. A series of developments, including the 1995 opening of the Aquarium, the 1996 debut of the Ice Palace and St. Pete Times Forum, awakened the area. Corporate interests began to develop the waterfront for commercial and industrial purposes. The opening of Channelside entertainment district in 2000 signaled a remarkable wave of investment and interest, especially in the number of condominium units. In the early twenty-first century, downtown Tampa continues to change and evolve. Condominiums have appeared on North Franklin Street, not far from the site where a young divinity student named Billy Graham preached to the homeless in the 1930s.

New arts and cultural centers also compete for space and attention. In the 1880s, visiting Shakespearean troupes entertained patrons at Branch's Opera House; by 1900, the Tampa Bay Casino was hosting lectures and concerts by Confederate generals and opera divas. When Elvis Presley came to Tampa in 1955, he performed at Fort Homer Hesterly auditorium. McKay Auditorium on the campus of the University of Tampa also played an important role in the city's cultural life. In 1965, Curtis Hixon Hall opened in the space off Ashley Street that had recently been home to warehouses. Modern Danish architecture and less-than-modern acoustics made the facility far from ideal. In 1987, officials opened the state-of-the-art Tampa Bay Performing Arts Center along the river.

During the 1970s, it became popular to endow sports teams and fine arts facilities with the name "Tampa Bay." Consequently, when Tampa acquired a professional team in the National Football League, the Tampa Bay Buccaneers debuted in 1976. The trend continued with the Tampa Bay Lightning, Tampa Bay Devil Rays, and Tampa Bay Storm.

The history of Tampa instructs and inspires. May Tampa's future be as interesting and fascinating as its past.

Tampa Robins

The robin laughed in the orange-tree:
"Ho, windy North, a fig for thee:
While breasts are red and wings are bold
And green trees wave us globes of gold,
Time's scythe shall reap but bliss for me
—Sunlight, song, and the orange-tree.

Burn, golden globes in leafy sky,
My orange-planets: crimson I
Will shine and shoot among the spheres
(Blithe meteor that no mortal fears)
And thrid the heavenly orange-tree
With orbits bright of minstrelsy.

If that I hate wild winter's spite—
The gibbet trees, the world in white,
The sky but gray wind over a grave—
Why should I ache, the season's slave?
I'll sing from the top of the orange-tree
'Gramercy, winter's tyranny.'

I'll south with the sun, and keep my clime;
My wing is king of the summer-time;
My breast to the sun his torch shall hold;
And I'll call down through the green and gold
'Time, take thy scythe, reap bliss for me,
Bestir thee under the orange-tree.'"

Sidney Lanier, 1877

View from the Outside

Observant entertainment fans have seen glimpses of Tampa in many popular films and television shows. In 1986, *Parent Trap II*, a made-for-television sequel to the popular Disney film, was produced in Tampa. Martin Scorsese's *GoodFellas* featured mobsters Henry and Jimmy (Ray Liotta and Robert DeNiro) dangling a gambler over the wall of the lion enclosure at Lowry Park Zoo. In 2004, John Travolta, Thomas Jane, and Rebecca Romijn came to Tampa to star in *The Punisher*, a film that featured many Tampa outdoor locations. Entertainment trivia experts can likely identify Tampa as the birthplace of actress Butterfly McQueen (*Gone with the Wind*), Brittany Snow (*Nip/Tuck*, *Hairspray*), Robert Gant (*Queer as Folk*), and Sarah Paulson (*Studio 60 on the Sunset Strip*).

Sports fans are familiar with the Tampa Bay Buccaneers, which came to Tampa as an expansion team in 1976. Bucs fans, who sometimes populated the stands wearing brown paper bags over their heads, sat through nearly two seasons before the team won its first home game in 1977. Tampa was host to Super Bowl XVIII in 1984, Super Bowl XXV in 1991, and Super Bowl XXXV in 2001. Patient fans were rewarded with the big prize, a Super Bowl–winning team, in 2003 when the Tampa Bay Buccaneers won Super Bowl XXXVII at the end of the 2002 season, defeating the Oakland Raiders 48–21 at Qualcomm Stadium in San Diego. Tampa will host its fifth Super Bowl, XLIII, on February 1, 2009.

Though seemingly an unlikely home for an ice hockey team, Tampa was awarded a franchise in 1991, the Tampa Bay Lightning. The Lightning enjoyed a strong first season. Absent from the playoffs for the next seven seasons, the team won a hard-fought series to defeat the Calgary Flames for Lord Stanley's Cup on June 7, 2004, the final game played on home ice in the St. Pete Times Forum. The Lightning is the southernmost team to win the cup. Sports trivia fans may know one extraordinary distinction for the team: Manon Rheaume was the first woman ever to play in an NHL game, taking the goalkeeper's place twice, in preseason play against the St. Louis Blues in 1992 and against the Boston Bruins in 1993.

In 1991, Tampa became home to the Arena Football League team Tampa Bay Storm when it moved from Pittsburgh. Winning the Arena Bowl in its first Tampa season, the team has won a total of five Arena Bowls. A Tampa team for the last eighteen years, the Storm is one of the two teams (with the Orlando Predators) to share the record of longest tenure in a single market.

Although not officially a "Tampa" team because the home field is across Tampa Bay in St. Petersburg, the Tampa Bay Devil Rays (now called the Tampa Bay Rays) played its first major league game in 1998. The franchise was awarded in 1995 as part of a MLB expansion. Though the team has yet to finish a season with an average above .500, diehard fans keep their fingers crossed, perhaps remembering the many years of suffering and ridicule the Bucs endured before prevailing. The Bay area has a rich history in baseball and is home to the New York Yankees spring training site, Legends Field. Many famous players were born in Tampa, including Derek Bell, Steve Garvey, Luis Gonzalez, Dwight Gooden, Tony LaRussa, Al Lopez, Tino Martinez, Fred McGriff, and Gary Sheffield.

Others who are not sports or movie fans know that Tampa is a subtropical paradise with warm, inviting temperatures virtually year round. Rarely does the thermometer dip below 60 degrees, and the chance of freezing temperatures is remote, with fewer than one chance of temperatures below 32 degrees every two or three years. In the long summer, Tampa experiences dramatic thunderstorms and is recognized as the lightning capital of the United States. Sunshine is the order of any day in Tampa, and at one time a local newspaper delivered free papers to every home the morning following a day without sunshine.

With weather so agreeable, it is no coincidence that there are a variety of outdoor festivals that make Tampa well known. For more than one hundred years, Tampa has celebrated an annual invasion, Gasparilla, known as the Mardi Gras of Tampa, led by pirate José Gaspar. Held on Mondays until 1988, Gasparilla, now held on Saturday to allow more participation from citizens, features a daytime parade, a children's festival, and a night parade through historic Ybor City. On invasion day, pirate ships invade the city with more than 300 private boats belonging to the flotilla. The krewes (private clubs made up of Tampa residents) march alongside floats in the parades and throw beads to the crowds. Annually, the event is attended by approximately 400,000 people.

Located near downtown Tampa, Ybor City is named for cigar factory owner Vicente Martinez Ybor, who, after moving from Spain to Key West, settled in Tampa in 1886. After other manufacturers of hand-rolled cigars followed, Tampa became the largest manufacturer of cigars in the world. Even today, the old cigar factories dot the landscape of Ybor City, known as a popular entertainment district with restaurants, concert venues, and shops.

Every October for more than twenty years, Tampa has celebrated its own take on Halloween with the Guavaween festival, named after the tropical fruit. This festival, which takes place in Ybor City, brings out the spirit of the season as participants dress up and take over the night. The Mama Guava Stumble Parade allows everyone to enjoy the sight of the revelers.

Without a doubt, outsiders know something about Tampa. This short list is but an introduction to the things that Tampa has to offer. But to truly understand this city, you need to come to the inside.

The thing I like most about Tampa is its diversity. There are so many opportunities to do different things. Whether you are looking for a night out on the town with theater, dining, and dancing, or you want to get back to nature with fishing, camping, and canoeing, it is all right at your fingertips.

Kenneth Gibbons, Tampa resident

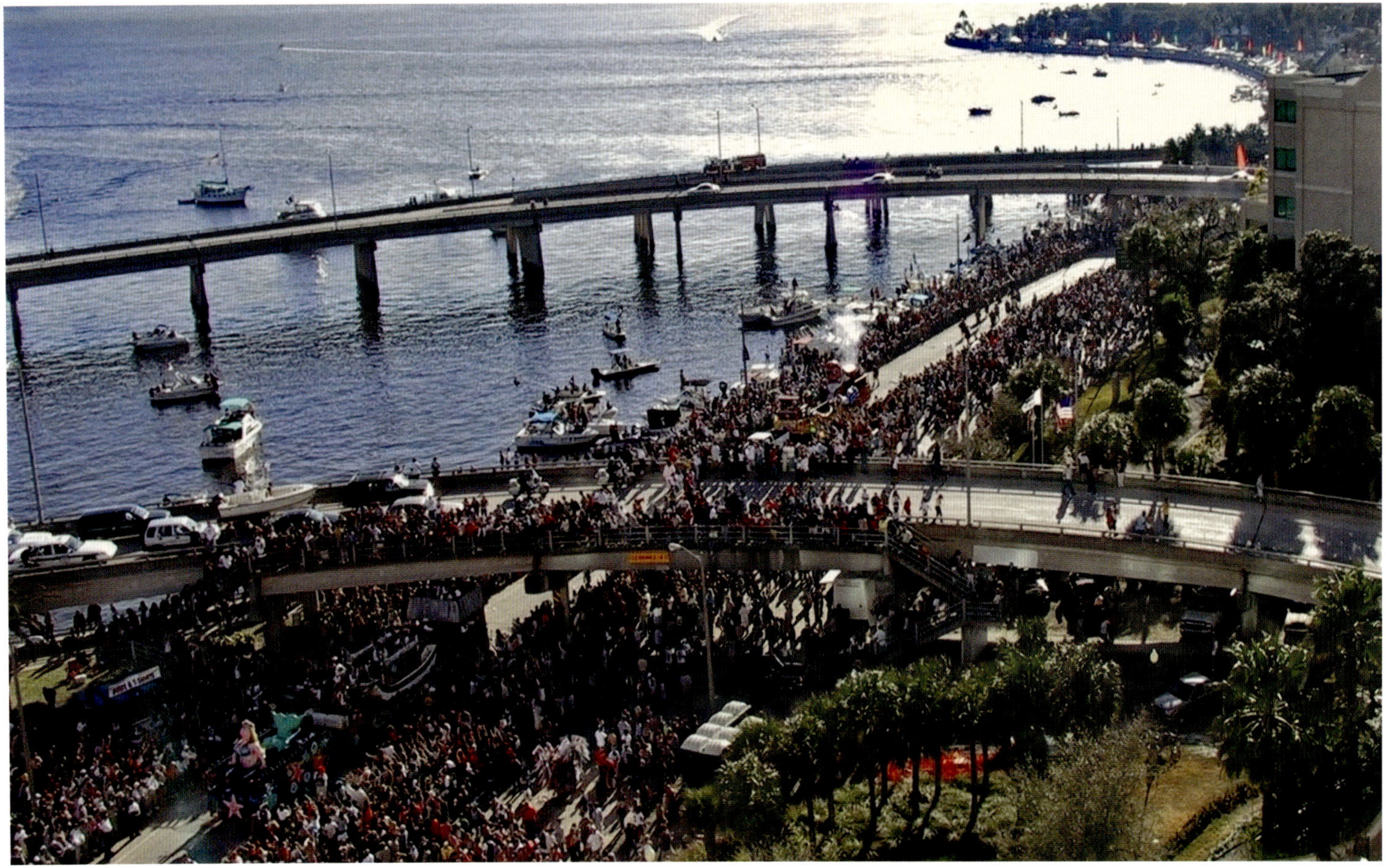

In 1904, Tampa businessmen put on an "invasion" of their city based on the increasingly popular figure of José Gasparilla. The original invaders dressed in pirate costumes and rode through the streets on horseback. The following year, all sixty of Tampa's automobiles kicked off a tradition that is still honored through an annual parade.

Photo by Ron Williams.

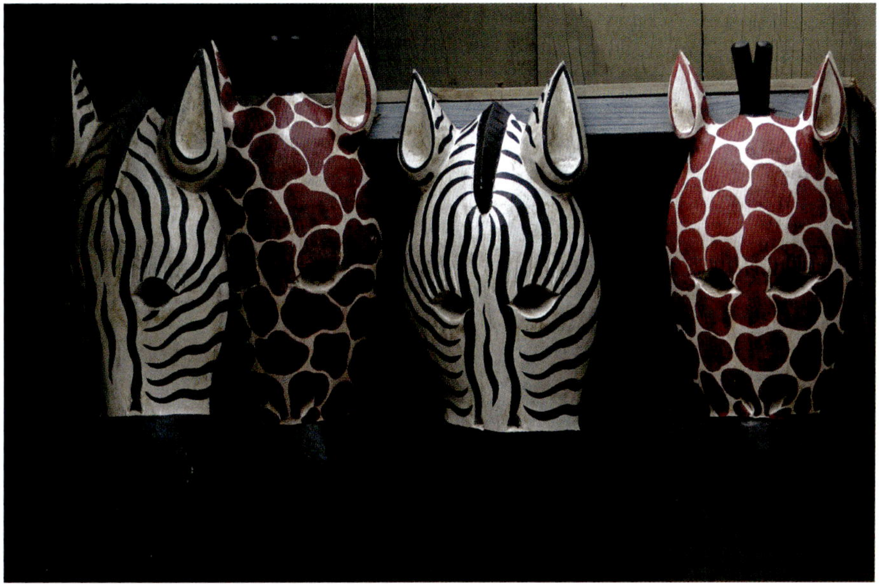

Tampa's Lowry Park Zoo is the region's only dedicated zoological garden. This kid-friendly space was recently voted the number one family-friendly zoo in America by *Child* magazine.

Photos by Ron Williams.

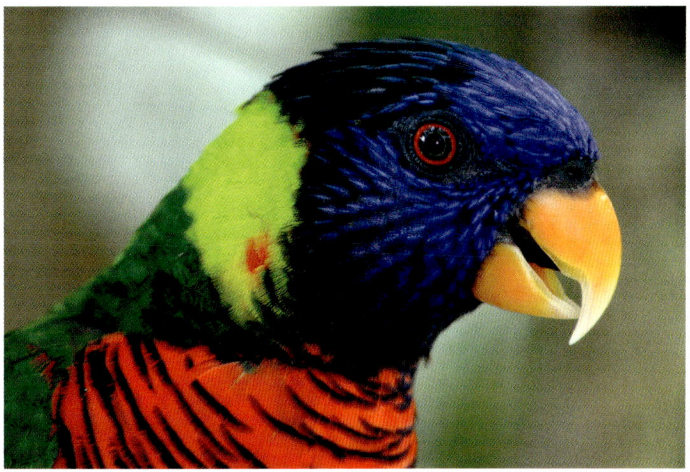

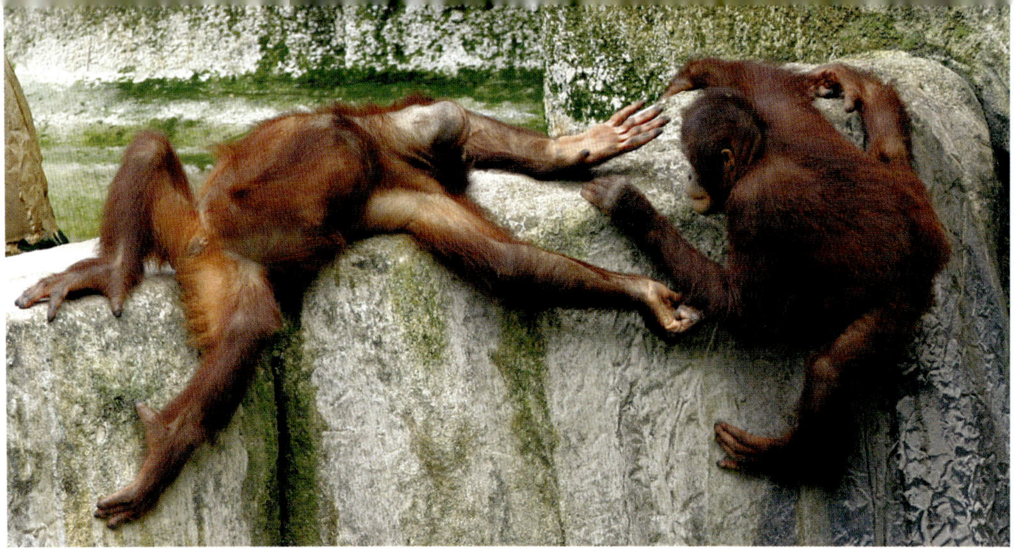

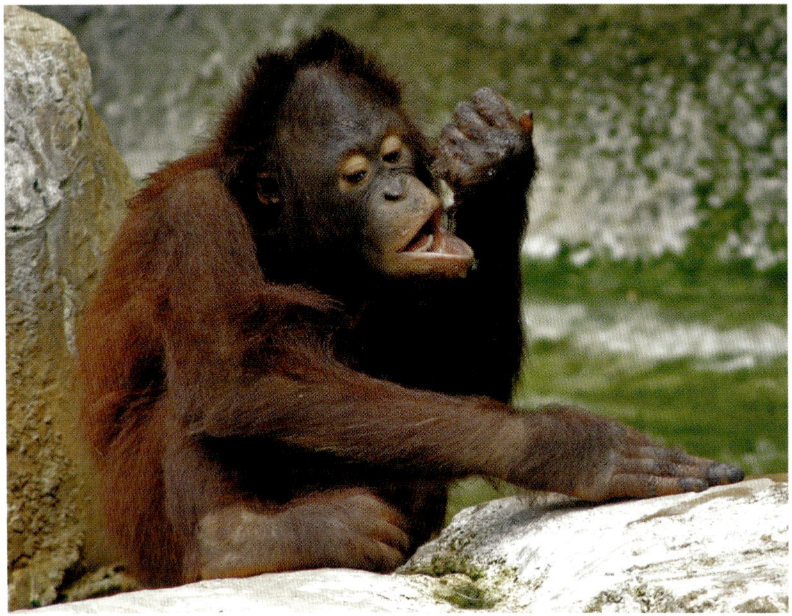

The Florida Environmental Education Center Zoo School, based at Tampa's Lowry Park Zoo, teaches more than 100,000 children annually the importance of sharing space with our animal neighbors.

Photos by Ron Williams.

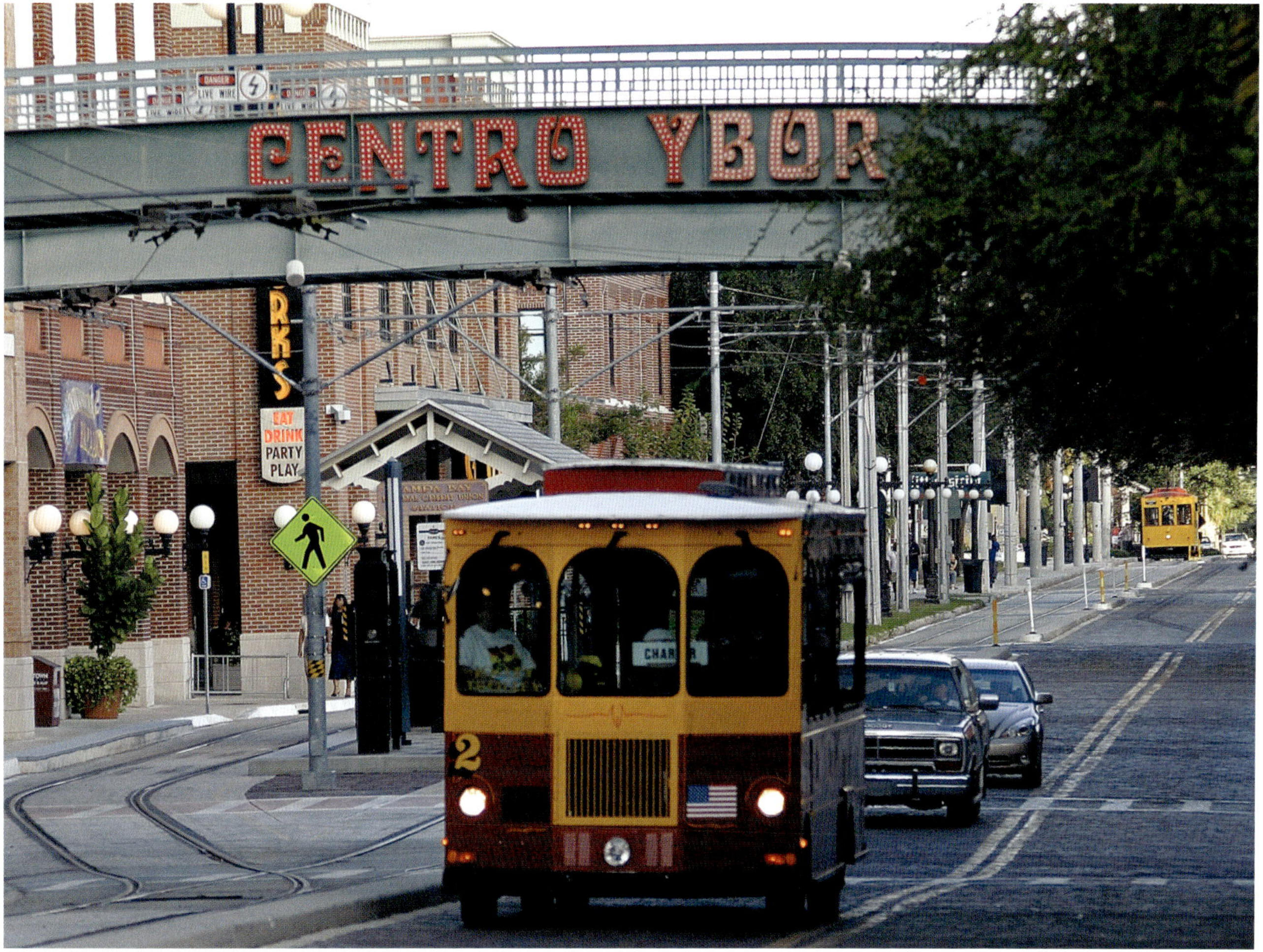

Local streetcar travels through Ybor City.
Photo by Ron Williams.

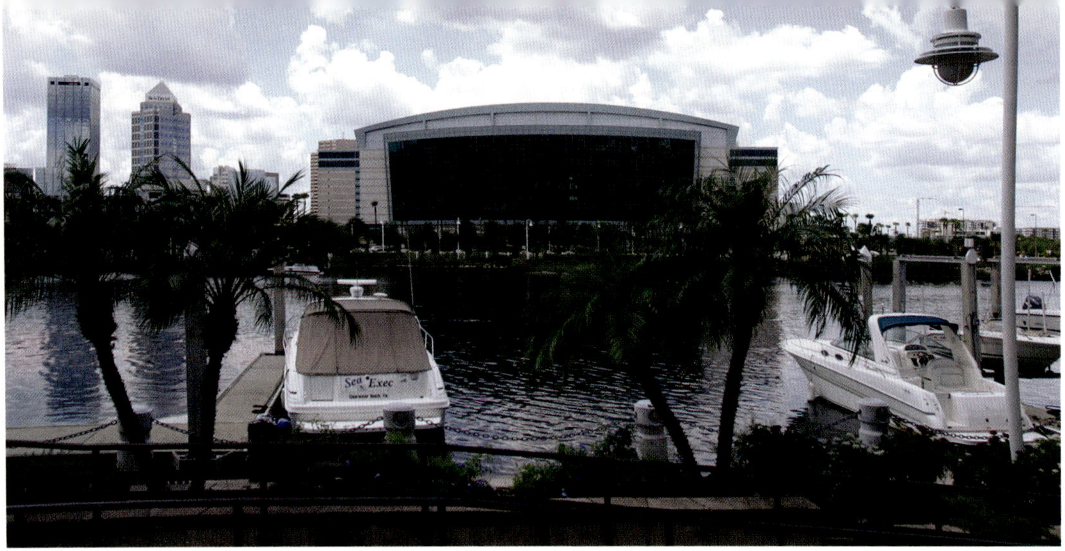

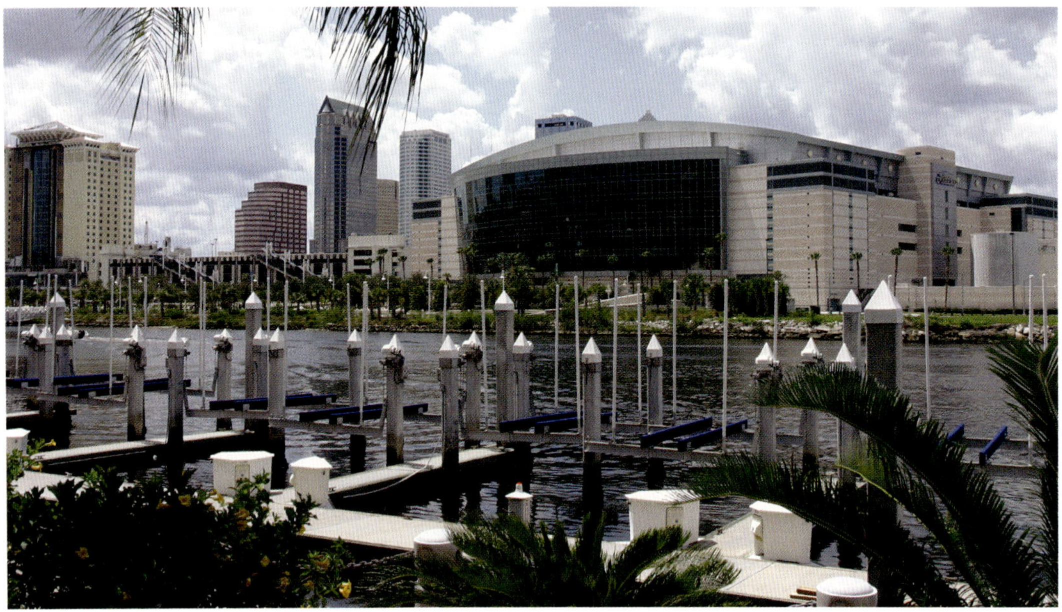

St. Pete Times Forum by the water.
Photos by Ron Williams.

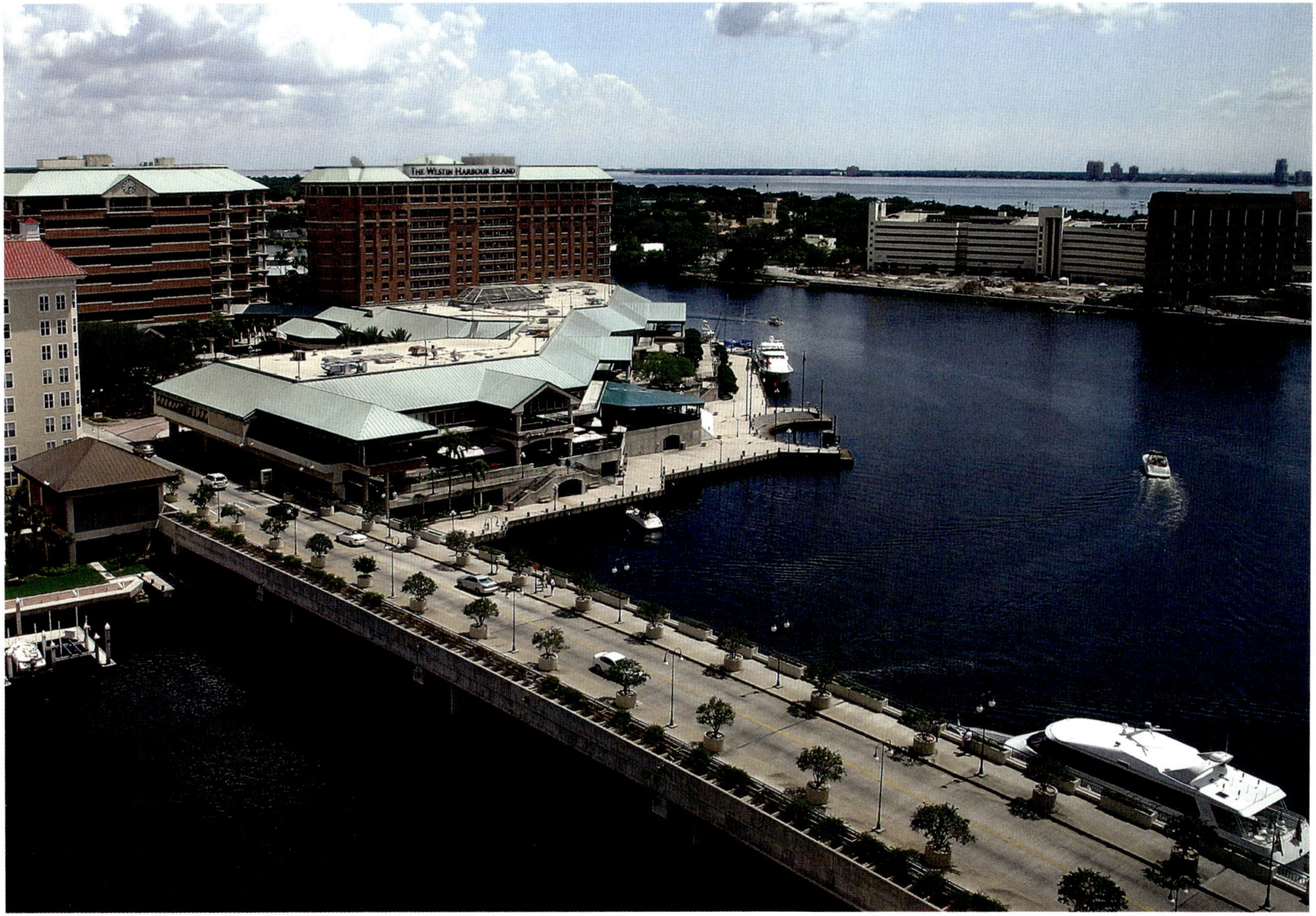

A short bridge connects Harbour Island to the downtown Tampa Convention Center. Harbour Island, a small island community, is home to the Westin Hotel, Jackson's Bistro, and dozens of independent businesses.

Photo by Ron Williams.

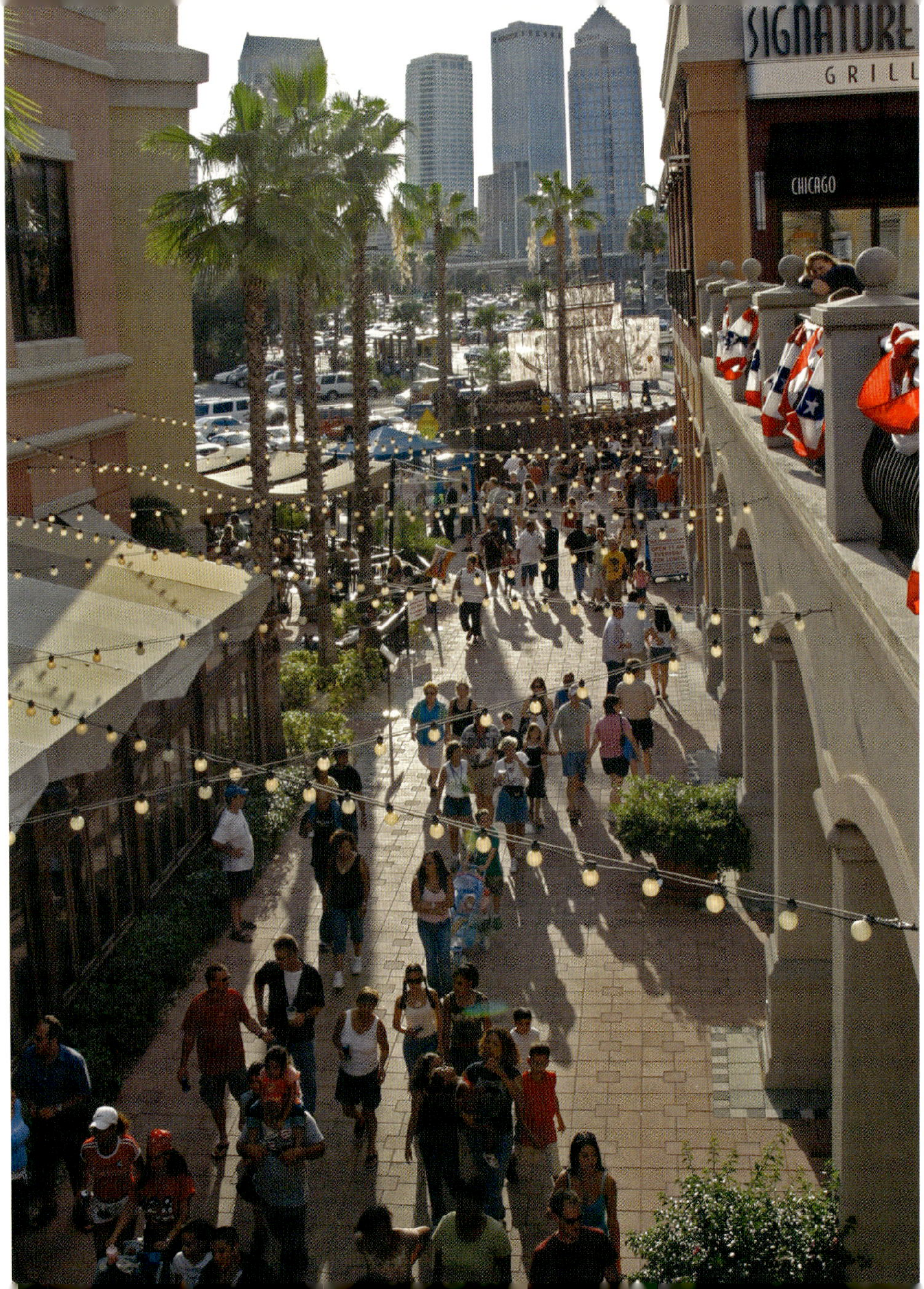

Busy Channelside with downtown in the background.
Photo by Ron Williams.

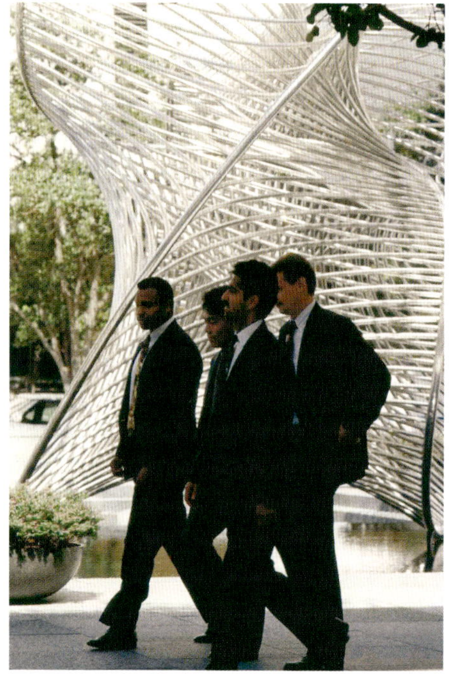

Businessmen walk past Tampa's public art downtown.
Courtesy of Tampa's Downtown Partnership.

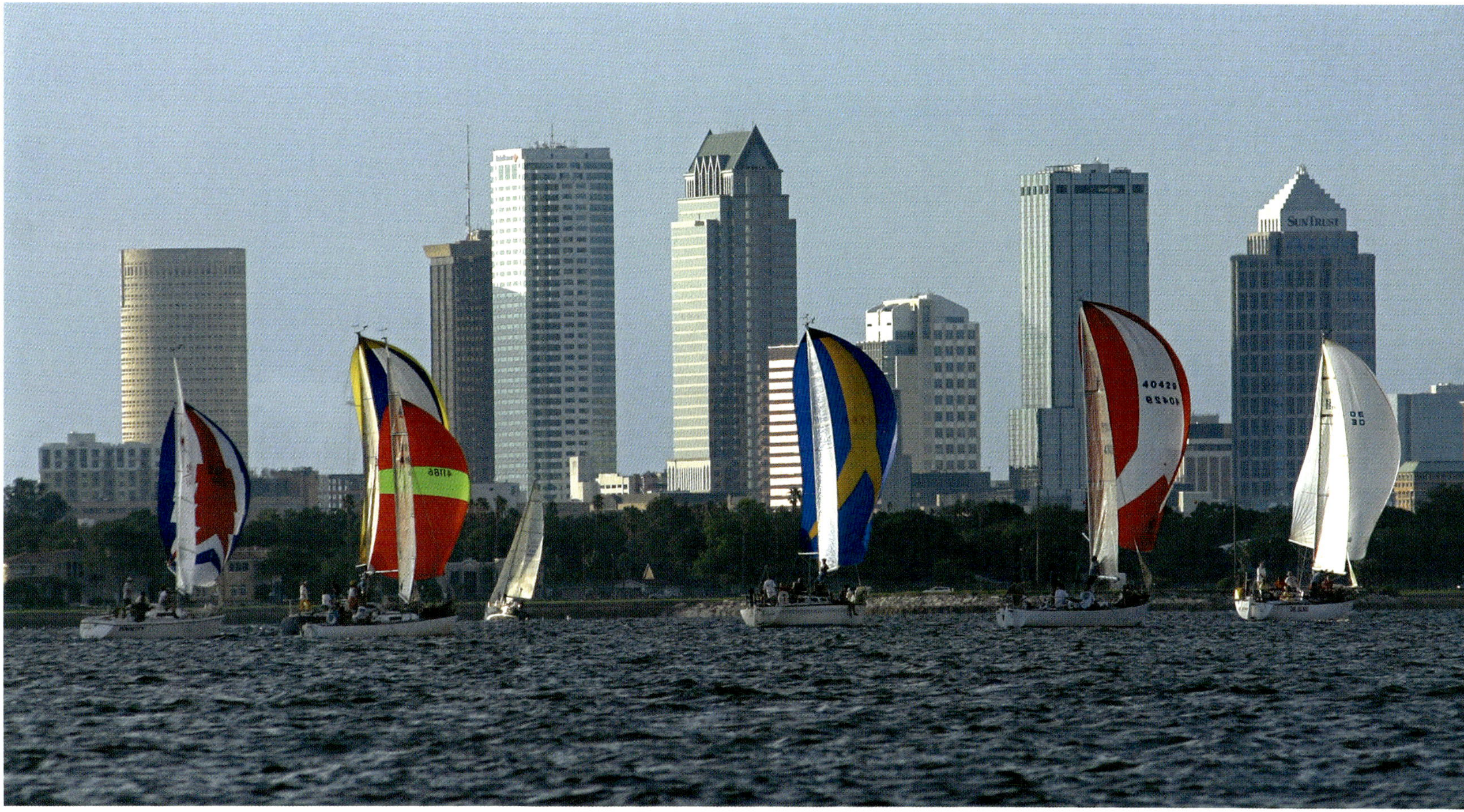

Tampa is a better place to live. It is a place where each day is too short for all the sights I want to see, all the fish I want to catch, all the fun in the sun I want to have, and all the people I want to meet.

Gerard Kedzie, Tampa resident

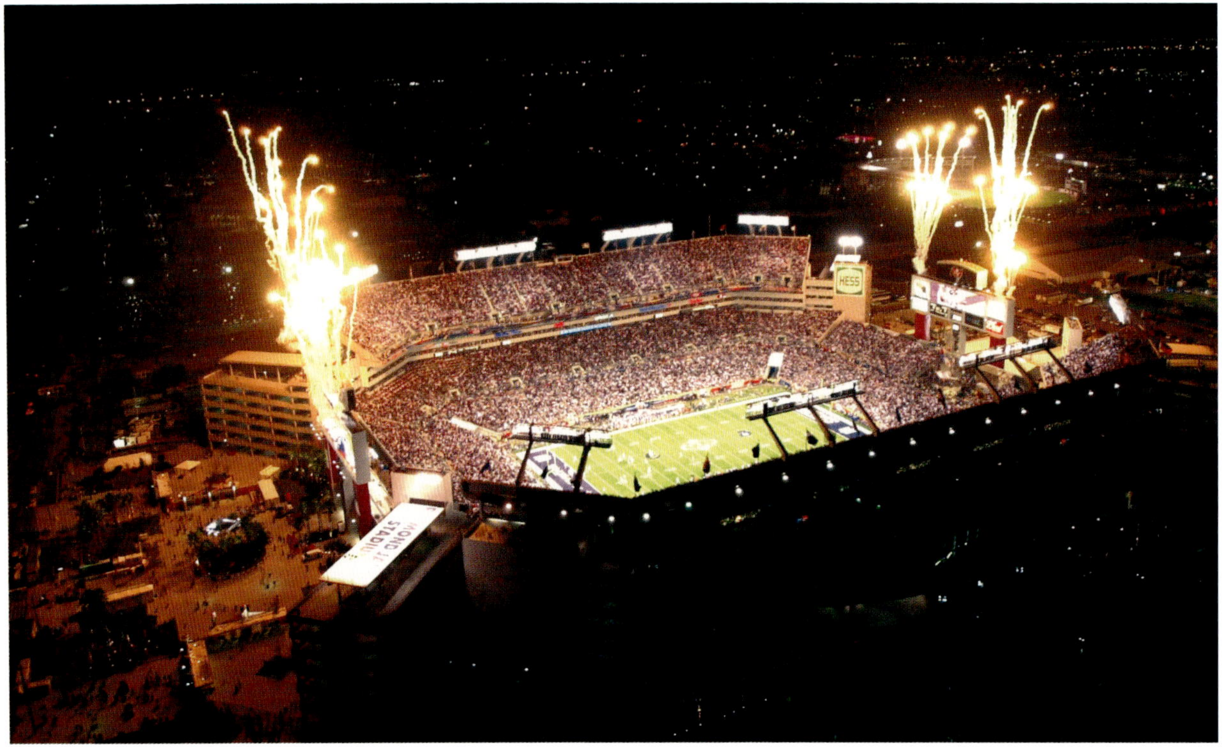

Fireworks erupt at Raymond James Stadium in Tampa after the Baltimore Ravens scored a touchdown against the New York Giants during Super Bowl XXXV on January 28, 2001. Tampa was chosen to host the 2009 Super Bowl in a vote by NFL owners. Tampa, which has hosted three previous championships, beat out finalists Atlanta, Houston, and Miami.

AP photo by the *St. Petersburg Times*, Skip ORourke.

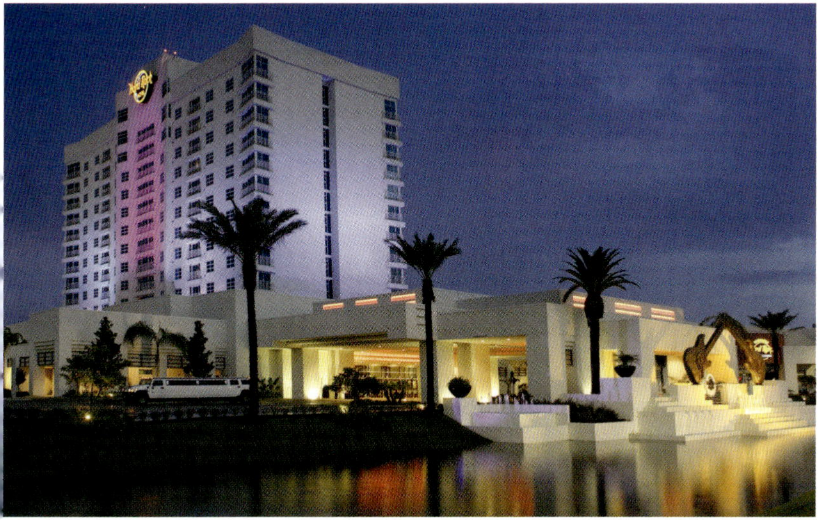

Tampa's dynamic Hard Rock Casino houses a 150,000-square-foot casino and a 250-room hotel. The AAA four-diamond rated resort promises impressive live entertainment, a full service spa, and a fitness center.
Image provided with permission of Hard Rock Casino.

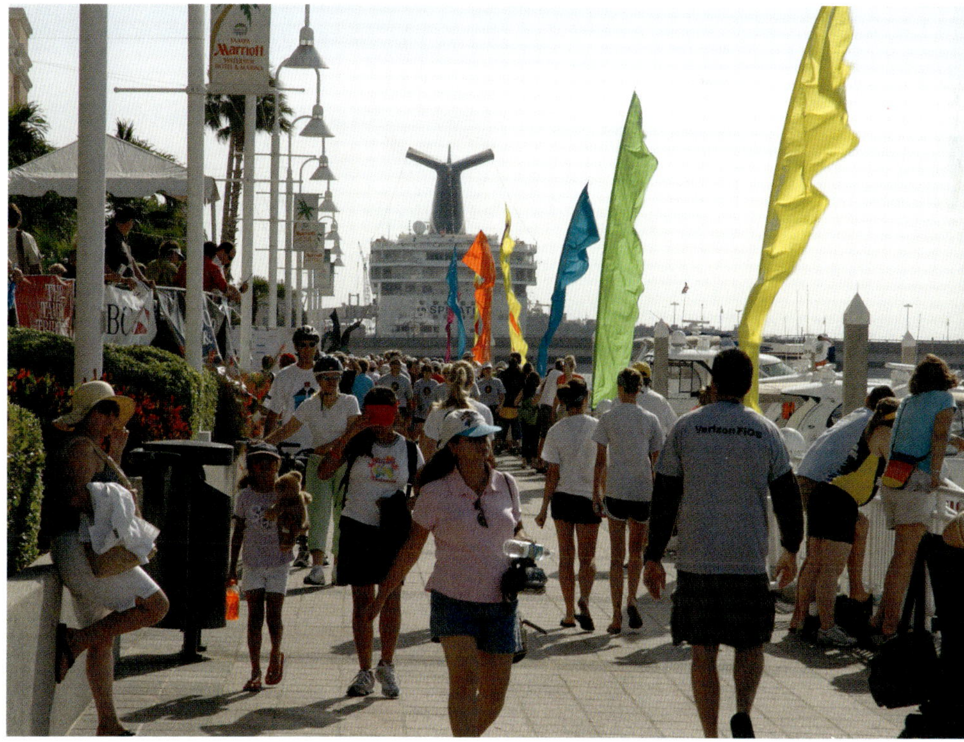

Pedestrians on a busy sidewalk with a cruise ship in the background.
Courtesy of Tampa's Downtown Partnership.

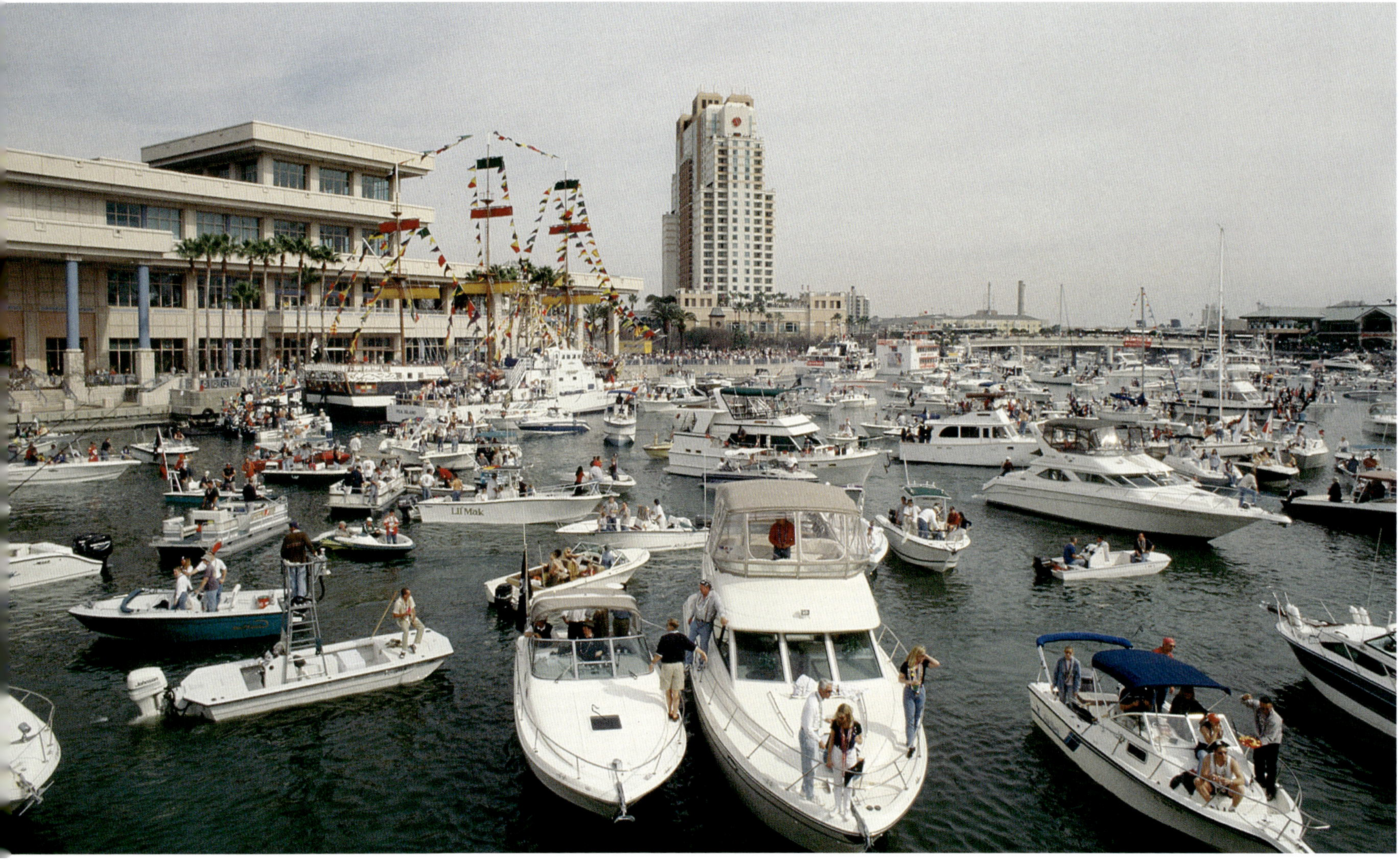

The Gasparilla Flotilla invades Tampa.

Courtesy of Tampa's Downtown Partnership.

View from the Inside

Tampa beckons you. Luring tourists with its comfortable warm breezes, subtropical climate, varied outdoor activities, vibrant art community, wild roller coasters, and beautiful waterfront, it offers all the opportunities of any sizable metropolis. Lapped by the blue waters of the Gulf of Mexico, it progresses, develops, and expands while maintaining its small-town warmth and charm. Many of Tampa's jewels have been displayed on the national stage; a number of hidden gems remain tucked away from the mainstream attractions, known by the locals but awaiting discovery by visitors.

This city has become home to more than 300,000 people. Many of its residents came seeking a new career, time with family, affordable housing, and access to some of the highest-rated schools in the country. The cultural plurality of Tampa is intimately connected to its past and its present. Early immigrants formed the clubs, churches, and commercial and community associations whose history is preserved in museum exhibits and cultural events today.

One of the key cities of the Sunshine State, Tampa also holds a place of distinction in the *Guinness Book of World Records*, having enjoyed 768 consecutive days of sunshine. Tampa treats enthusiastic golfers to a range of diverse courses, sports fans to championship teams, and nature lovers to a wide variety of stimulating activities. Its parks include welcome surprises for locals and visitors alike. With dozens of private hideaways to choose from, curious souls will find miles of trails and bike paths, as well as alligators, birds, and turtles. Equally picturesque are the countless water lilies, swamp hibiscus, and old cypress trees surrounding lakes and rivers that wind through quiet neighborhoods and stretch toward Tampa Bay. With hundreds of acres of Florida wildlife to explore, park-goers can enjoy a day of kayaking, hiking, picnicking, and fishing within minutes from downtown. Filled with verdant parks, historic sites, and palm-lined avenues, Tampa possesses a colorful landscape that is an explorer's paradise.

Those who desire less strenuous daytime activities can enjoy the rich cultural experiences that Tampa has to offer. With informative historical centers like the Tampa Bay History Center and the Ybor City Museum, guests have ample opportunity to acquaint themselves with our rich cultural heritage. Likewise, the Henry B. Plant Museum captures the charm and interest of turn-of-the-century Tampa Bay Hotel and the lifestyles of America's Gilded Age. Tampa residents also celebrate their heritage through dozens of annual festivals, which honor their Hispanic and European roots.

The Museum of Science and Industry is one of the largest in the South. This impressive facility boasts a diverse collection of educational exhibits that entertain astronomers and children alike. Its More than Meets the Eye exhibit compares naked-eye views of celestial objects with the views from binoculars, telescopes, large observatories, and, in some cases, space probes. MOSI is especially proud of the popular Kids in Charge! exhibit, which teaches children the value of learning through play. This center, which is currently the largest children's science center in the country, came into existence through the careful supervision of an advisory board of twenty-six children.

Regular cultural festivals include popular events like Cigar Heritage, Guavaween, and the Tampa International Gay & Lesbian Film Festival. Wine aficionados enjoy Bern's Steak House and SideBern's Annual Winefest, while families take pleasure in MacDill Air Force Base's Air Fest. The two-day event is one of the largest air shows in the country and features the U.S. Special Operations Command Jump Team, the U.S. Navy's Demonstration Team, and the Blue Angels, who perform aerial maneuvers.

When the sun sets, nightlife calls, and Ybor City is a hotbed of activity. This National Landmark Historic District has welcomed U.S. presidents at such fine establishments as the Columbia Restaurant and Tropicana. Cigar shops, tattoo parlors, nightclubs, and coffee houses trumpet Ybor's fondness for all types of amusements. Ybor's sidewalks bustle with people, whether they're shopping, seeing the sights, or enjoying one of the area's warm sunny days.

Residents of Tampa enjoy a rich history and a high standard of living. According to *Southern Business Development*, Tampa Bay is one of the most attractive places to operate a business in the United States. At the end of the work day, Tampa residents commute past long stretches of water, dine under impressive sunsets, and open their homes to visitors from across America. The city's urban skyline blends with the area's lush natural environment, lending the city a personality all its own. With historic bungalows and modern condominiums, it is a great place to call home for all budgets and lifestyles. And when residents need to travel, they fly in style. Official Airline Guide Worldwide ranks Tampa International Airport among the world's top five airports.

Schools and universities turn out first-class graduates. The University of South Florida is the third-largest university in the Southeast and among the top twenty largest in the nation. The School District of Hillsborough County was ranked as one of "the most outstanding school districts in the United States." Hillsborough High School, with its beautiful Gothic construction and clock tower, ranked as the tenth-best high school in a survey conducted by *Newsweek*. Hillsborough Community College is ranked fifteenth nationally for the number of AA degrees awarded and fourth for AA degrees in nursing. Moreover, *Kaplan's Unofficial, Unbiased Guide to the 328 Most Interesting Colleges* has ranked the University of Tampa, with its towering minarets, high on the "Hot and Trendy" list.

The armed forces also recognize Tampa's many attributes. MacDill Air Force Base, home to the U.S. Central Command Post, benefits from close proximity to deep-water harbors and long summer nights, making Tampa an ideal home base for practicing air, sea, and land operations. MacDill also serves as an alternate landing site for NASA and is home to National Oceanic and Atmospheric Administration's fleet of weather-tracking and research aircraft.

Tampa has its own unique identity, shaped by history, by the people who settled here, and by the nature of the surrounding area. Tampa's residents are easy and cordial with strangers. Peoples who live in Tampa fully appreciate that they live on the edge of paradise, and their hospitable nature is a testament to the warm Florida lifestyle.

The Red Baron Squadron entertains Tampa residents, performing loops, barrel rolls, and hammerheads. These flying feats have helped make the Red Baron Squadron flight team the longest-serving nonmilitary air show team in the history of aviation.

Photo by Ron Williams.

Tampa has something for everyone. It is one of the few places where home connects snarled oak trees with big city nightlife and calming waters. Tampa is a wonderful place to call home.

Jennifer Thayer, Smith & Associates

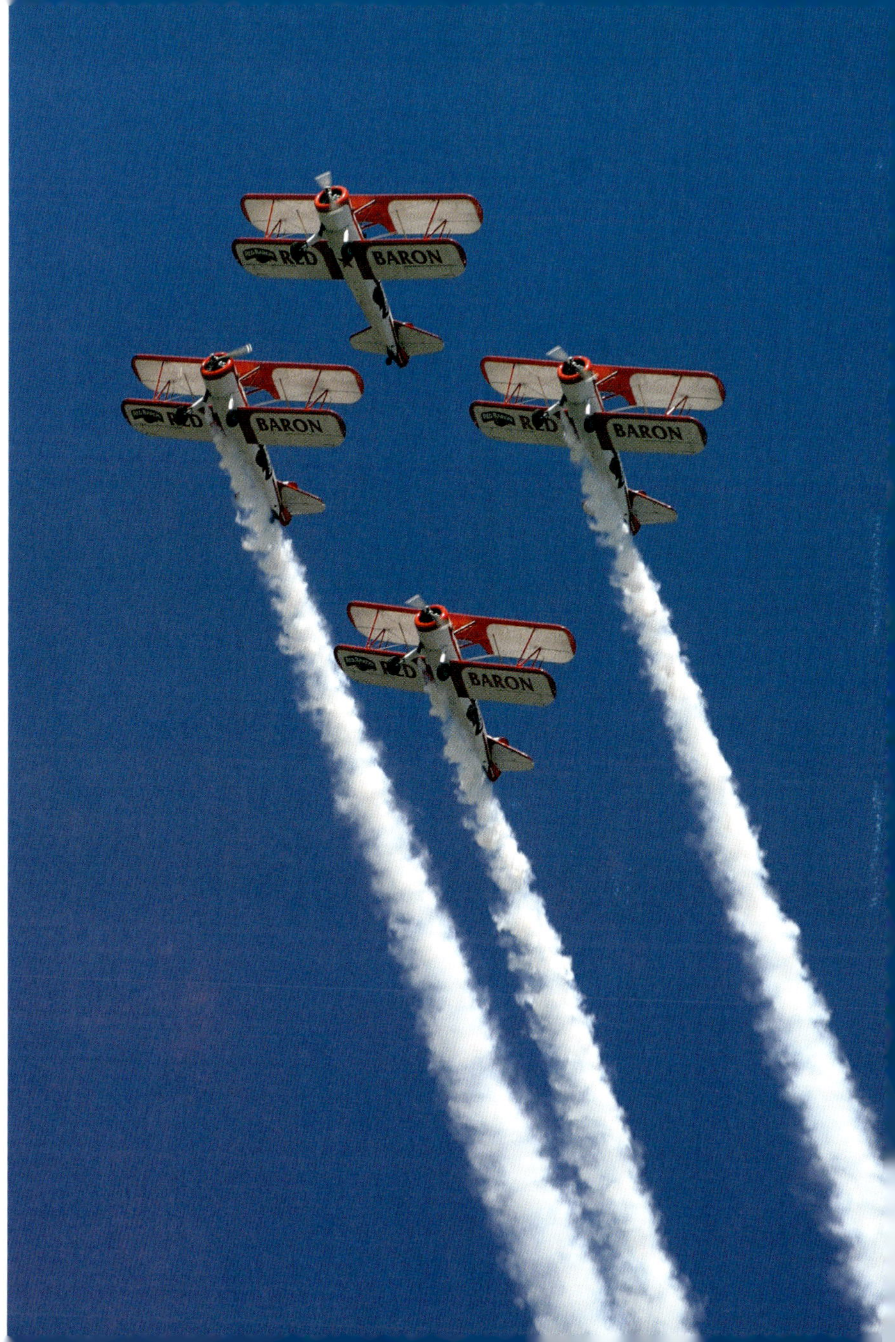

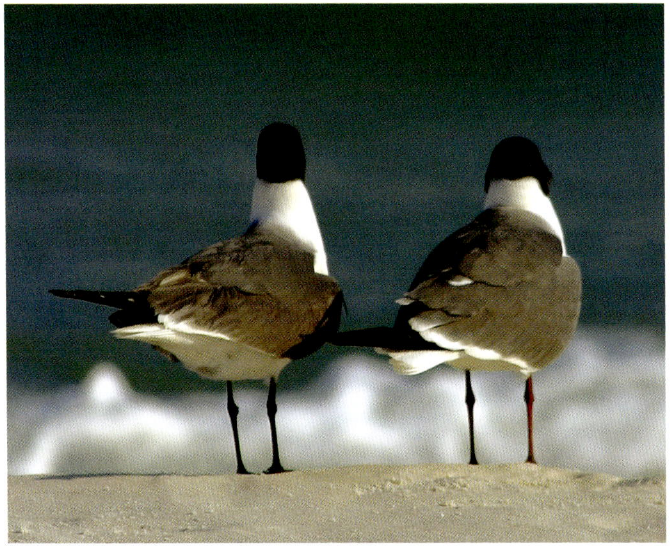

Just another perfect day in paradise for black-headed gulls enjoying a day at the beach.

Photo by Ron Williams.

Tampa's wetlands are home to thousands of plants and animals. In one sanctuary, a little blue heron hunts for fish.

Photo by Ron Williams.

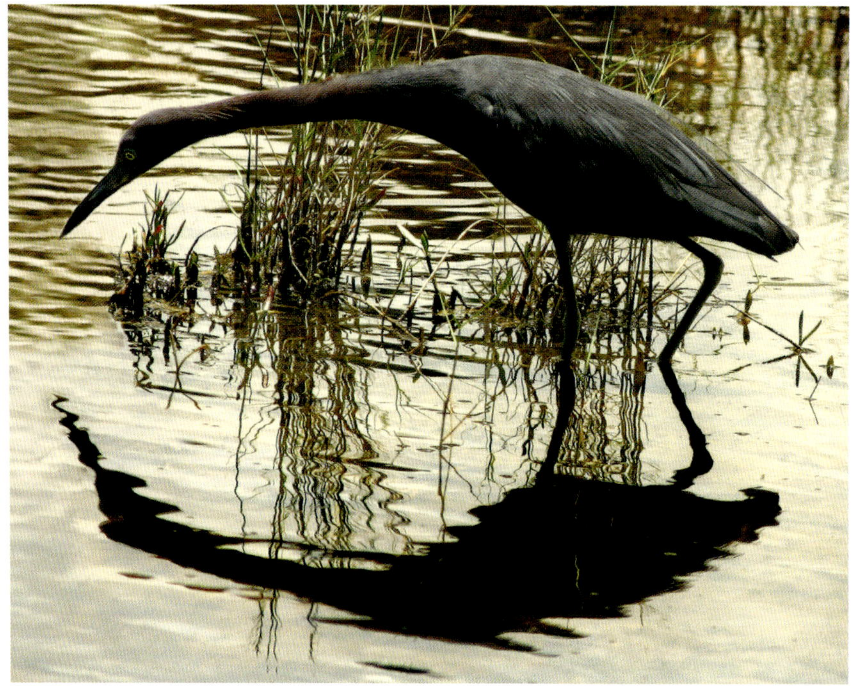

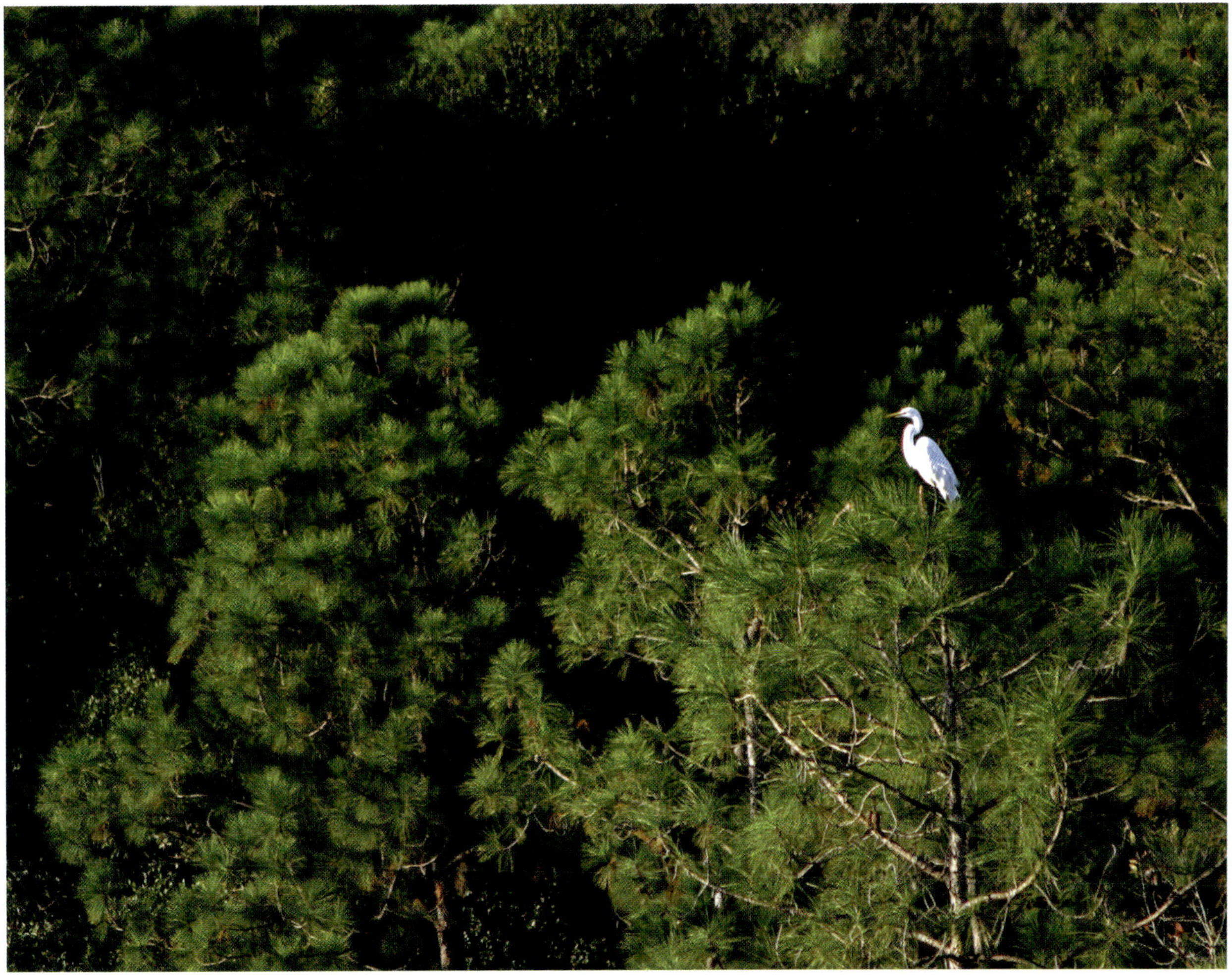

North Tampa woods provide safe havens for a wide variety of wildlife.
Photo by Ron Williams.

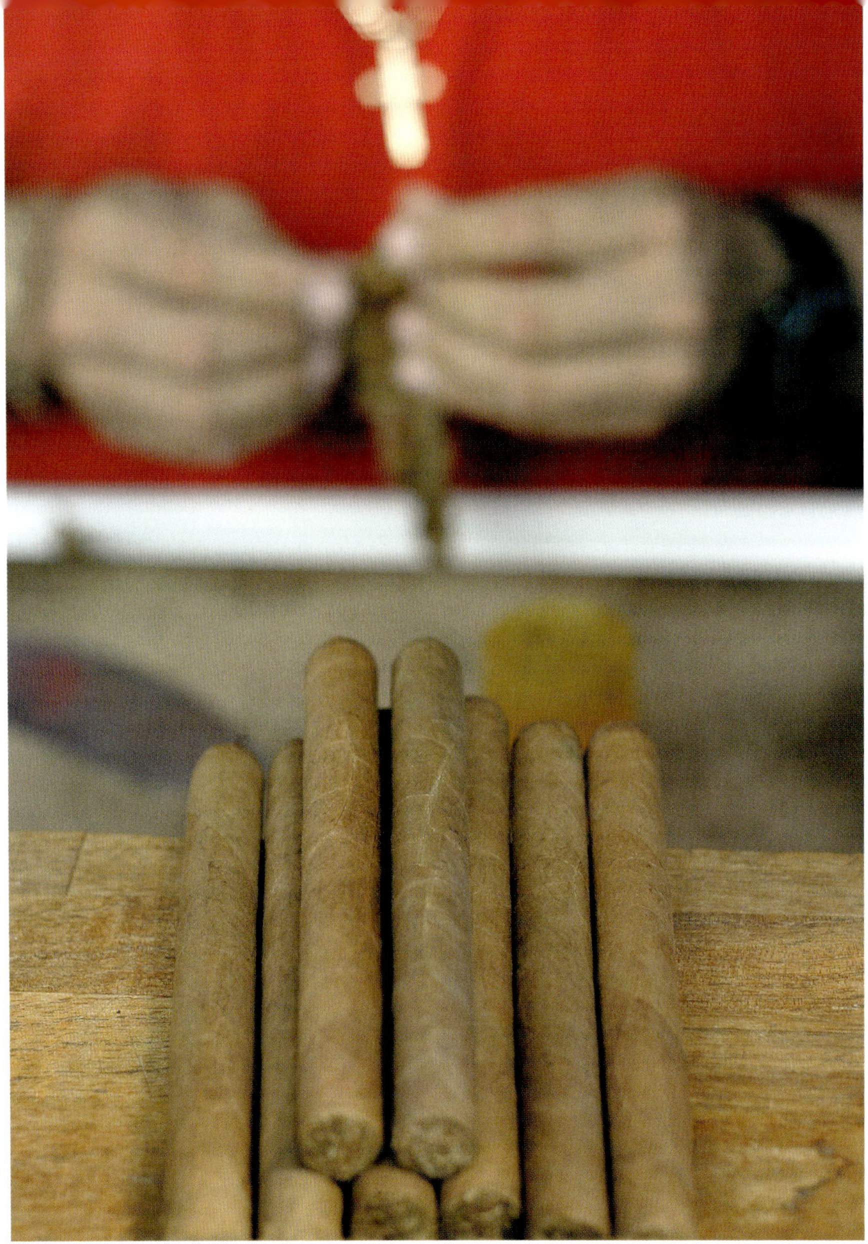

Ybor City was once the cigar capital of the world. Even today, Tampa is still famous for its excellent hand-rolled cigars.
Photo by Ron Williams.

Cigar makers provide me with an inexhaustible source of material. In any case, I had to write about them, for I feared that this community, which of necessity had to die out, would be forgotten, a part of America no one would get to know.

José Yglesias

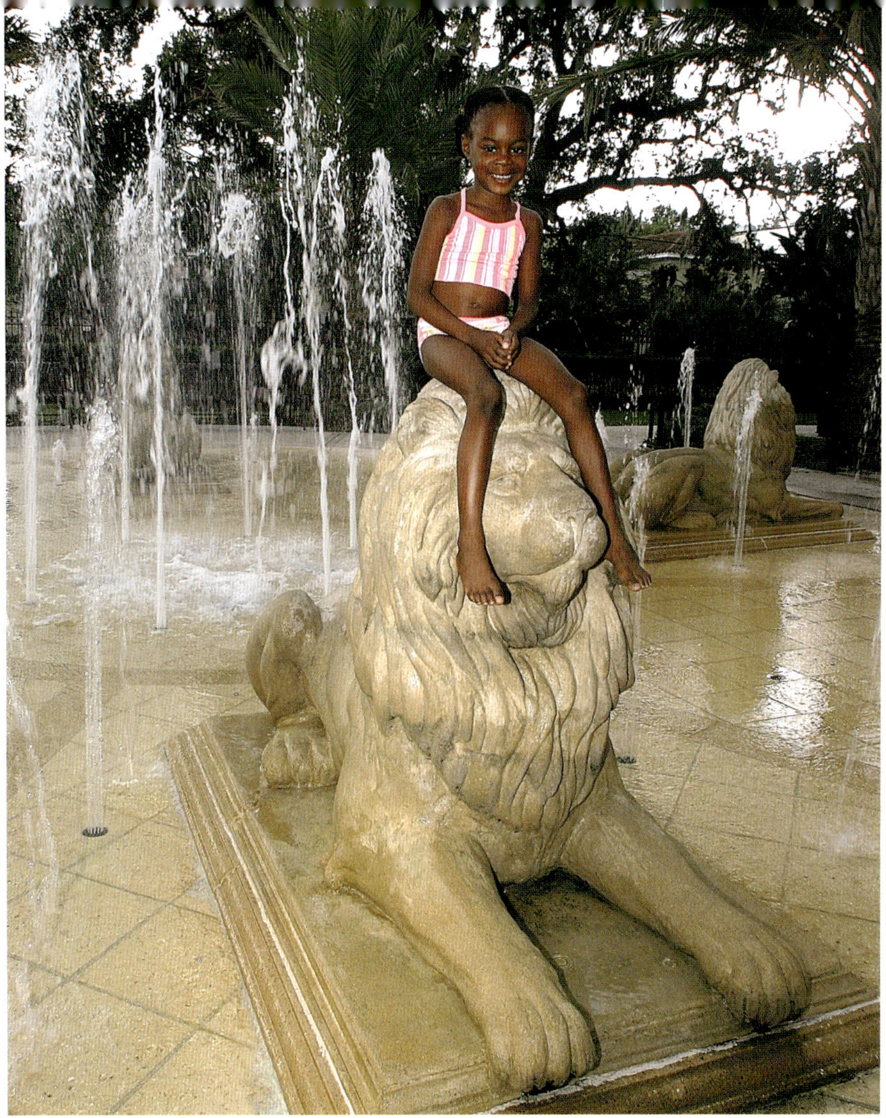

Hyde Park is more than a great place to grab lunch or a concert by the fountain; it is also a favorite with the city's youngest residents. This local girl is enjoying the Kate Jackson Center playground on Rome Avenue.
Photo by Ron Williams.

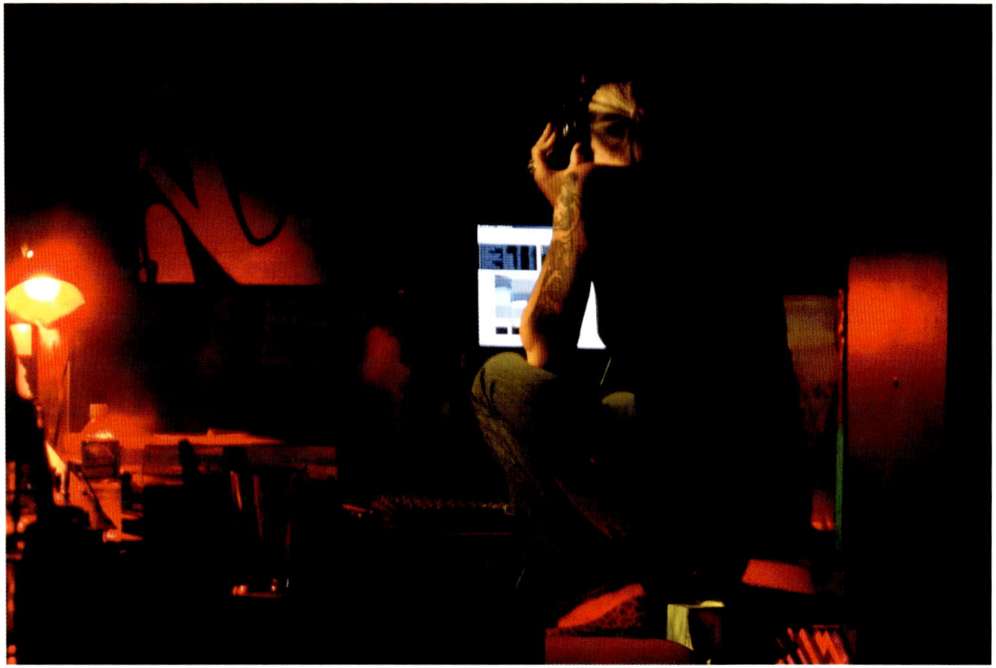

I am the DJ. One of the all-electro DJs in the Red Room at Czar nightclub in Ybor City.
Photo by Sean Birdsell.

Home to Tampa's only maritime reading room, the Port Tampa City Library is a historic treasure that enjoys wide community support.
Photo by Ron Williams.

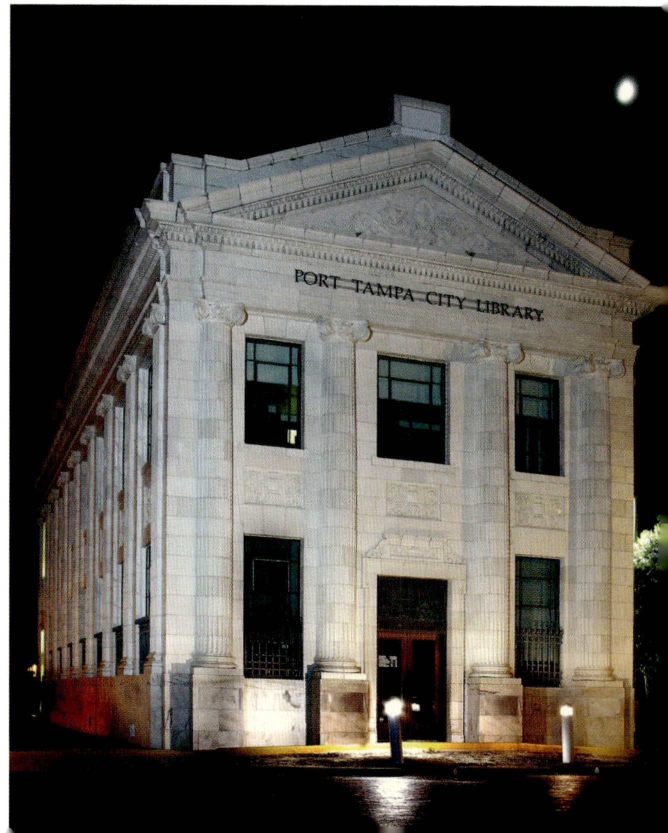

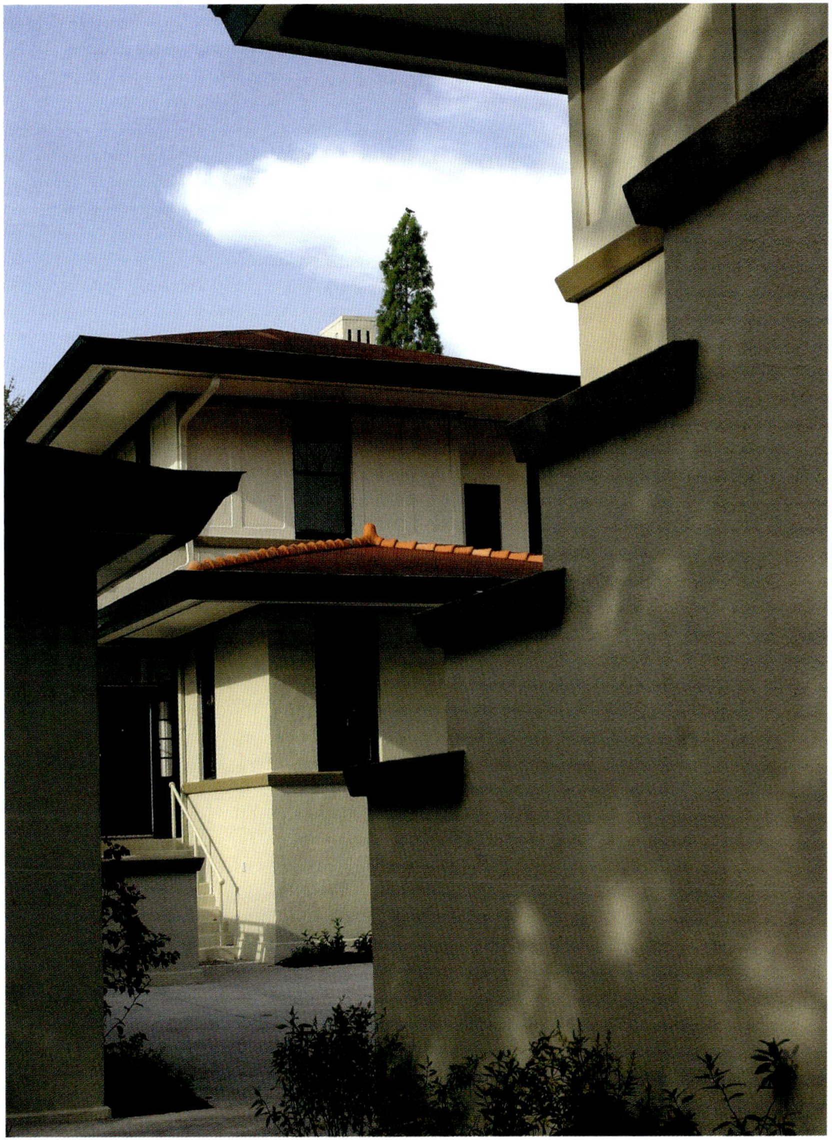

Art meets style in this Hyde Park home designed by students of Frank Lloyd Wright. Tampa residents enjoy unique architectural designs in quiet neighborhoods near the water.

Photo by Ron Williams.

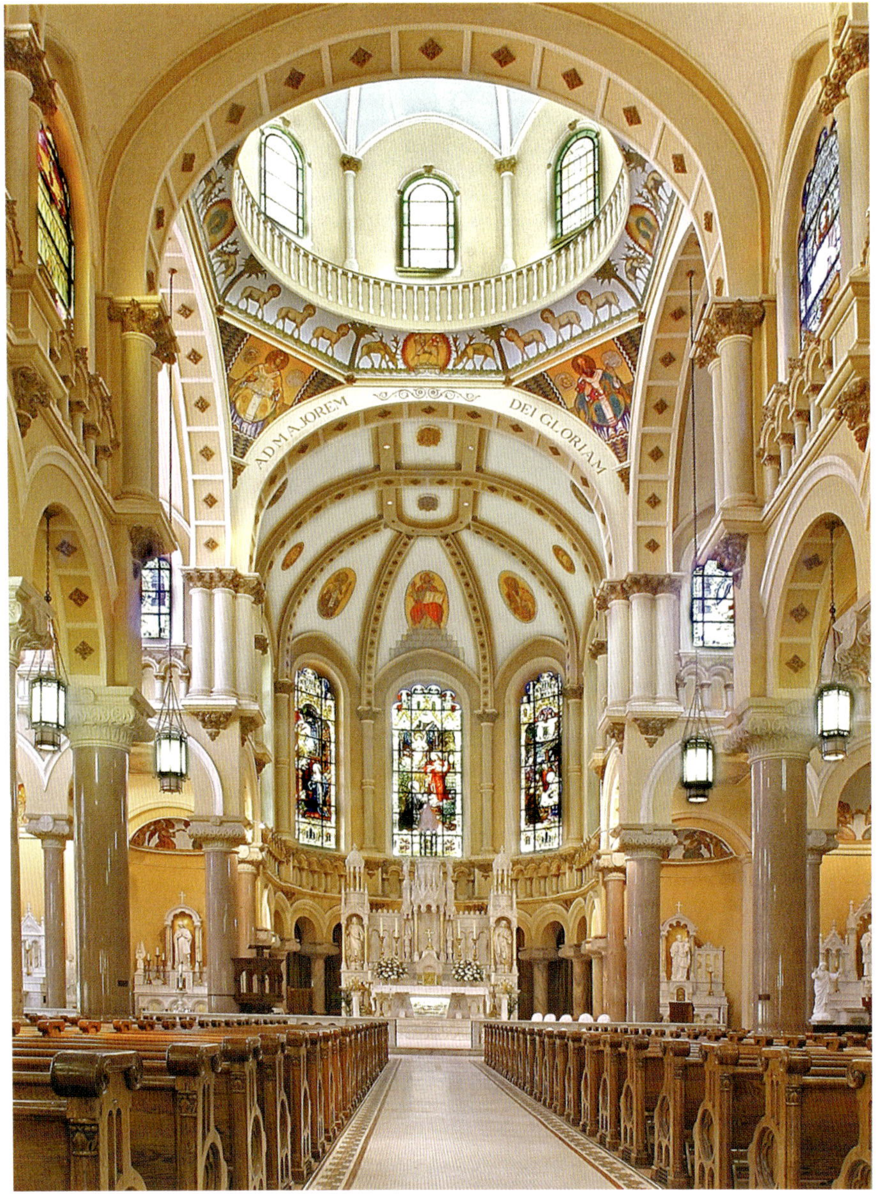

Dedicated in 1905, the Sacred Heart building has maintained its historical charm for more than 100 years. The current parish serves at least 1,400 families spread across the Tampa Bay area.
Photo by Ron Williams.

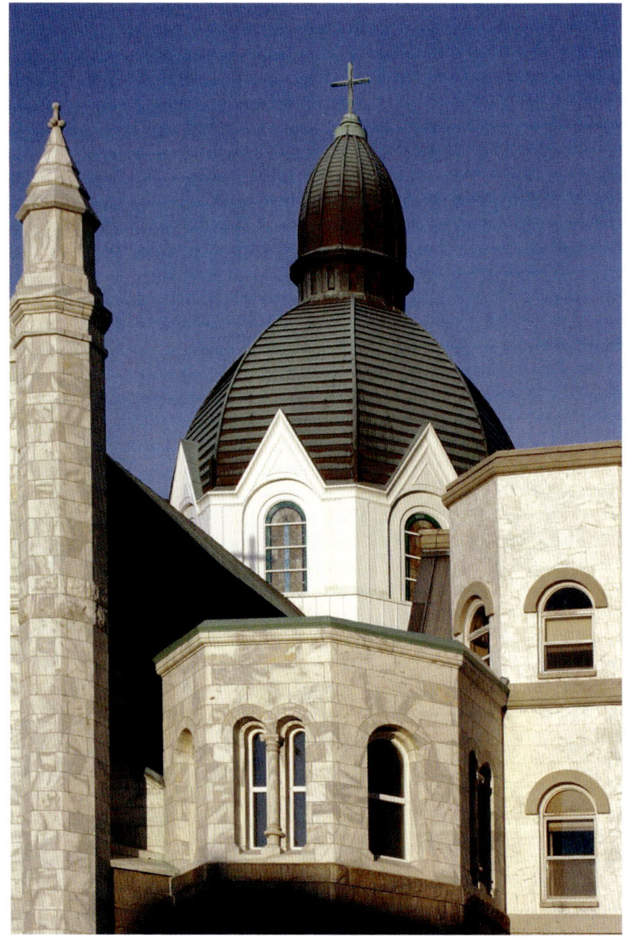

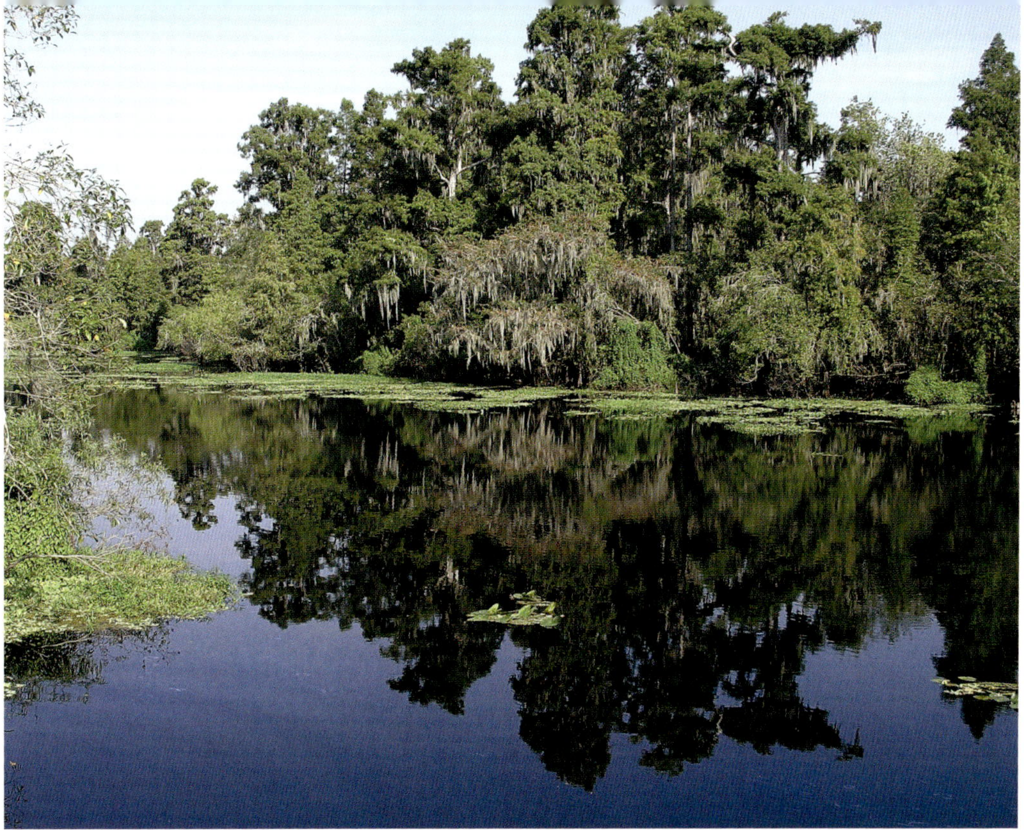

Tampa is home to more than 140 parks that are well suited for hiking, fishing, and camping. Lettuce Lake Park is particularly well known for its scenic pine flatwoods, sprawling cypress swamps, and extensive boardwalk.
Photos by Ron Williams.

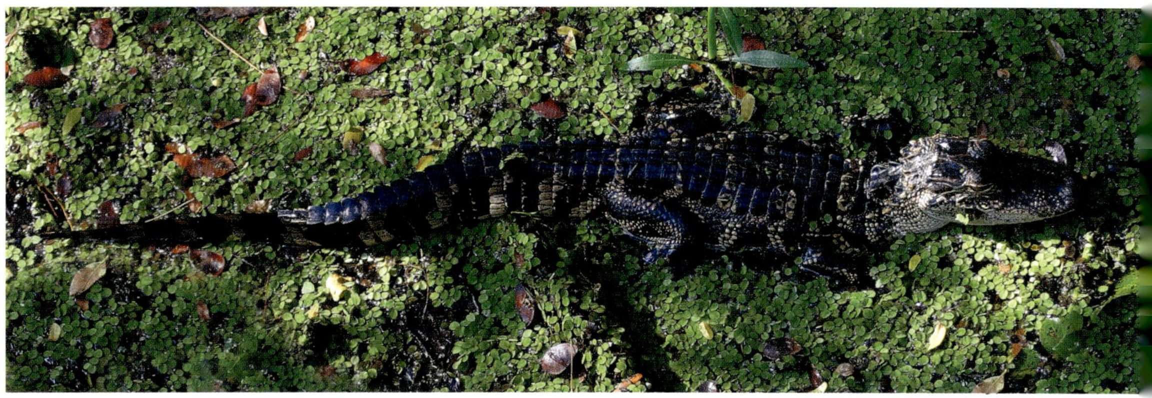

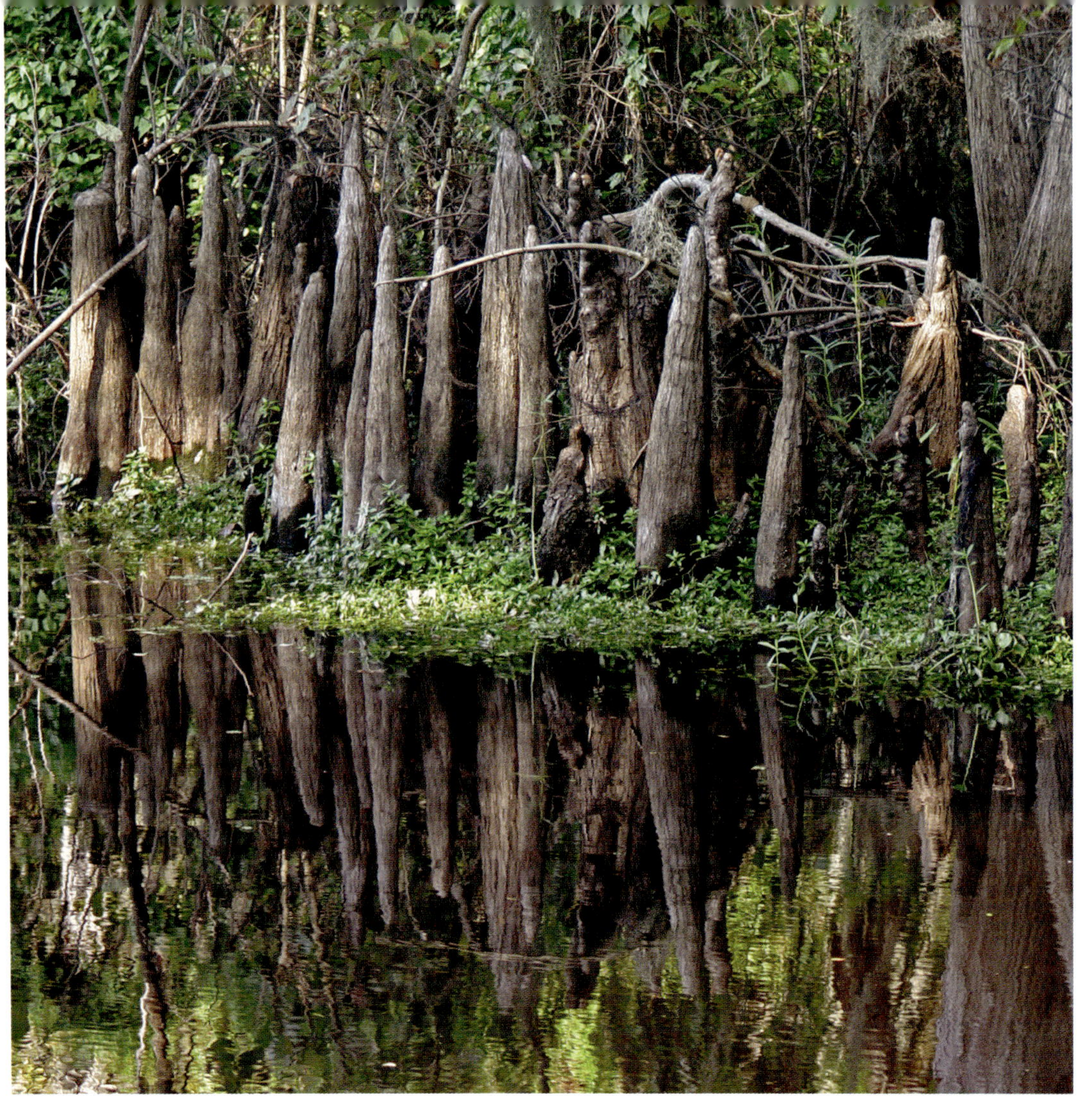

Cypress knees emerge from the water in one of Flatwoods Wilderness Park's scenic trails. Such sights are common to North Tampa along bike paths and horseback riding trails.
Photo by Ron Williams.

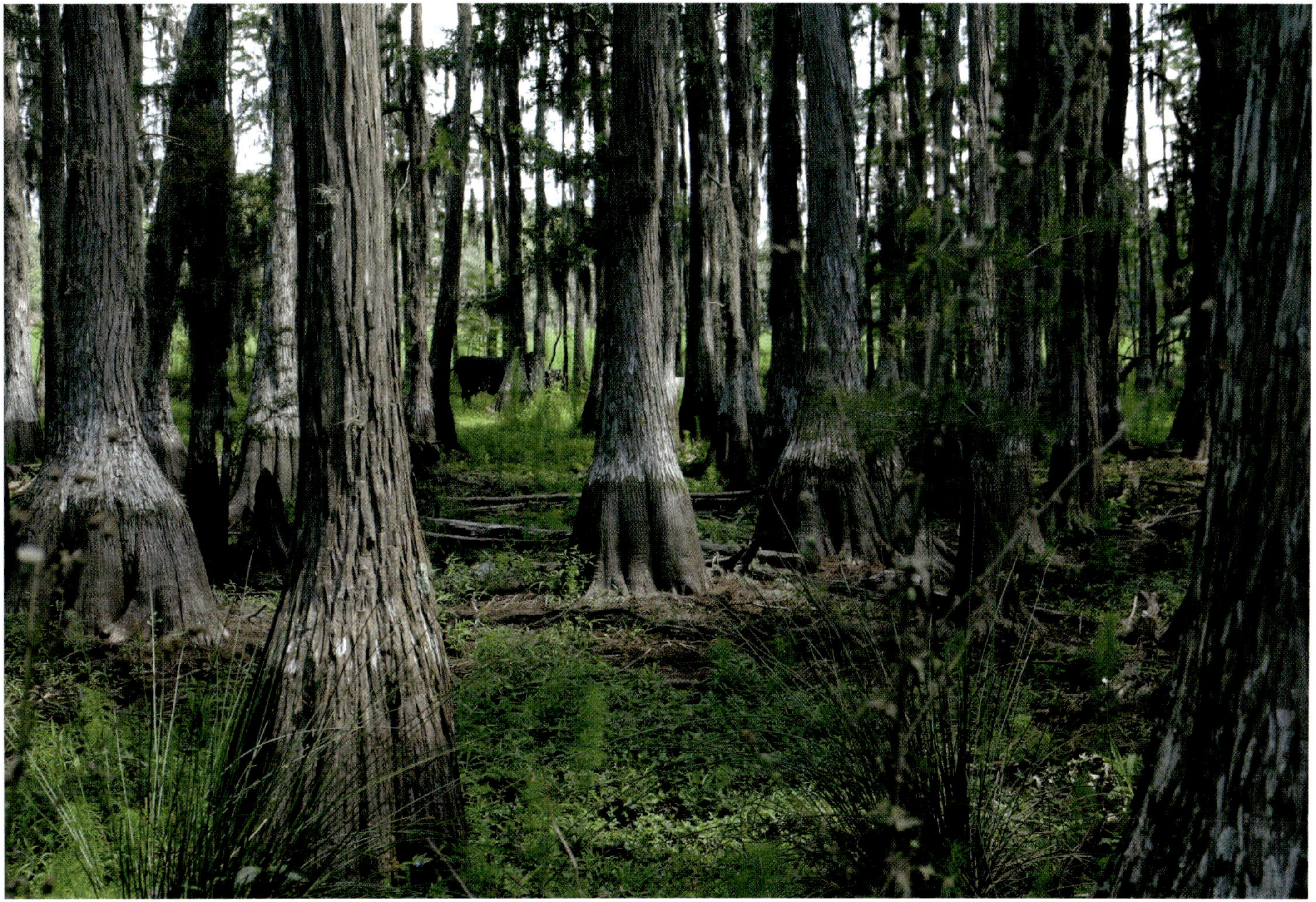

North Tampa is home to rolling hills, scattered lakes, and cattle ranches. Here, one cow is found in North Tampa's scenic woods.
Photo by Ron Williams.

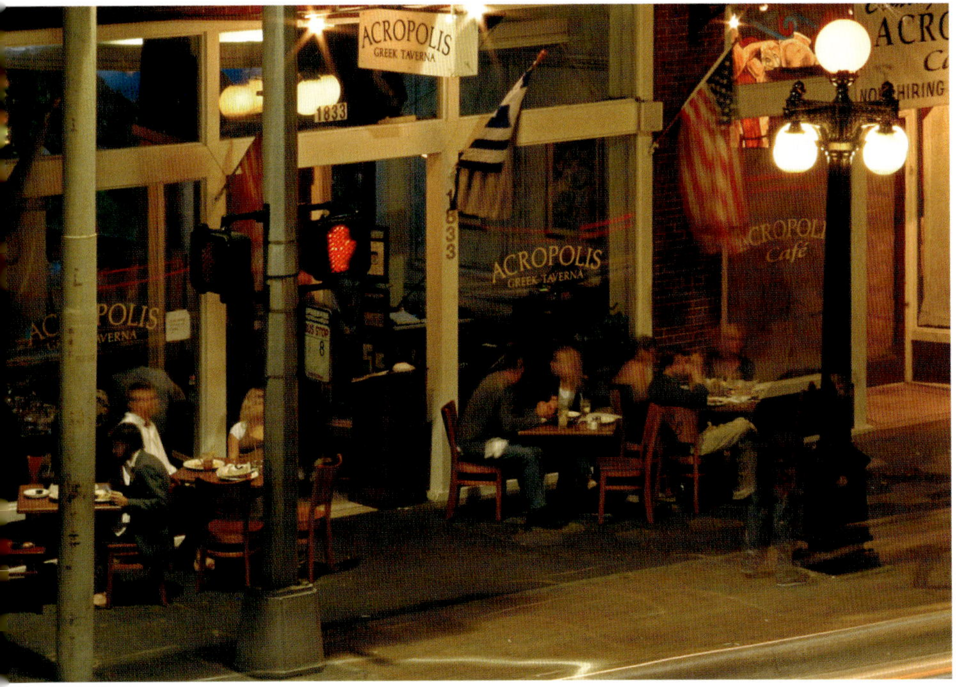

Diners enjoy an evening at Ybor City's Acropolis, complete with traditional music, plate breaking, and belly dancing. Ybor City lights up at night with restaurants, shops, and clubs dotting its pedestrian-friendly avenues.

Photos by Ron Williams.

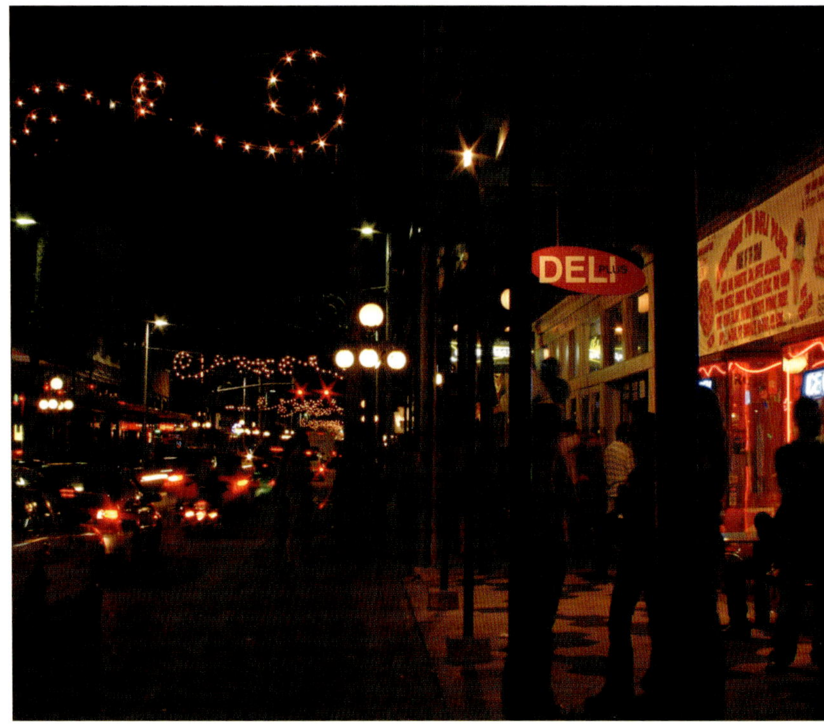

Ybor City is a vital part of our history—not just locally but nationally. Ybor was at the center of world events during the turn of the twentieth century, playing a key role in the Cuban independence movement and the Spanish American War. Ybor is a unique place, historically, architecturally, and culturally.

Manny Leto, Cigar City Magazine

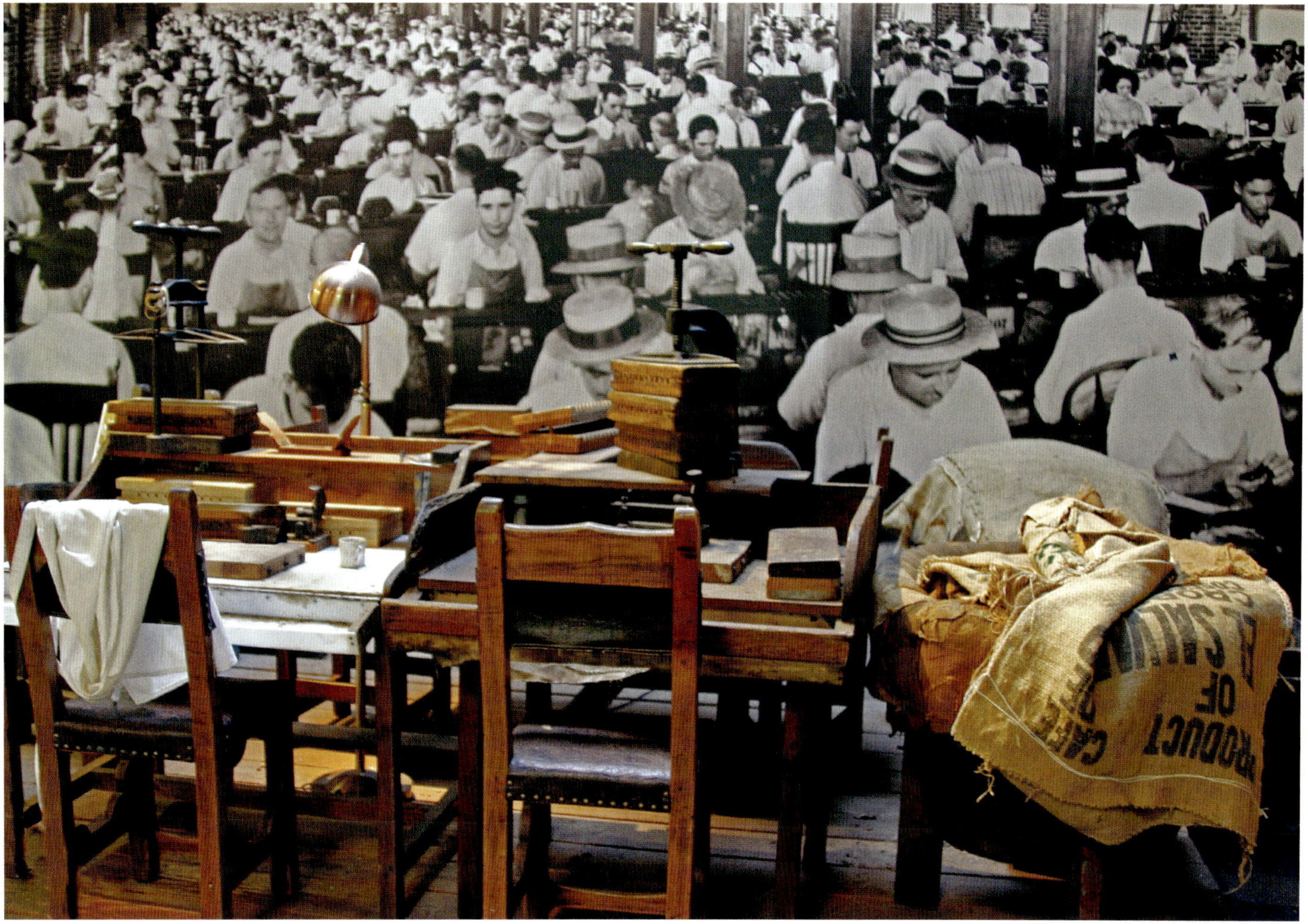

Ybor honors its long history and its proud Cuban heritage. This early photograph of Tampa's cigar workers is positioned behind the work station of a modern cigar roller.
Photo by Ron Williams.

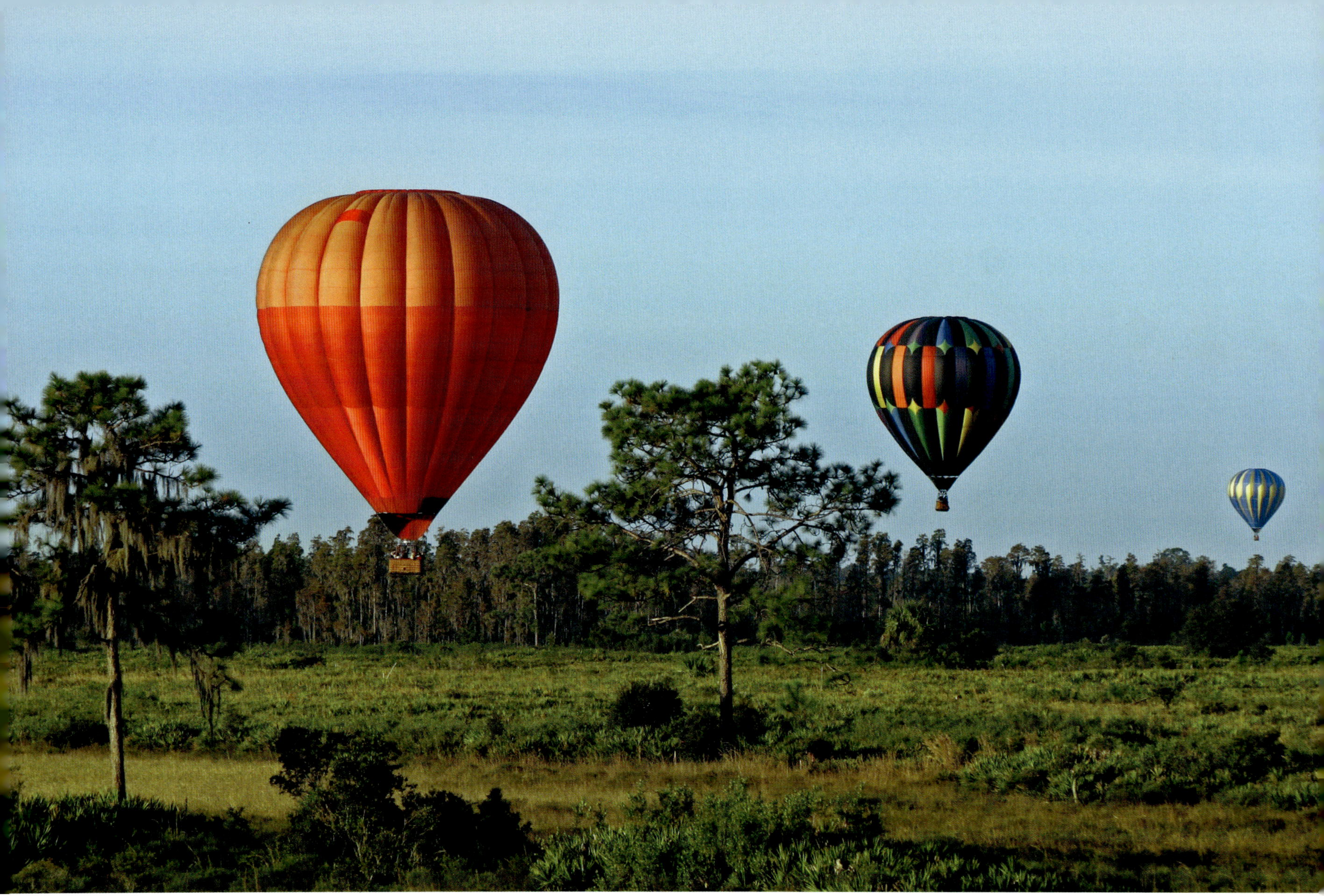

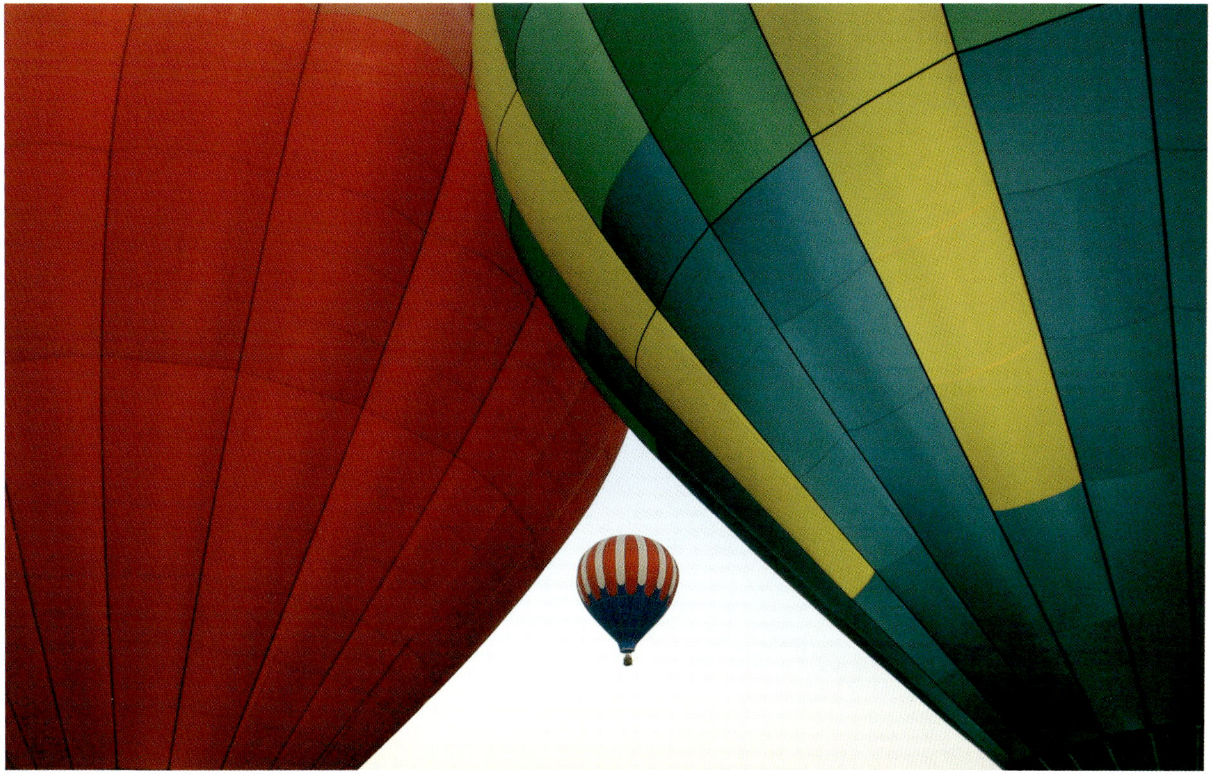

Hot-air balloons depart just after sunrise. Flying from treetop to 1,000 feet high, they offer passengers a breathtaking view of the Tampa skyline, Tampa Bay, and often the Gulf of Mexico.

Photos by Ron Williams.

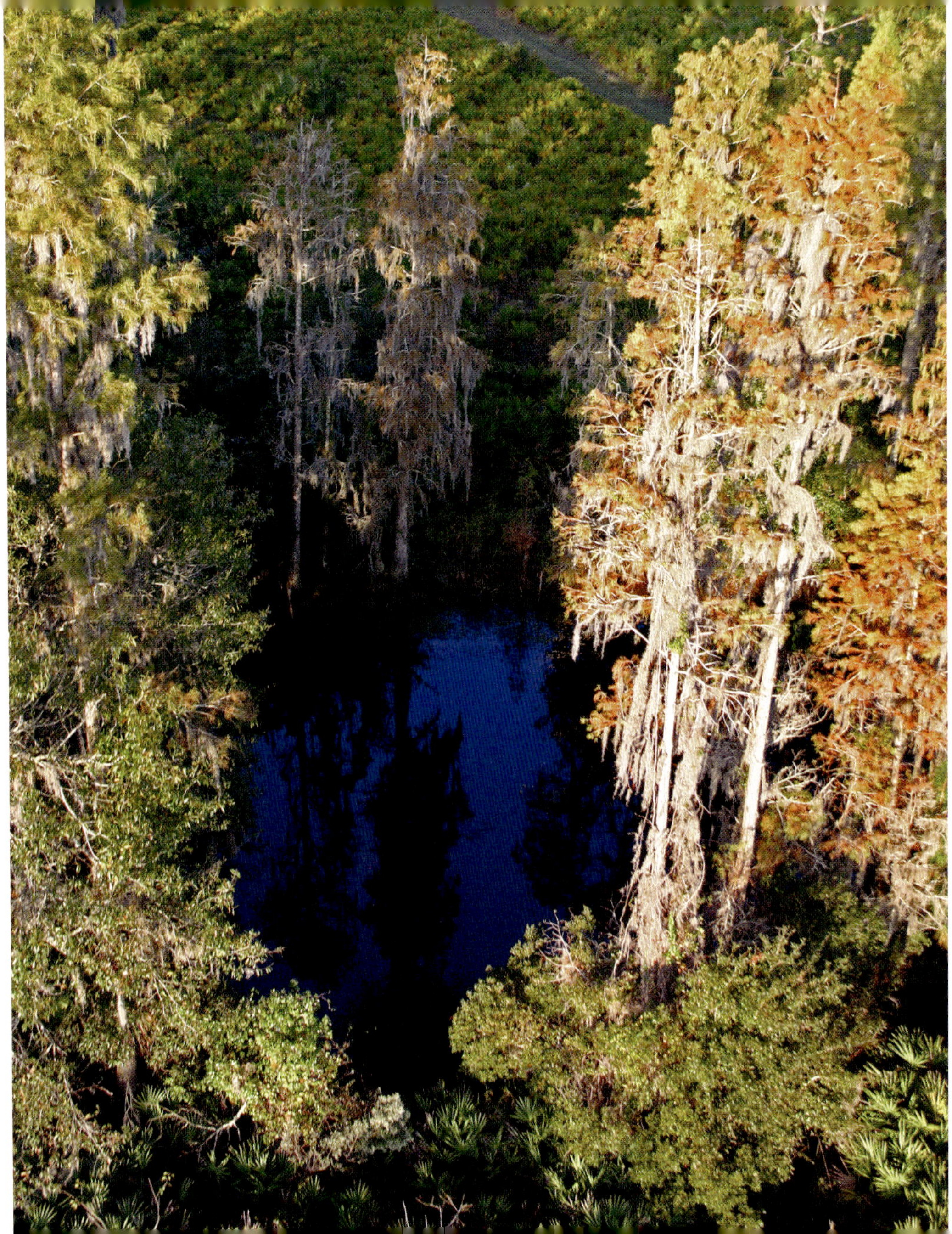

Below a hot-air balloon, tall cypress trees delicately laced with Spanish moss cast their reflections on picturesque lakes.
Photo by Ron Williams.

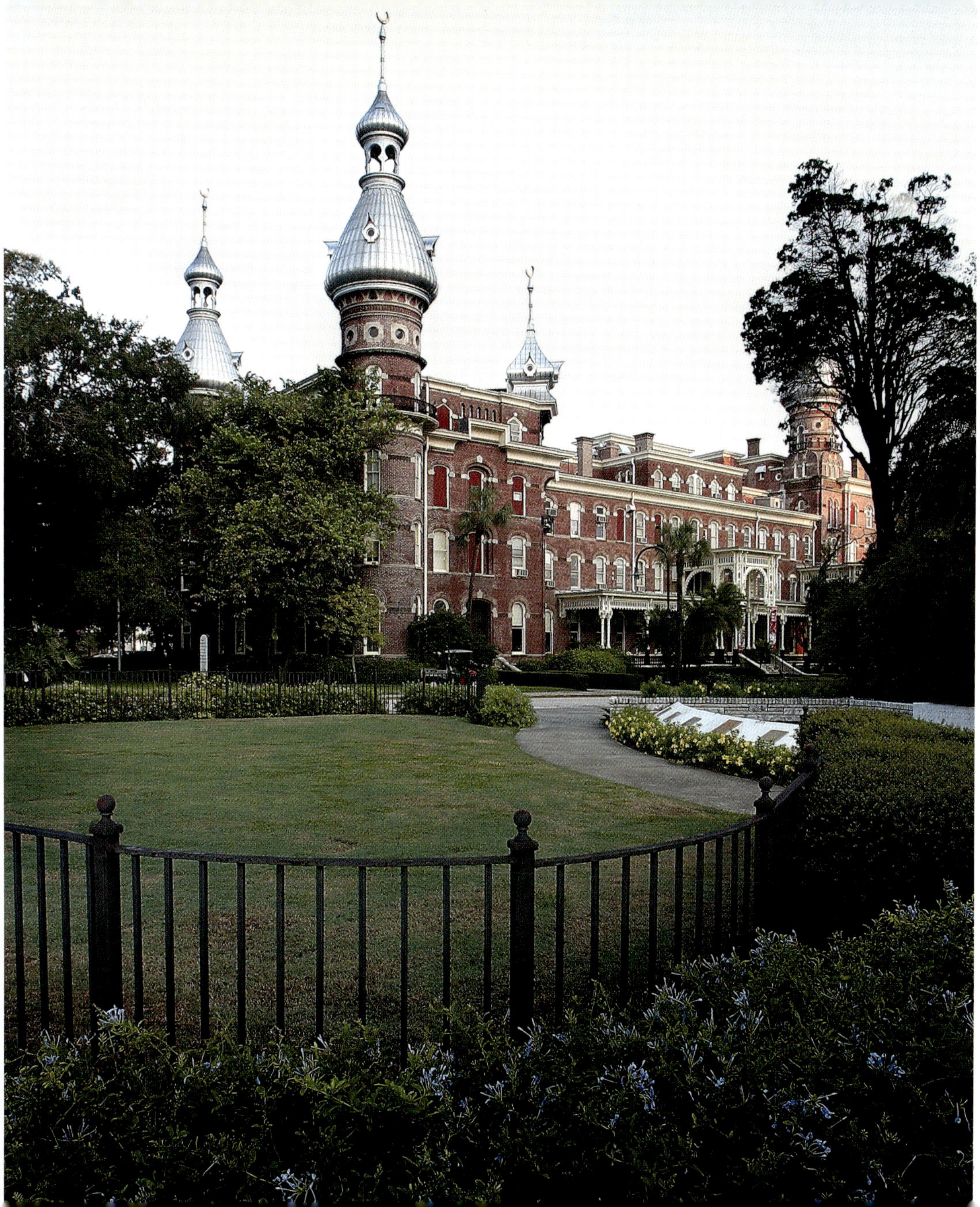

Formerly the Tampa Bay Hotel, Plant Hall stands as the academic and administrative center of the University of Tampa.
Photo by Ron Williams.

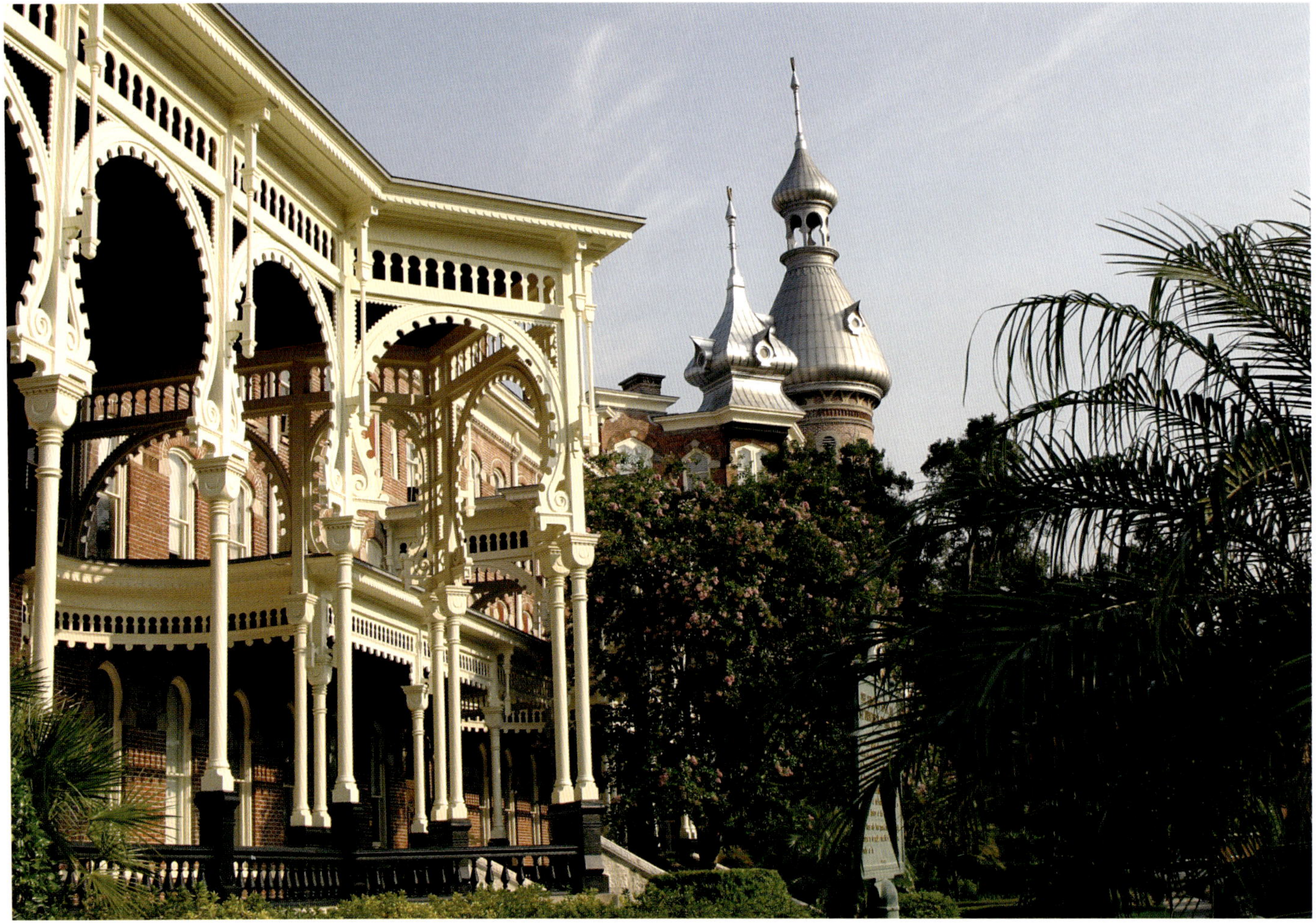

U.S. News & World Report ranks the University of Tampa as one of America's best colleges.
Photo by Ron Williams.

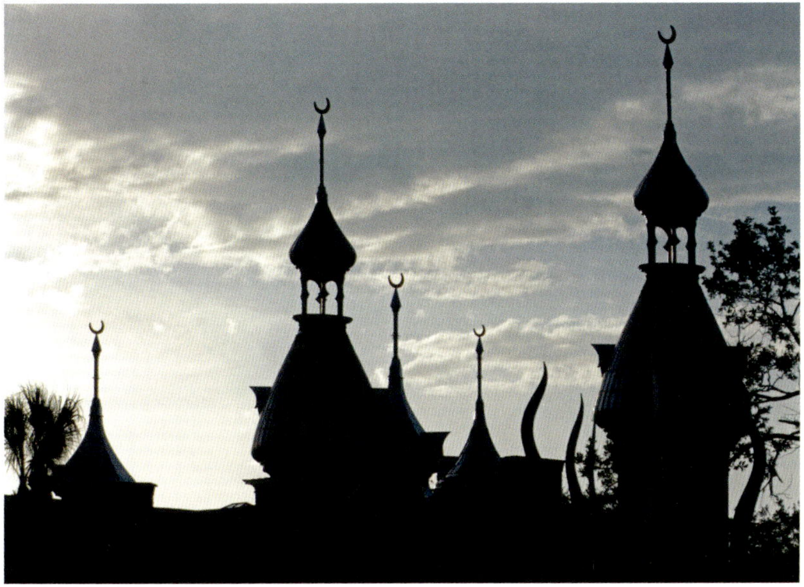

The University of Tampa spires have become a familiar icon of one of the oldest buildings in the city.
Photo by Ron Williams.

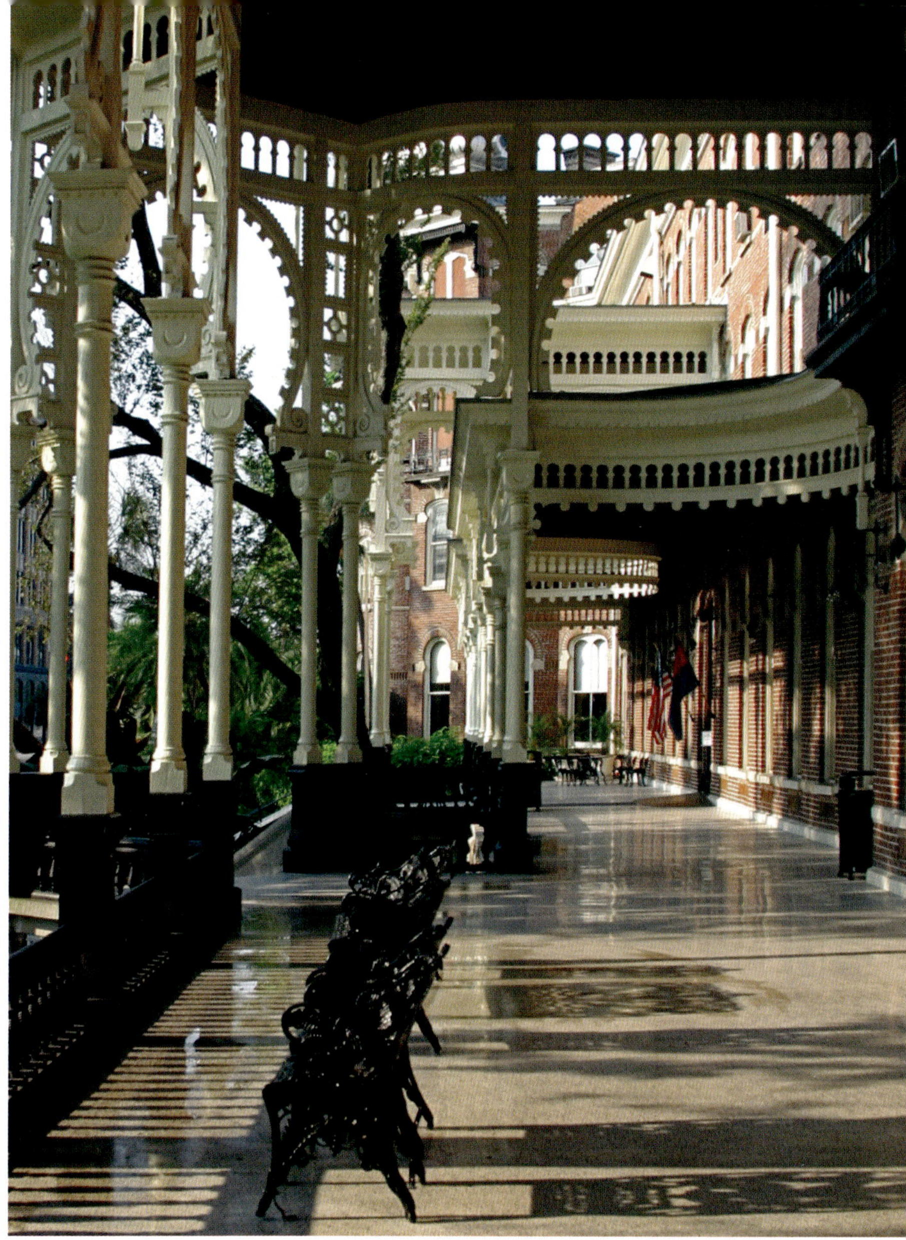

Outdoor corridor at the University of Tampa.
Photo by Ron Williams.

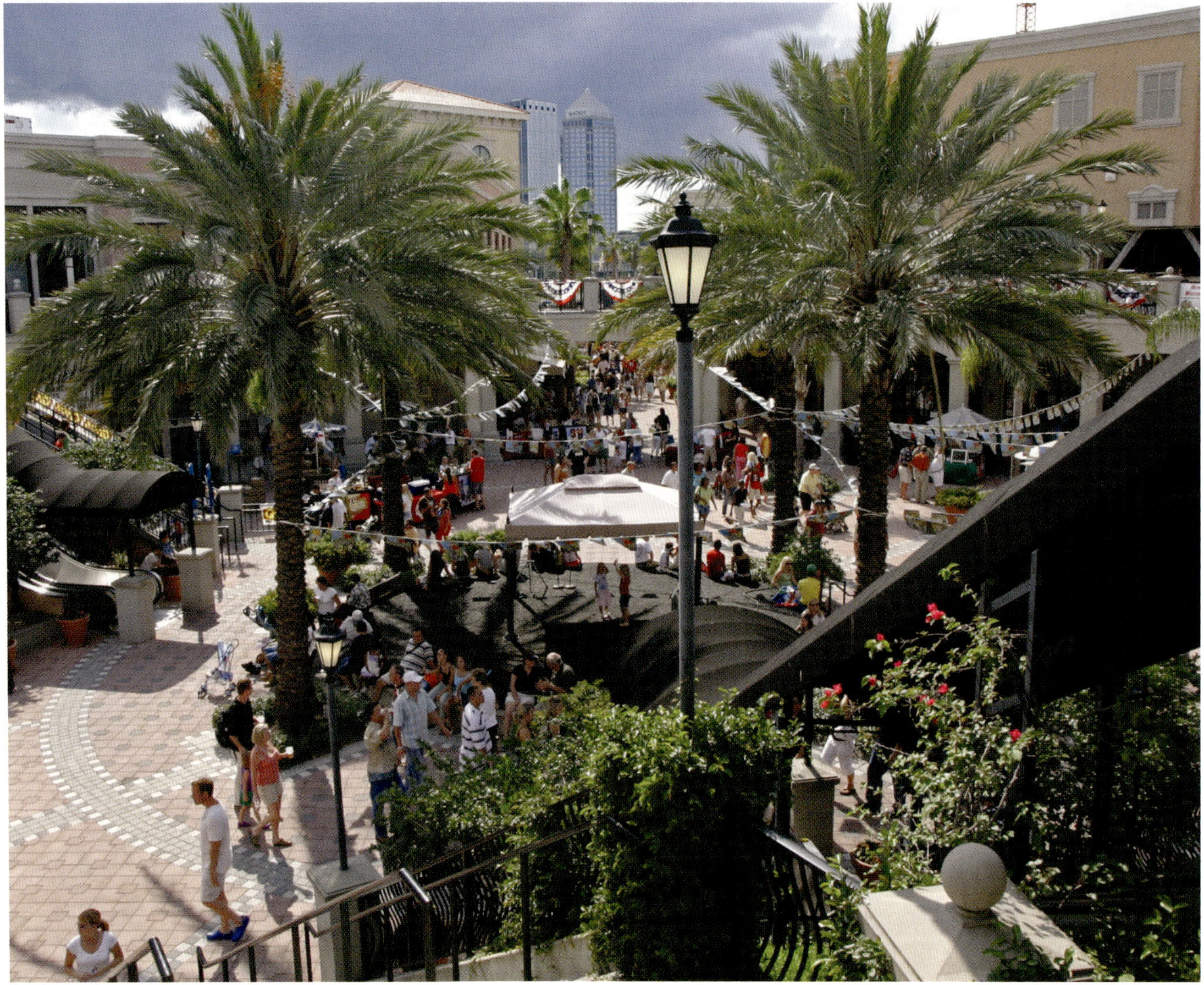

A view of Channelside on an active afternoon.
Photo by Ron Williams.

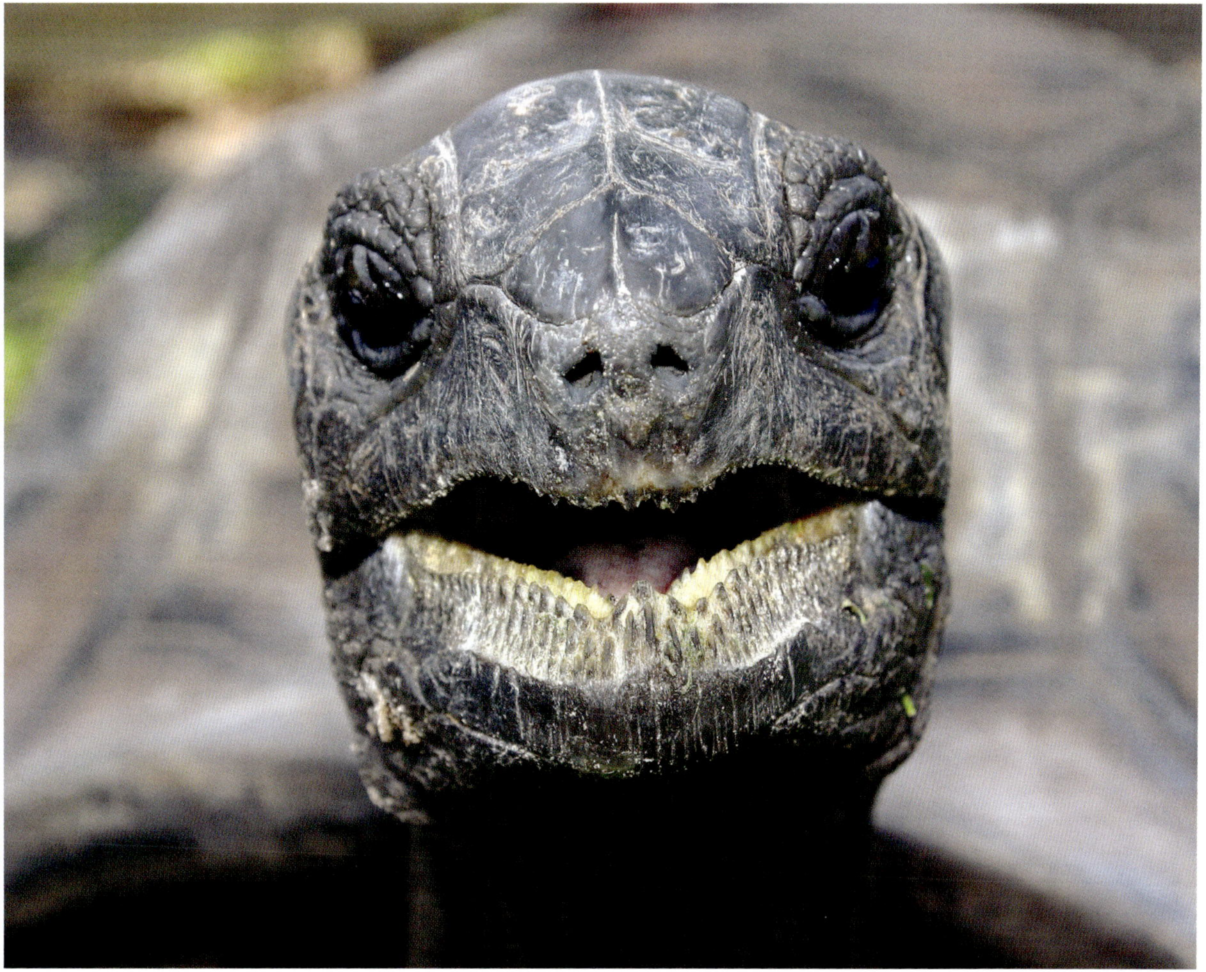

One of Lowry Park Zoo's most famous residents smiles for the camera. Tampa's zoo is recognized by the State of Florida as a center for Florida wildlife conservation and biodiversity.
Photo by Ron Williams.

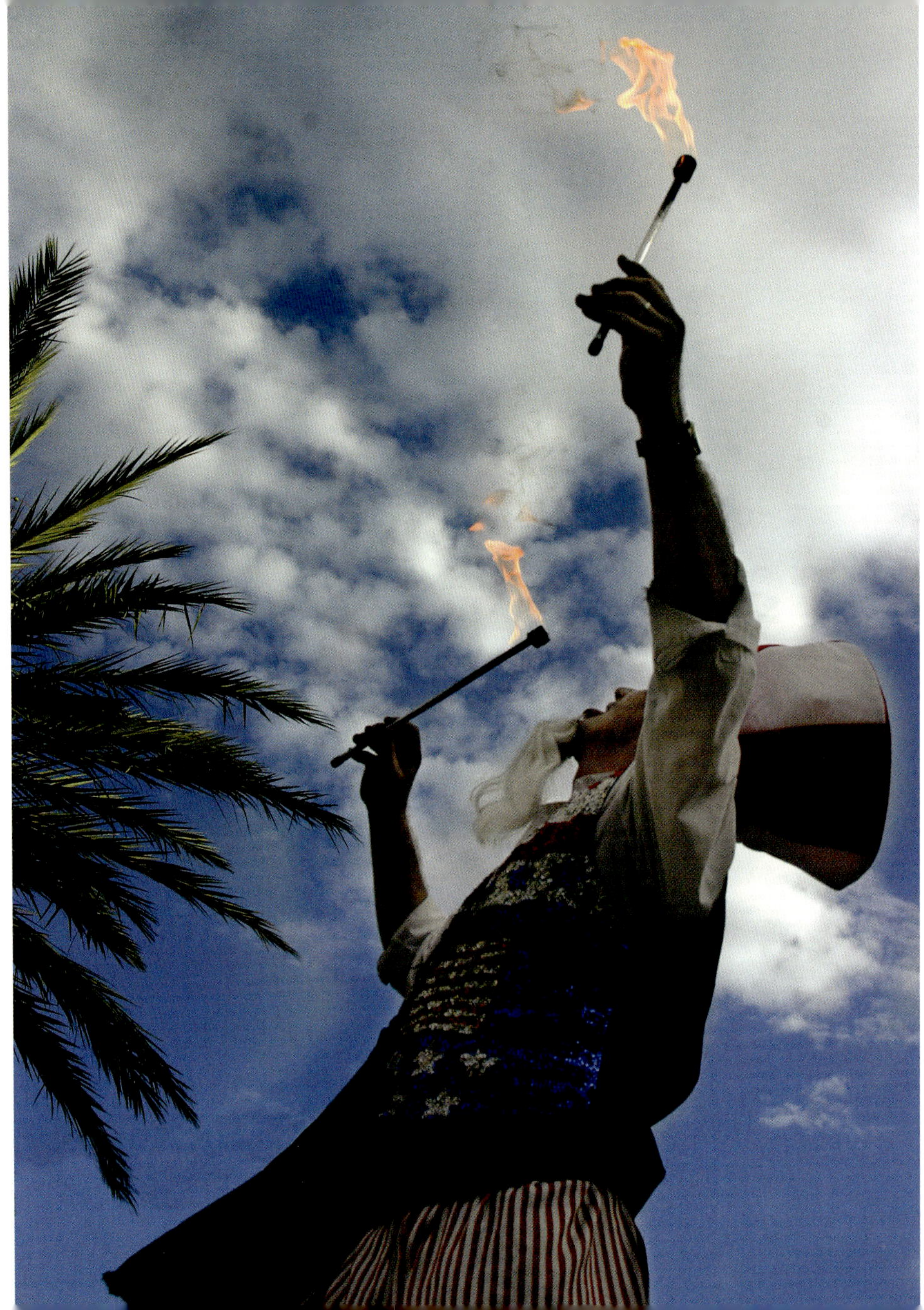

A fire-breathing Uncle Sam pays a visit to Channelside on the Fourth of July.
Photo by Ron Williams.

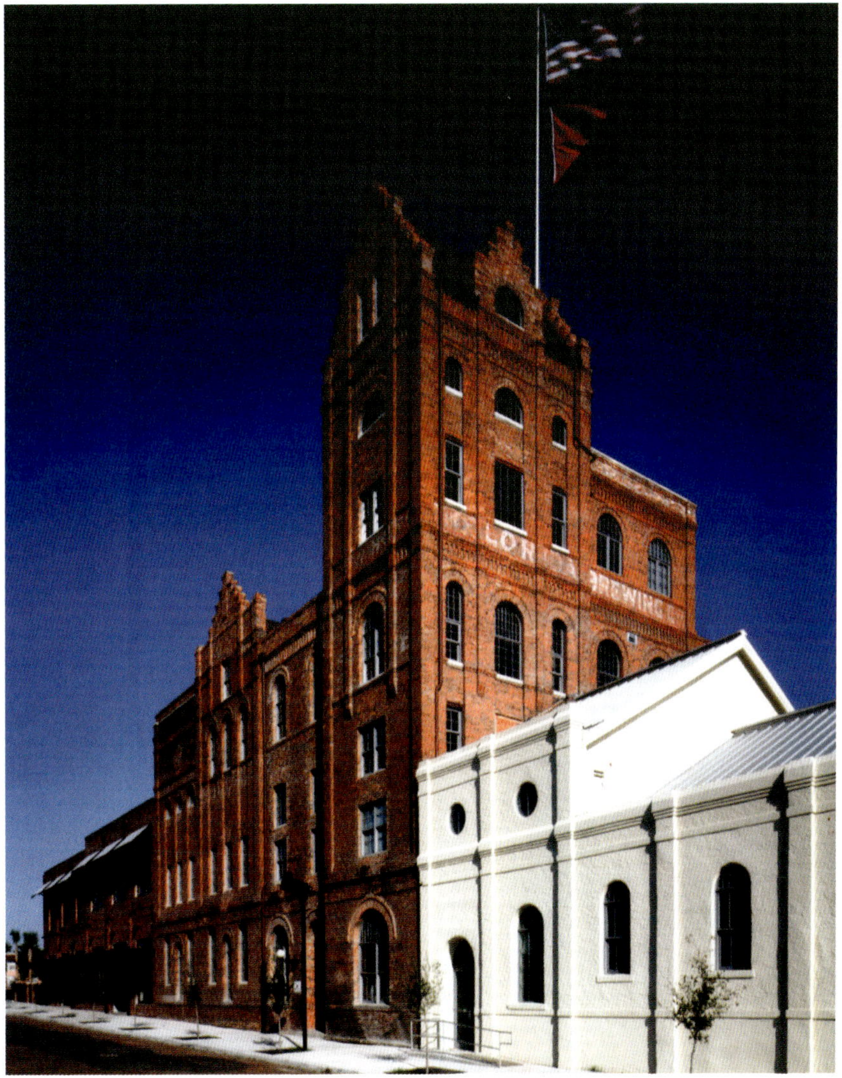

Swope Law Group has worked hard to restore the Tampa Florida Brewery. Today, lawyers not only enjoy a stylishly modern workspace in a historic gem, but they get a little extra company. Employees tell tales of a drunk but jolly ghost who haunts the old laboratory, laughing and muttering late at night.

Photo by George Cott/Chroma Ink. Image provided by Swope, Rodante P.A.

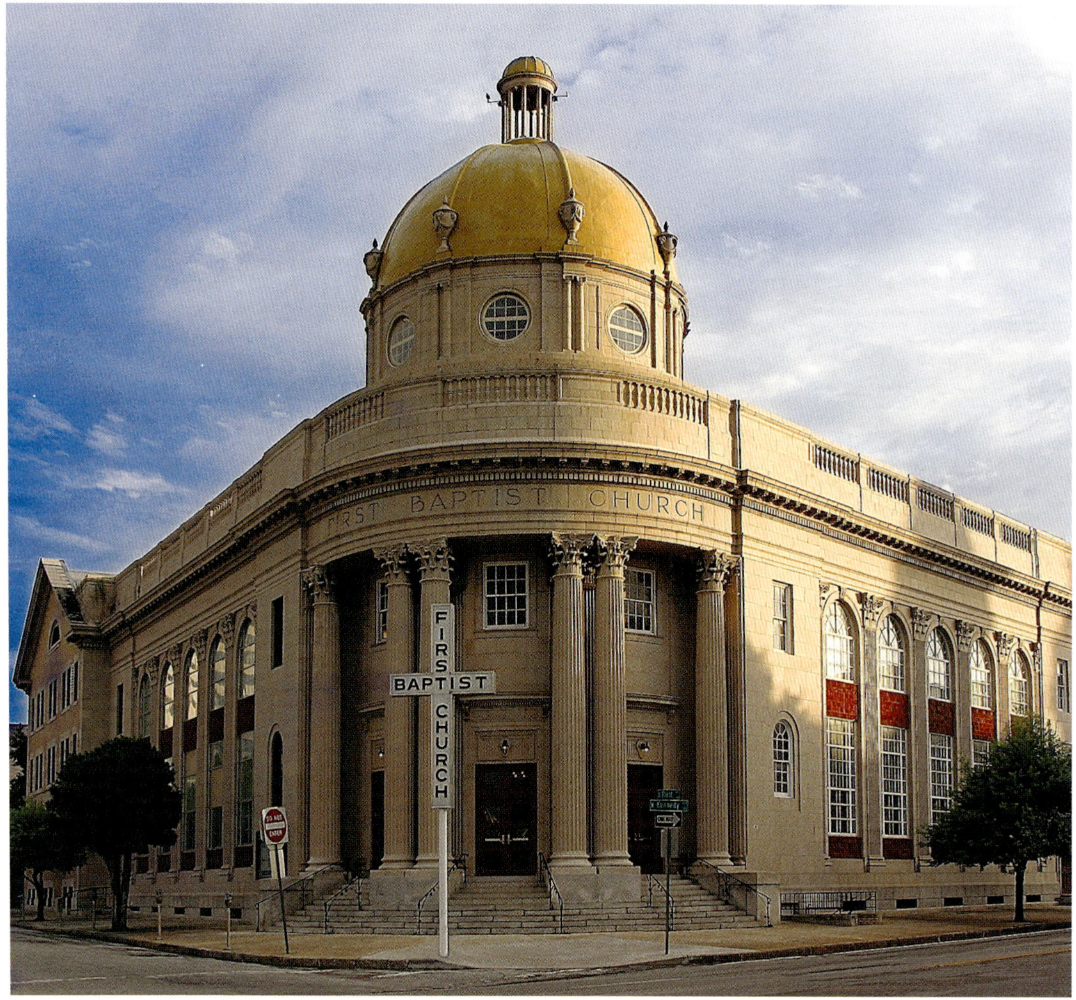

Tampa's active religious community offers spiritual guidance to a diverse population from all parts of the globe. The First Baptist Church of Tampa has served the Tampa community since 1859.
Photo by Ron Williams.

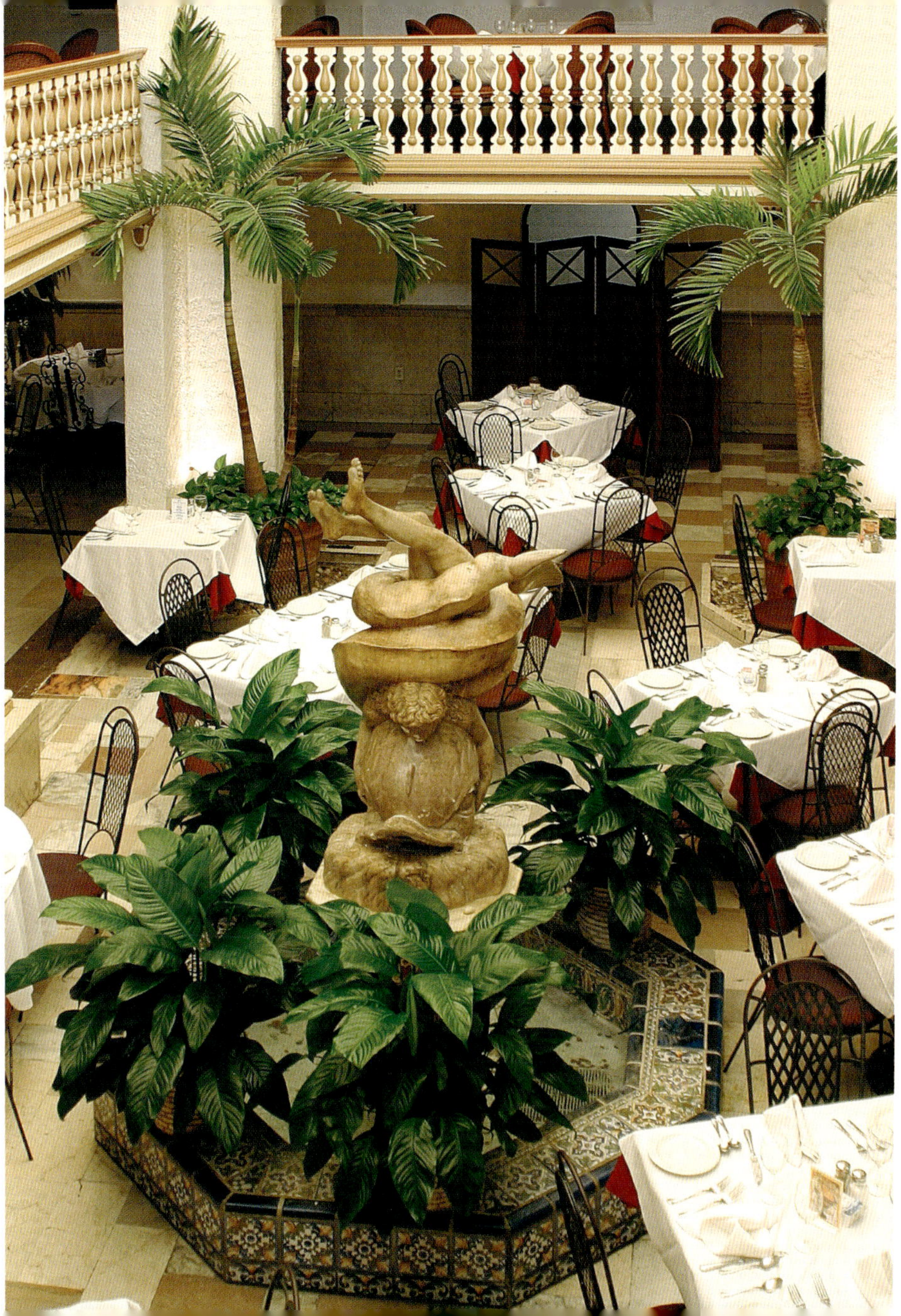

The legendary Columbia Restaurant, located in Ybor City, has earned the Distinguished Restaurants of North America Award of Excellence. Opened in 1905, the Columbia is Florida's oldest restaurant and the largest Spanish restaurant in the world.
Photo by Ron Williams.

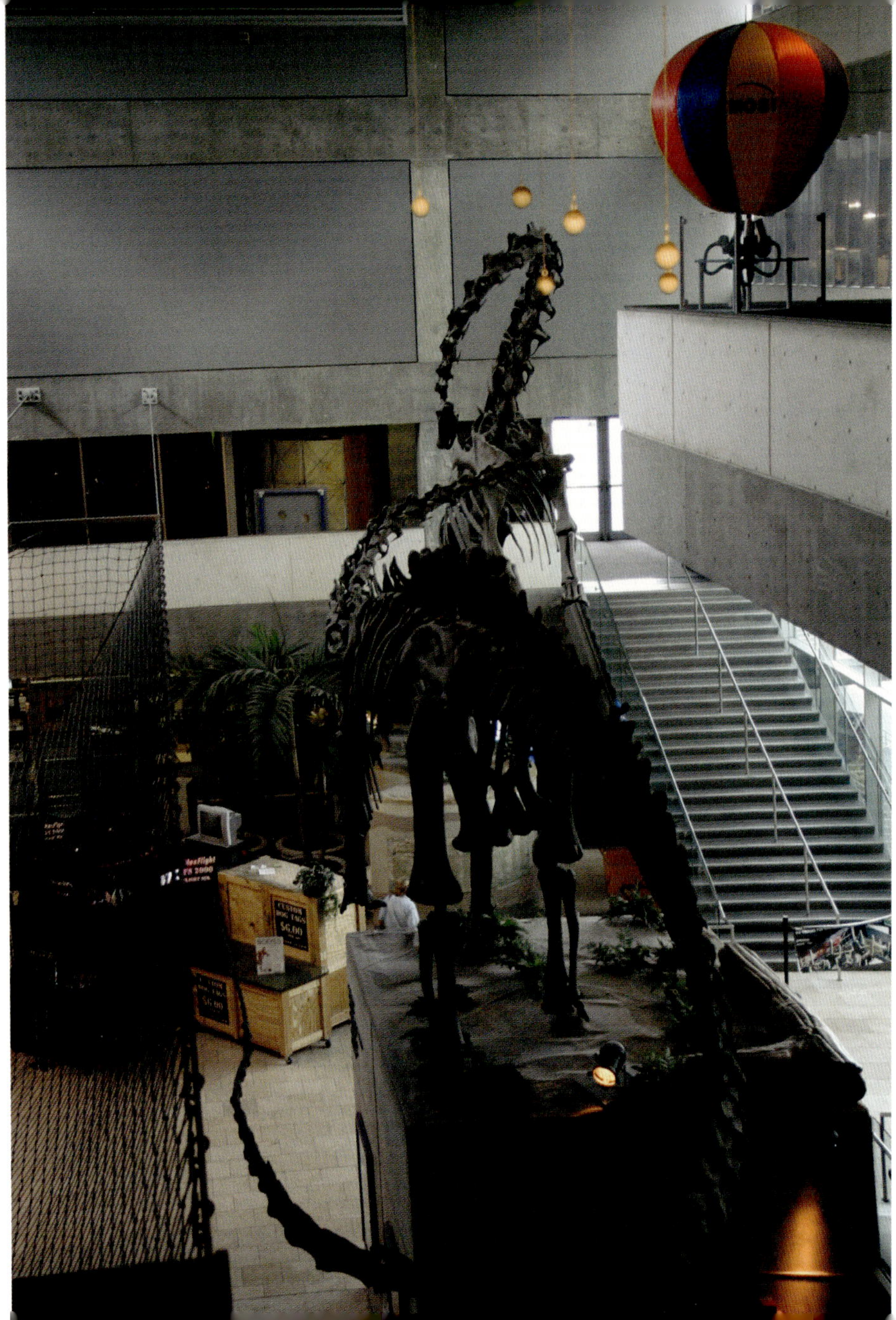

Dinosaur bones on display at the Museum of Science and Industry.
Photo by Ron Williams.

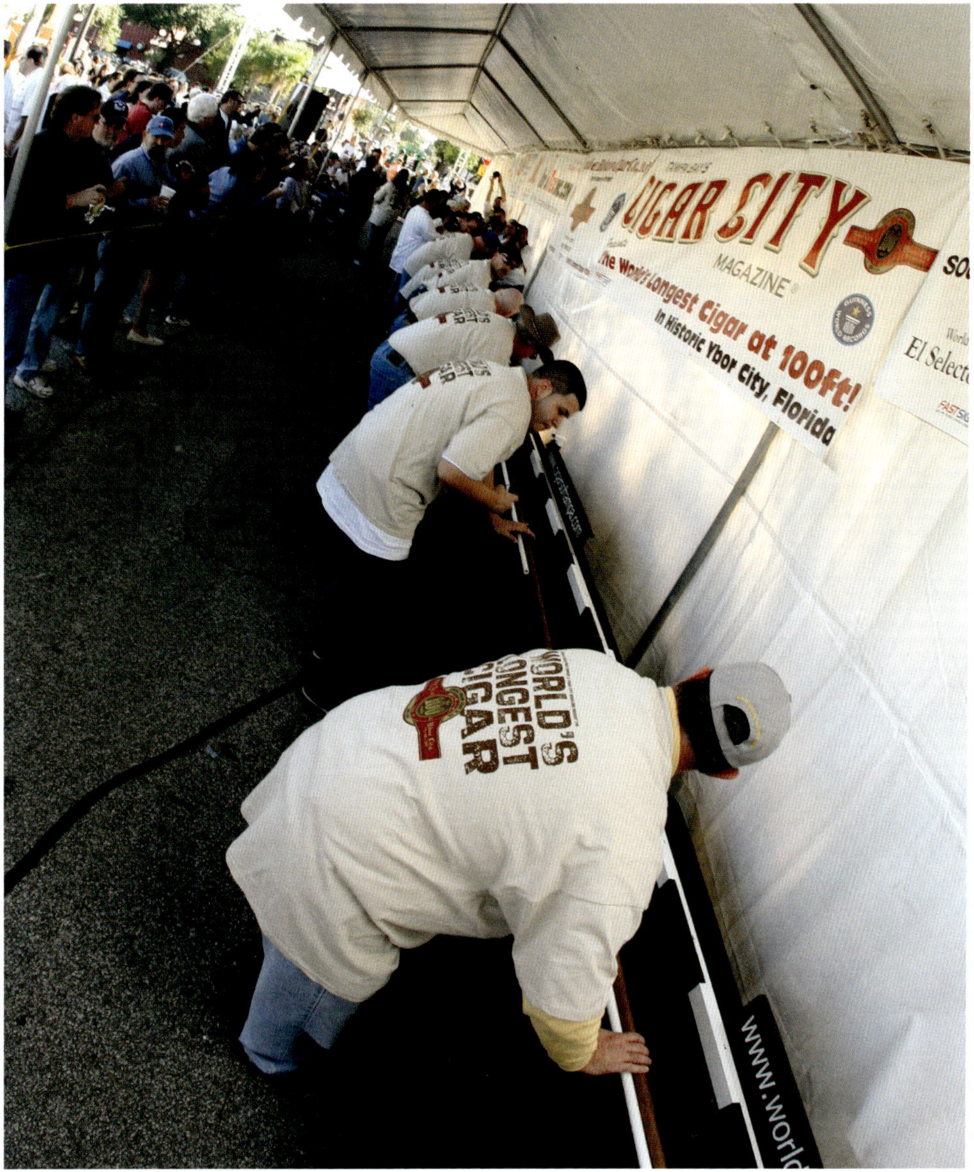

In 2006, Tampa cigar rollers rolled the longest cigar in the world. The 101-foot cigar was rolled under the tobacco license of Gonzalez Habano Cigar Co. and recorded by the *Guinness Book of World Records* at the Tampa Cigar Heritage Festival.
Photo by Ron Williams.

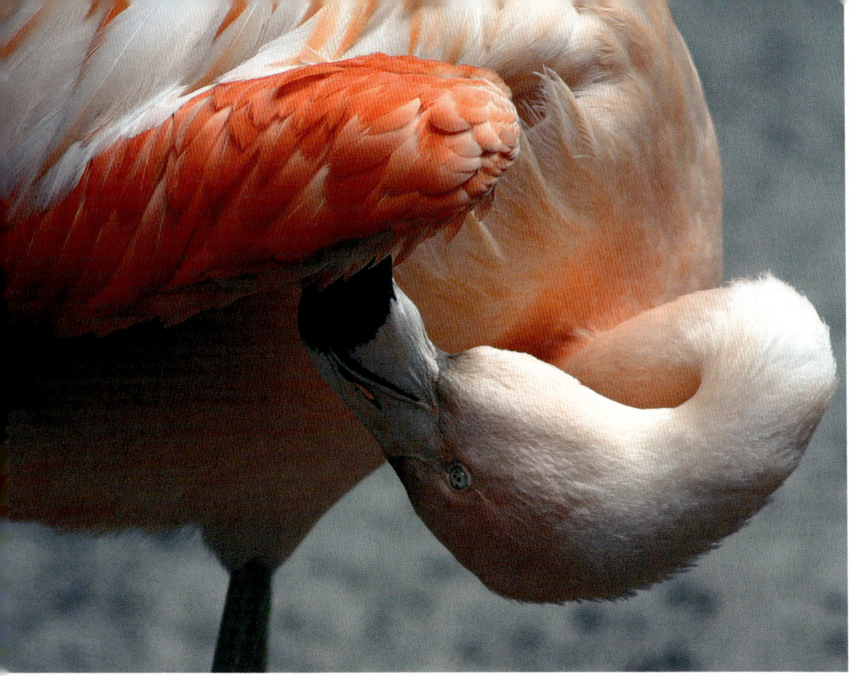

This Lowry Park flamingo is maintaining her beauty—not too surprising given the elaborate courtship these monogamous birds engage in. When trying to impress a potential mate, flamingos will march, dance, bob their heads, and twist their necks to gain attention.
Photo by Ron Williams.

Tampa Bay's maze of mangroves, salt marshes, and mudflats attract more than 125 species of birds each year.
Photo by Ron Williams.

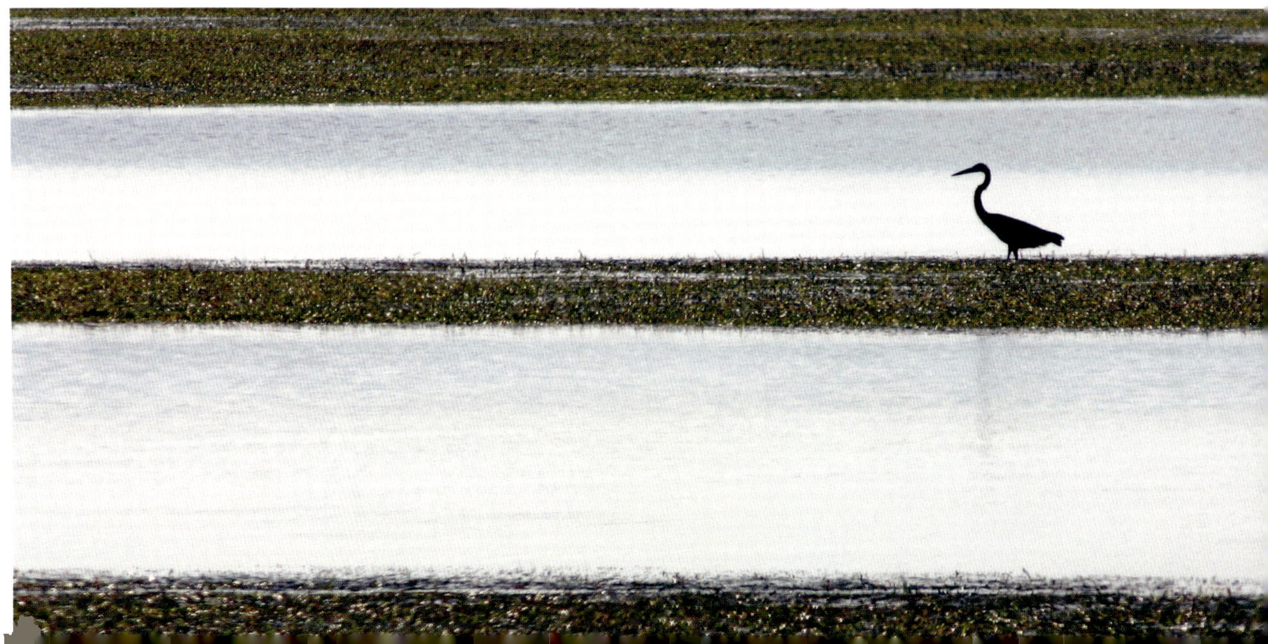

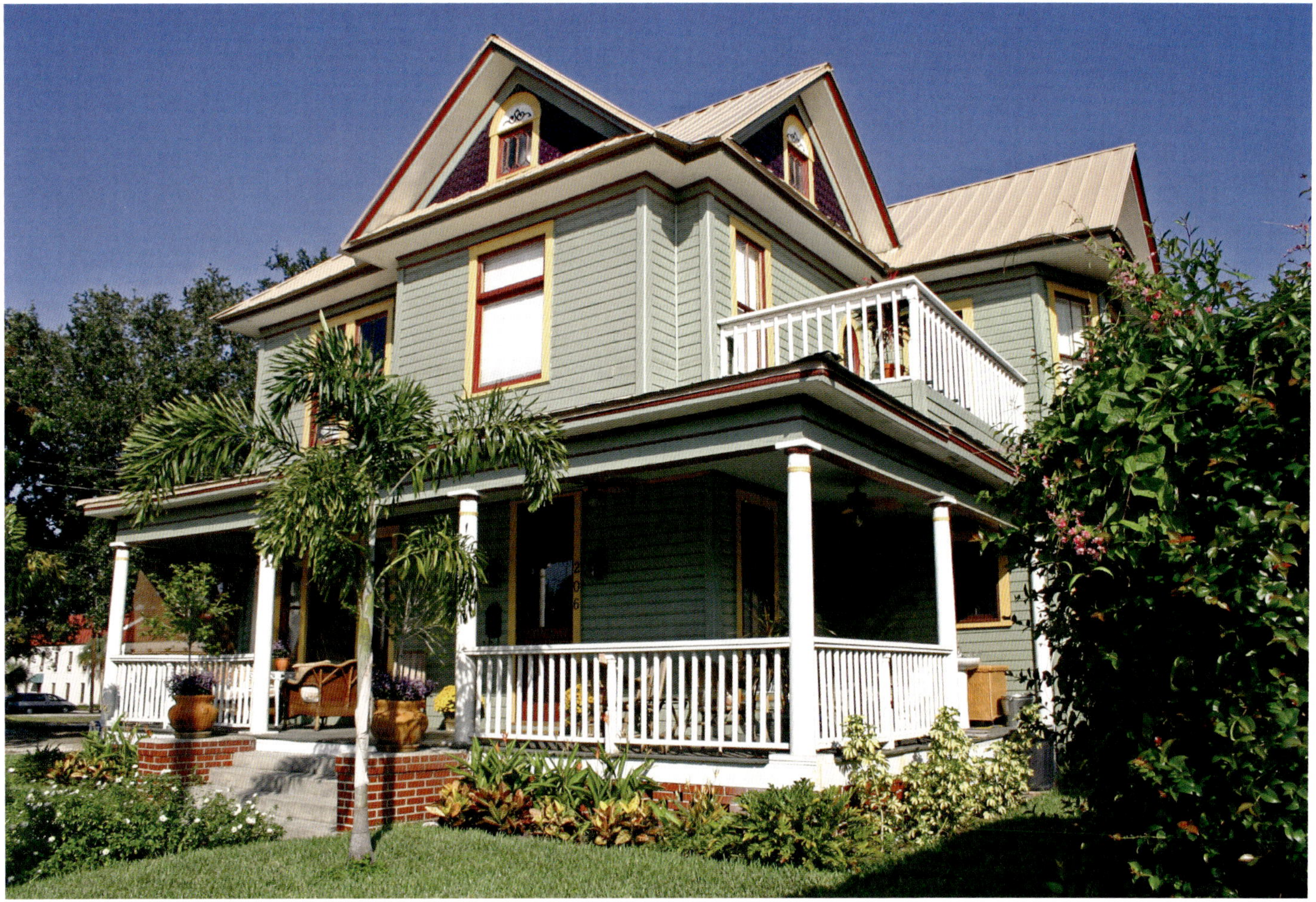

David Purnell and Steve Johns are two of many Tampa Heights residents who have restored charming Victorian homes to their former glory.
Photo by Ron Williams.

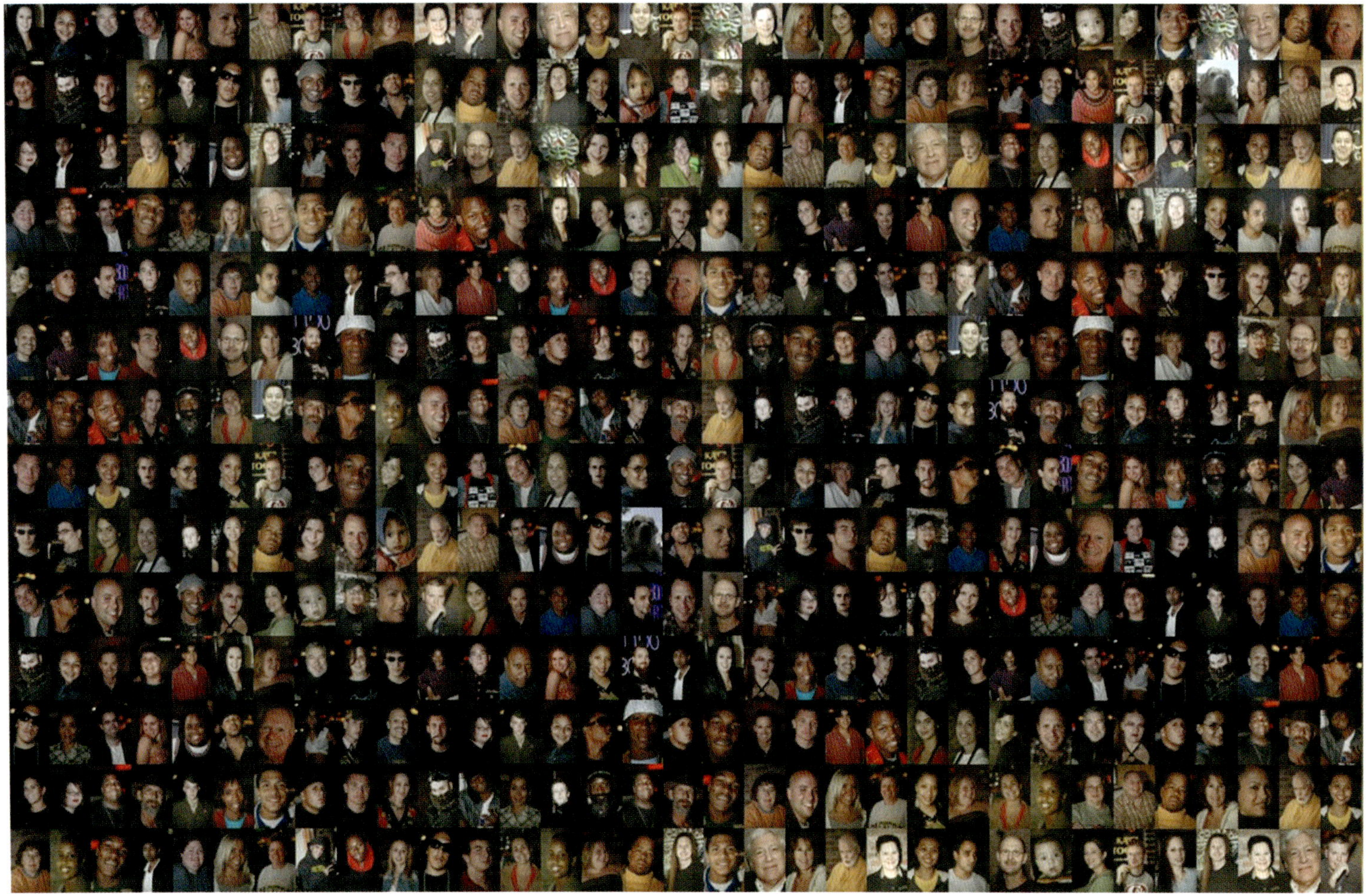

Marcos Ceruto, *Faces of Ybor*, 2007. Photograph collage of Ybor residents and visitors, with images taken by photographer Ron Williams.

Photo by Ron Williams.

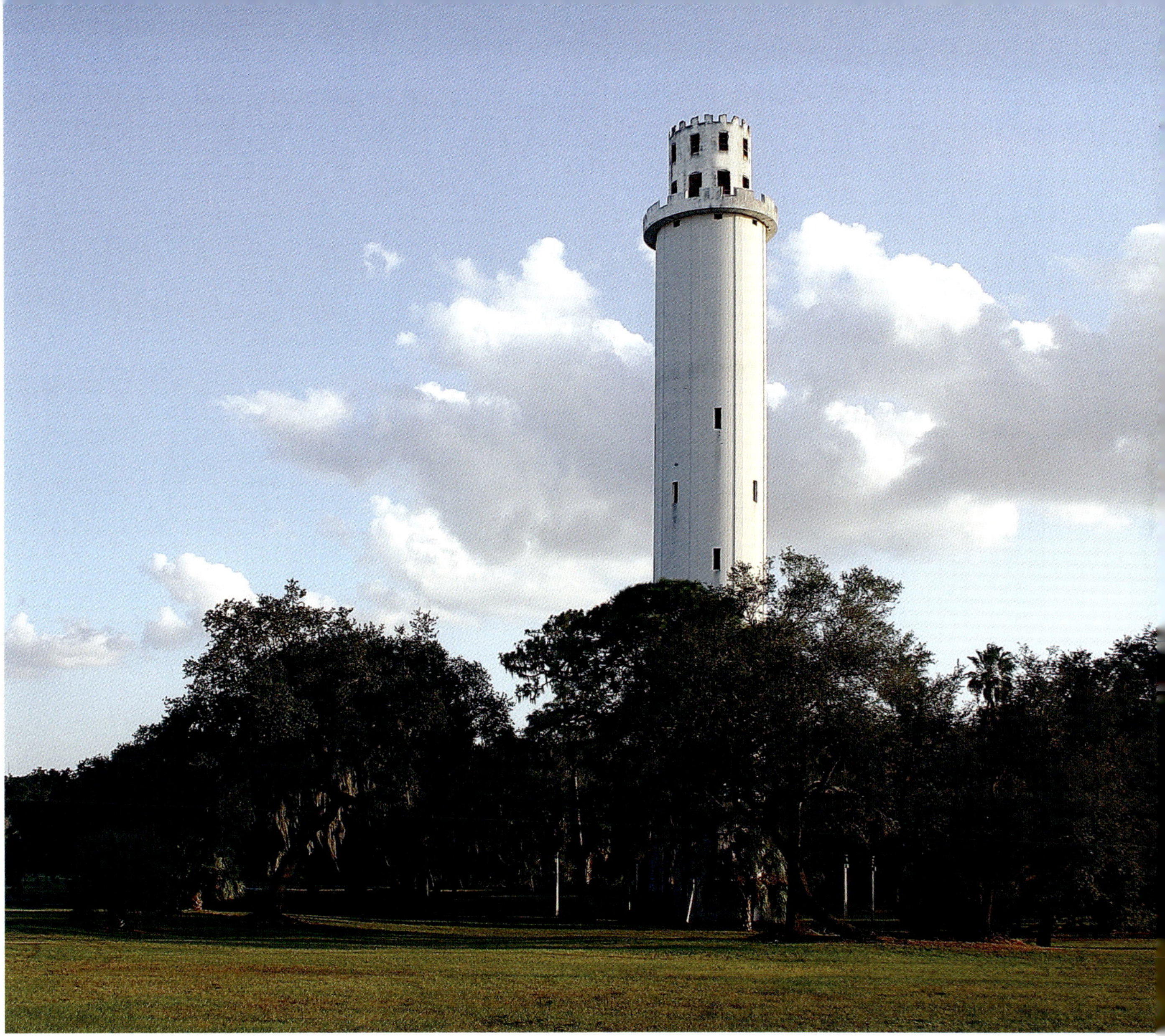

The Sulphur Springs Water Tower was built in 1927 by developer Josiah Richardson who hoped that it would serve as a local attraction. He also needed a water supply for his amusement park, alligator farm, and shopping arcade.
Photo by Ron Williams.

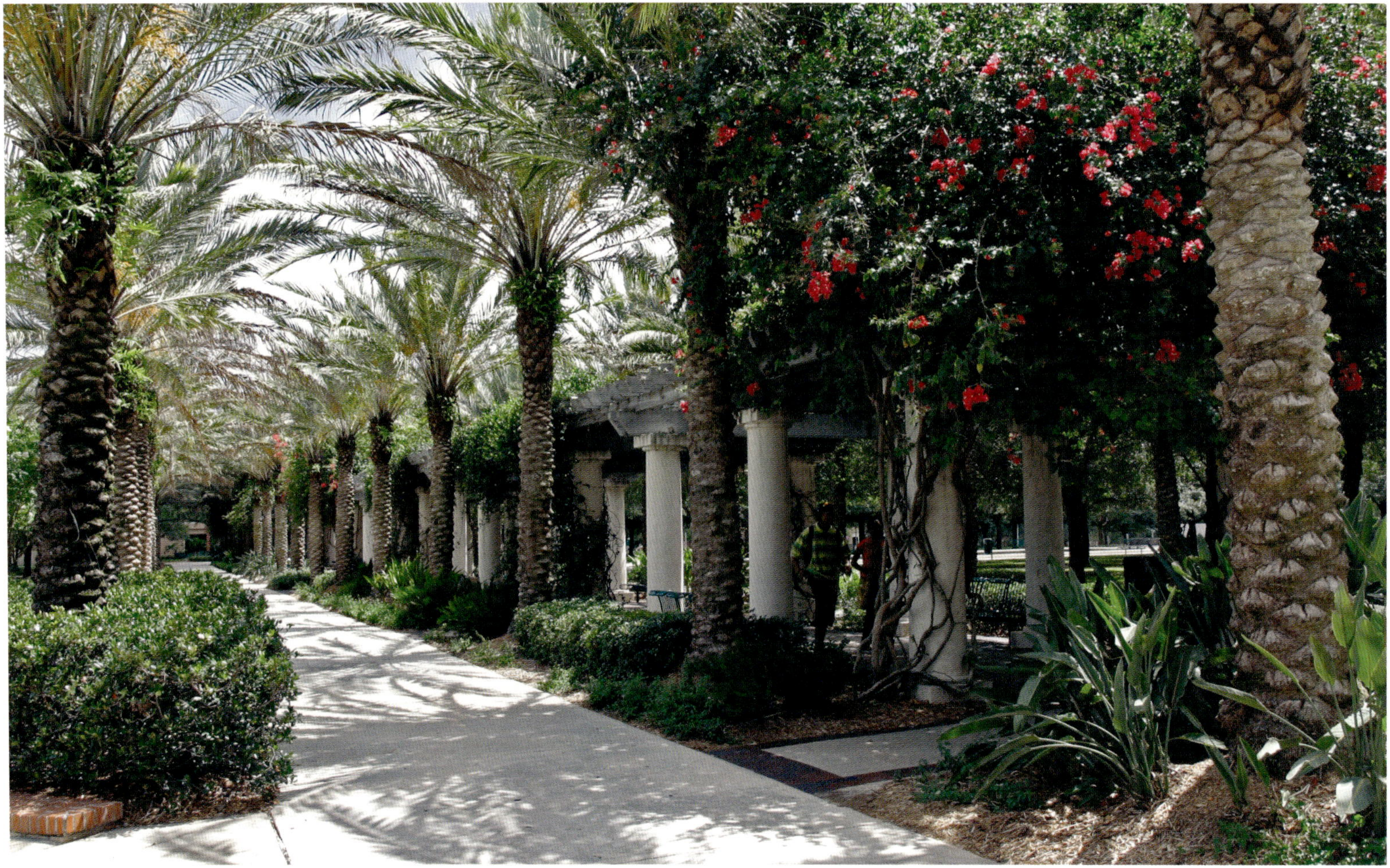

This tropical outdoor walkway is a signature feature of the University of South Florida landscape.
Photo by Ron Williams.

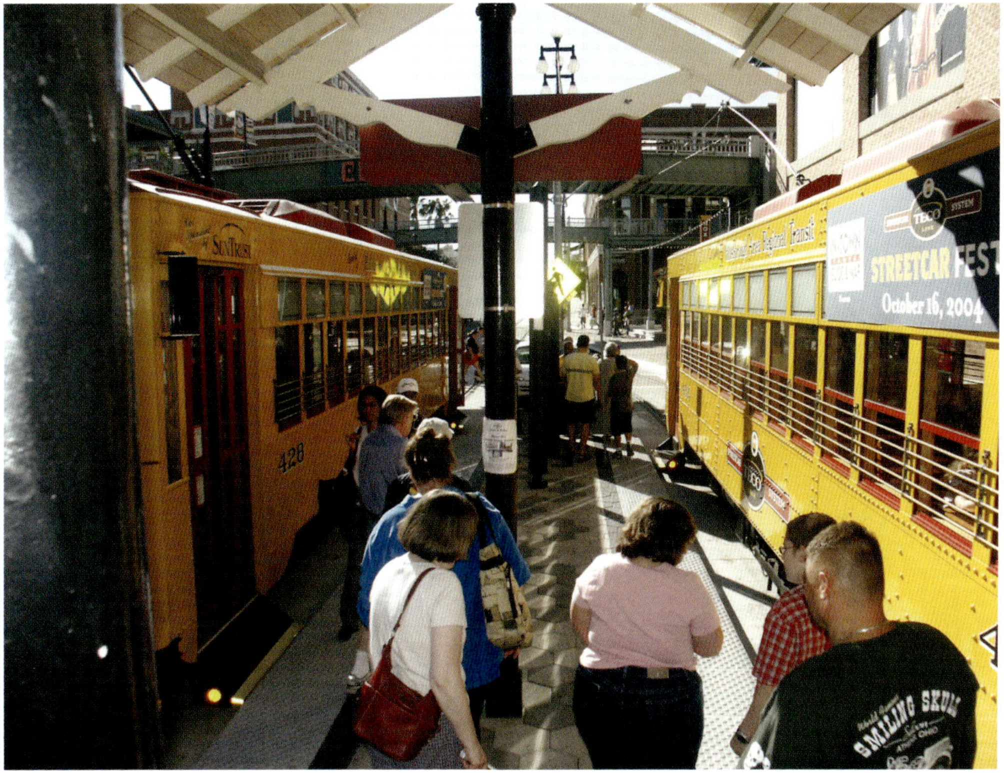

Pedestrians enter and exit streetcars in Ybor City.
Courtesy of Tampa's Downtown Partnership.

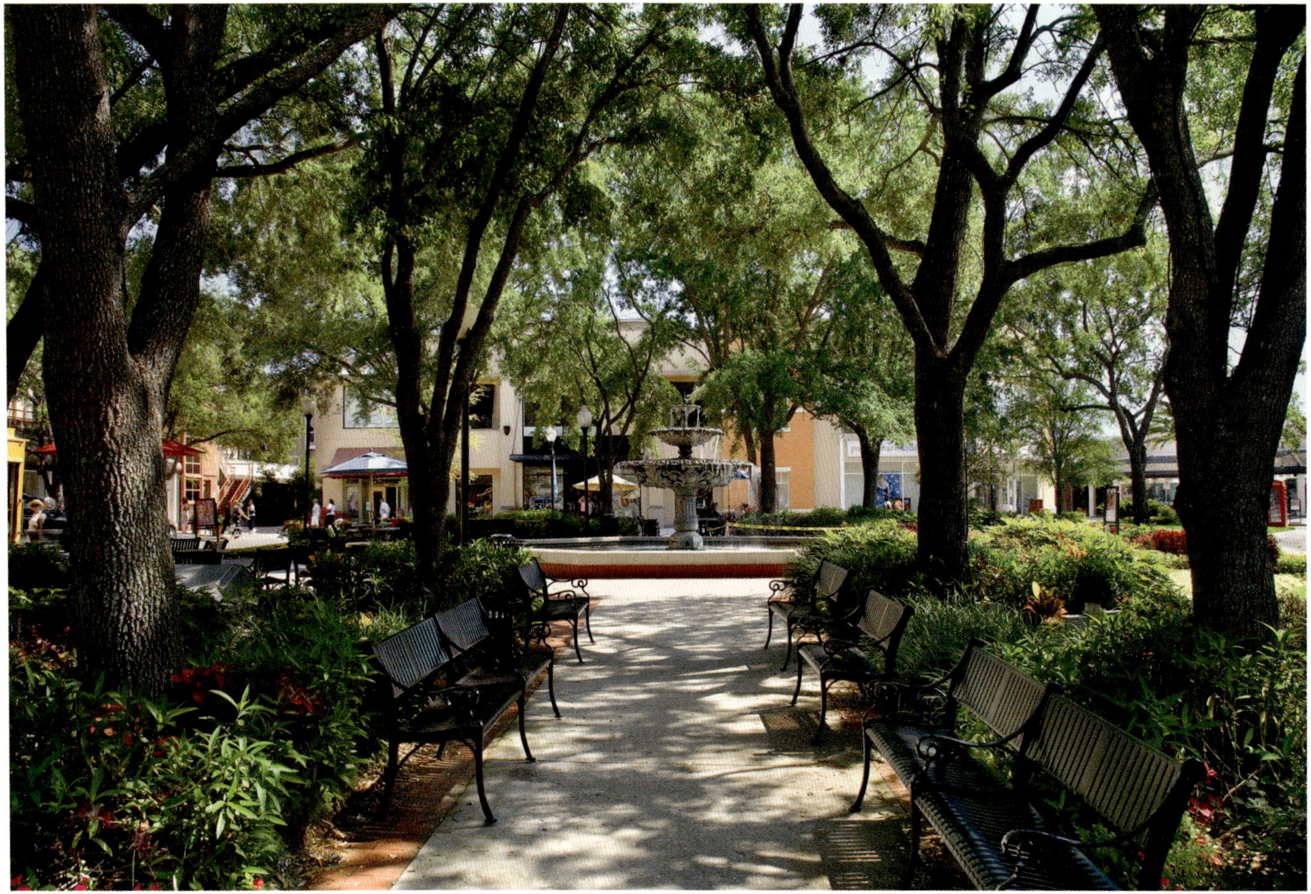

Hyde Park Village is home to shops, restaurants, arts festivals, a live music series, and annual Christmas tree lightings.
Images provided by Hyde Park Village.

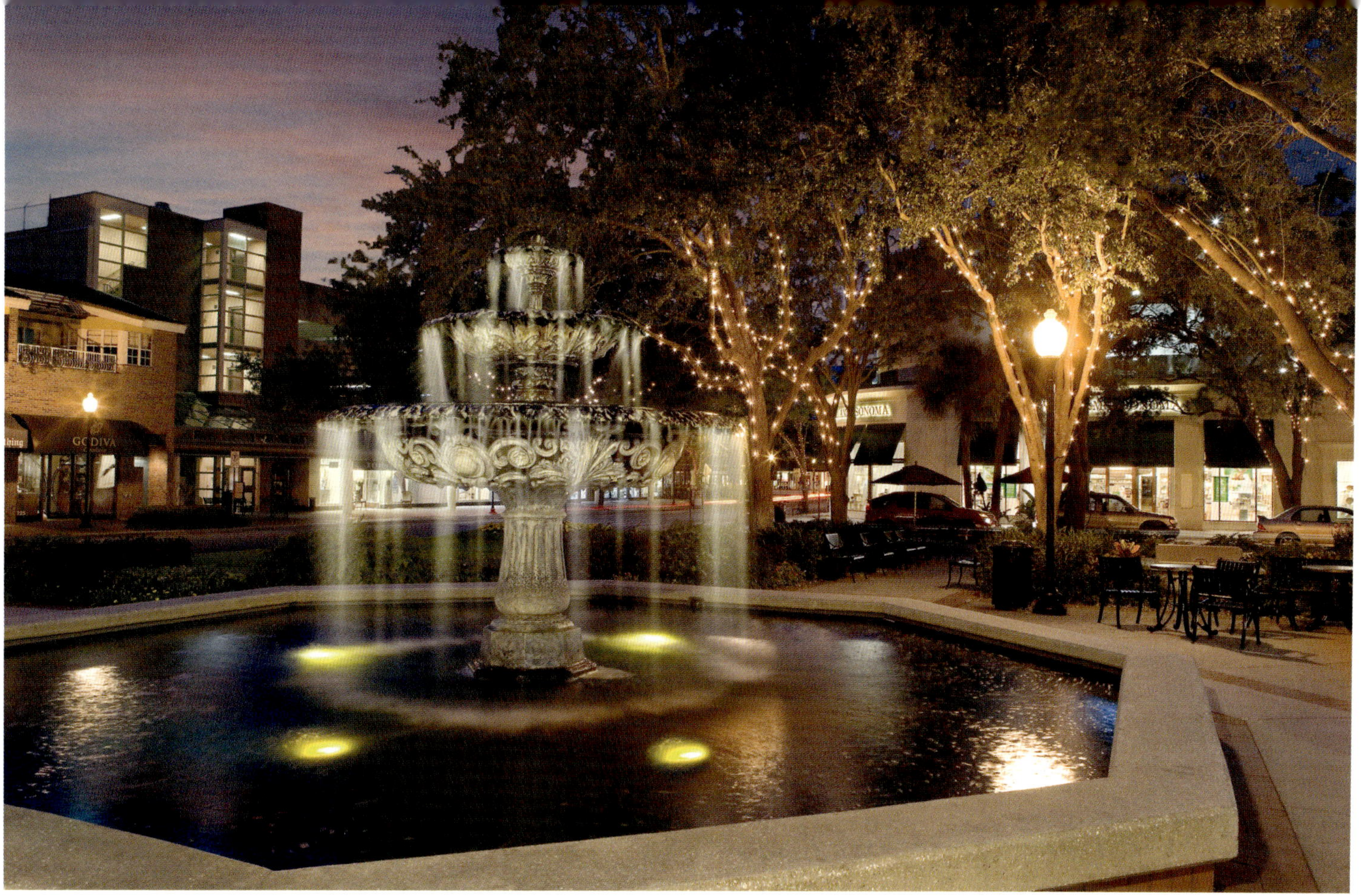

Tampa is like a tree from its roots of historical neighborhoods, solid core for the arts, to its blossoming canopy for business and commerce.

Seamus Gallagher, Tampa resident

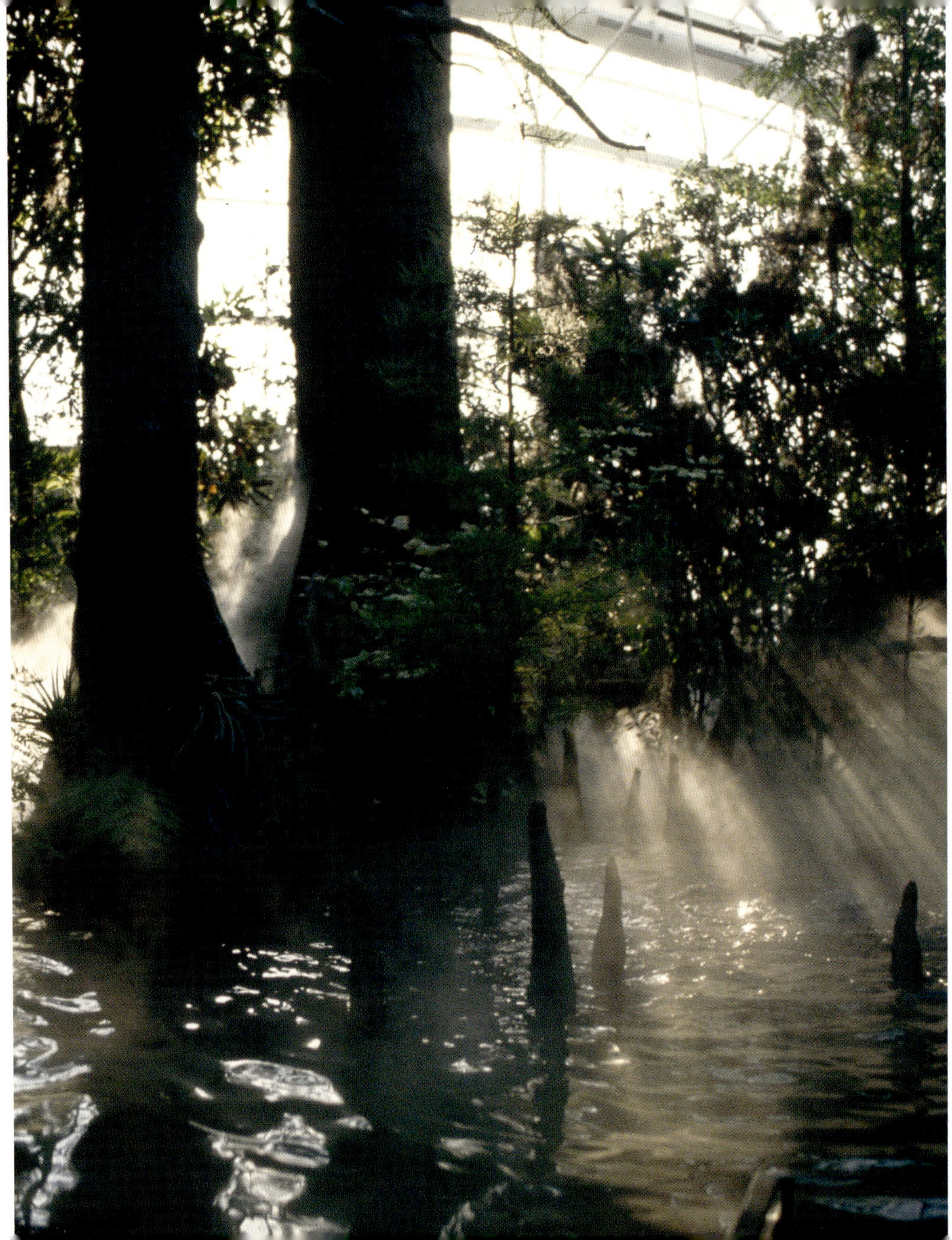

Cypress trees as tall as 28 feet reach for the sky inside the Florida Aquarium's signature glass-panel dome. The Wetlands Gallery houses a variety of living plants and animals, including river otters, alligators, snakes, and turtles.
By permission of the Florida Aquarium.

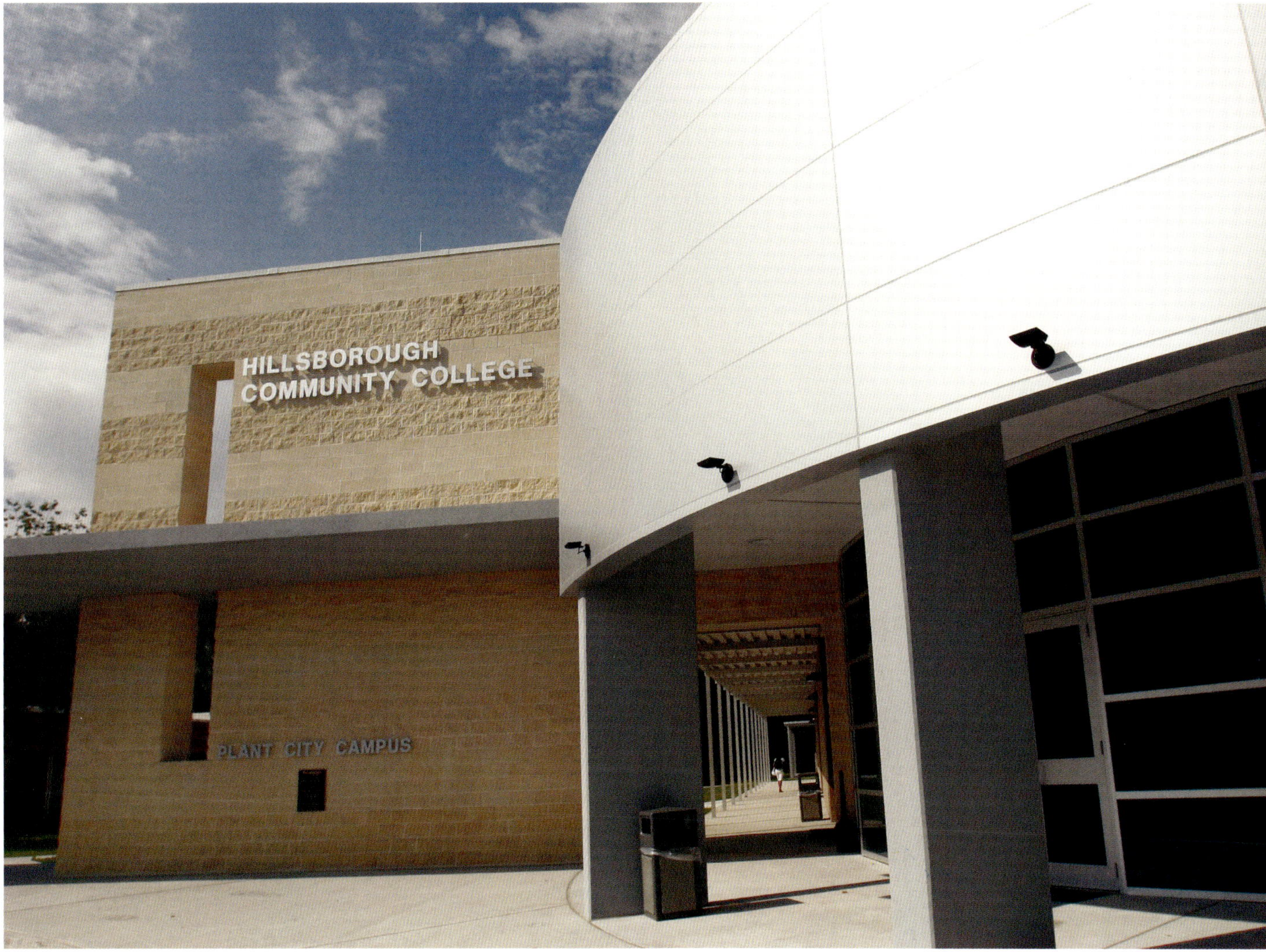

The Trinkle Building at Hillsborough Community College. HCC serves a large student base of more than 40,000 and is home to nine Fulbright scholars.

Image provided by Hillsborough Community College.

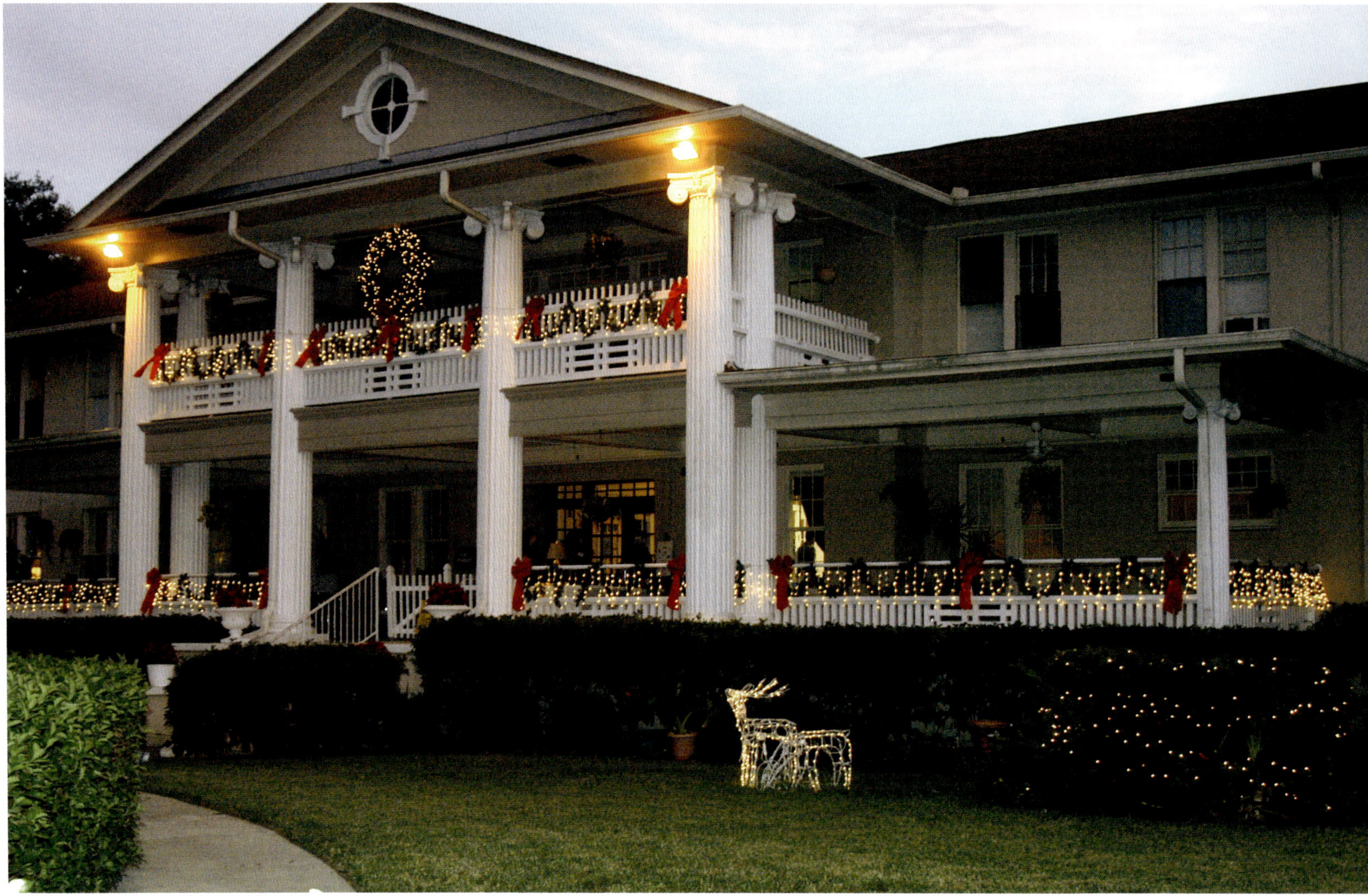

Christmas at the Home Association. The Home Association is a long-established nursing home on a six-acre private park in Tampa.
Photo by Al Allen.

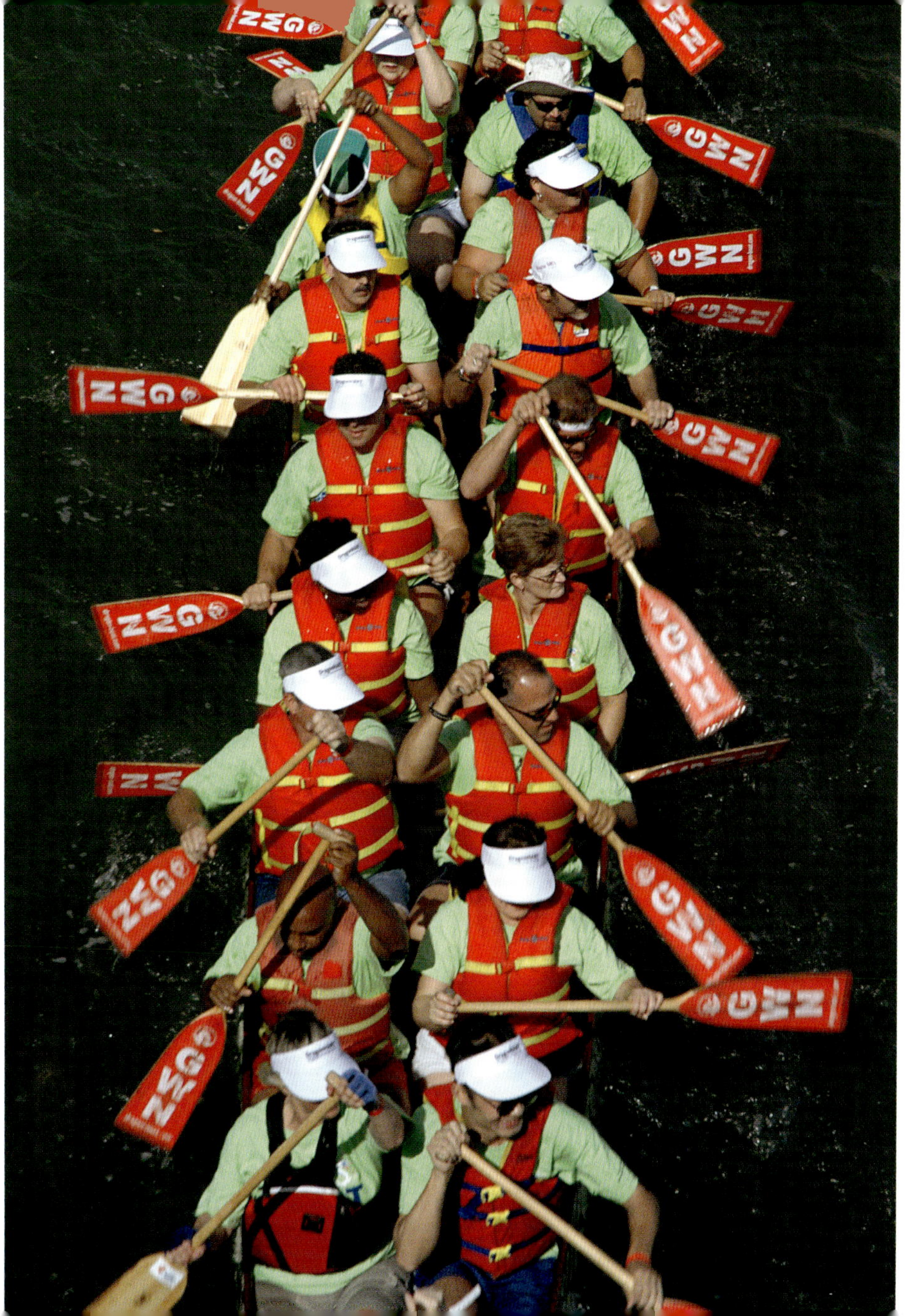

Rowers on the Hillsborough River.

Courtesy of Tampa's Downtown Partnership.

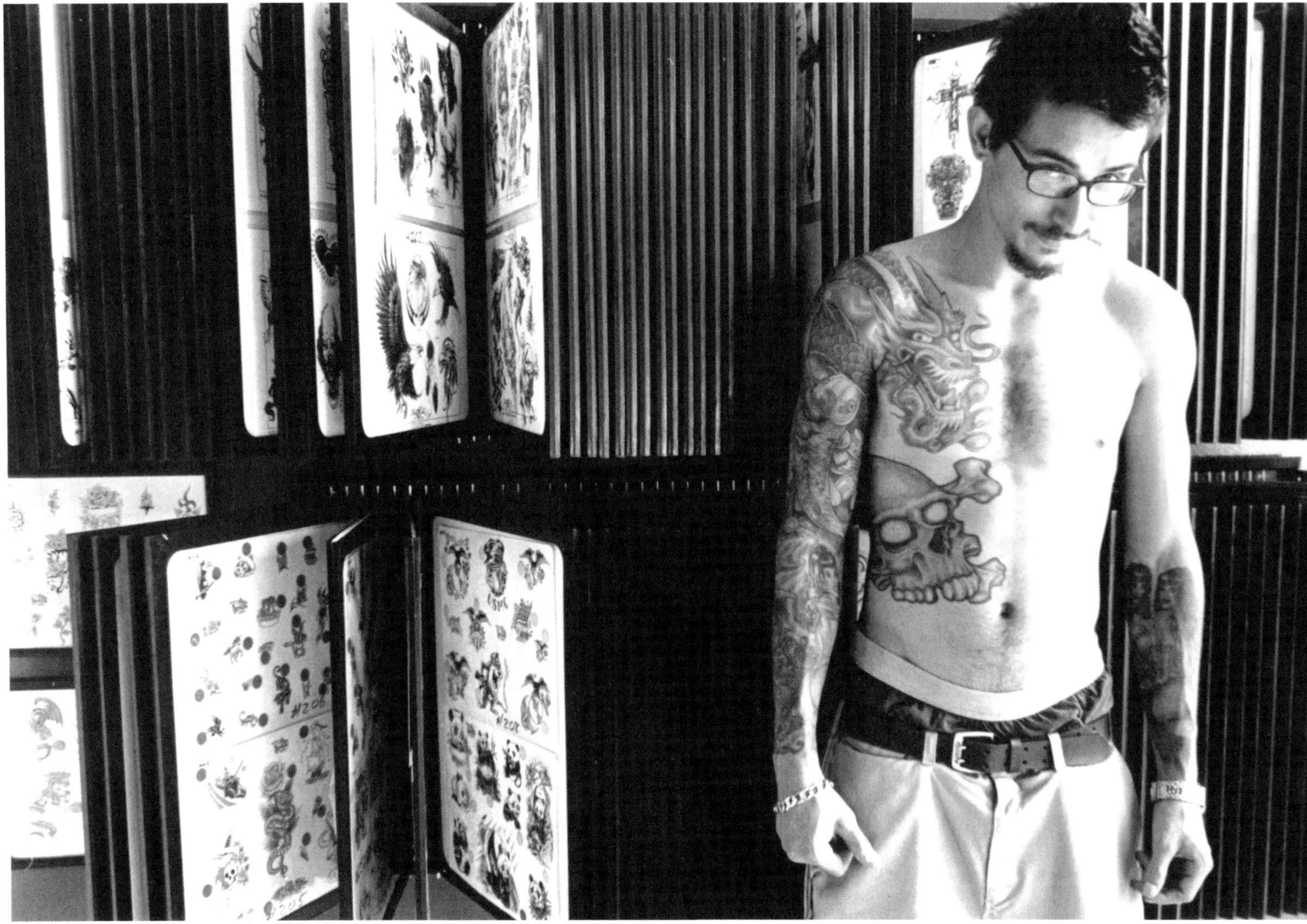

An Ybor tattoo artist at the Las Vegas Tattoo parlor.

Image provided by Las Vegas Tattoos.

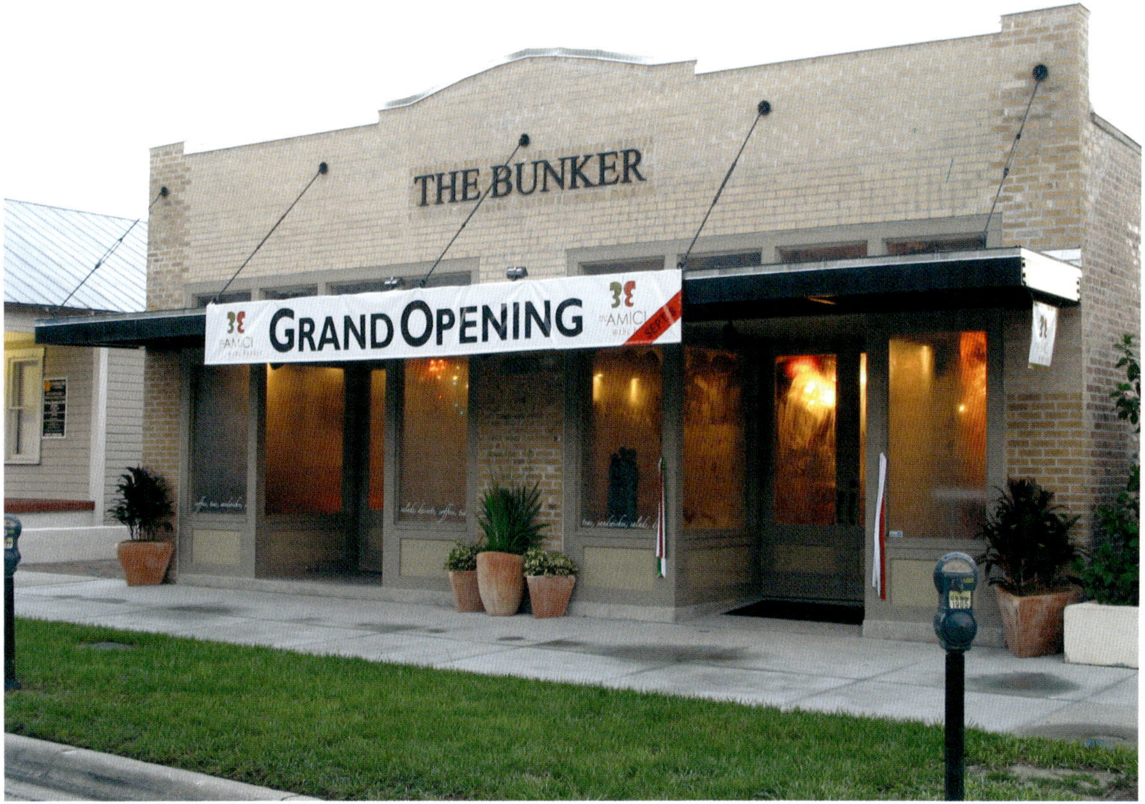

Tre Amici @ the Bunker. This popular coffee and wine bar is nestled into a skillfully restored casita in Ybor City.
Photo by Jessica Stehlik.

City of the Arts

On any given Tampa evening, residents and visitors can take in a play, dine to improvisational comedy, view showings of fine art, hear a spoken-word performance, enjoy a concert, or attend a Broadway musical. There is no shortage of cultural offerings in this city of the arts. The citizens of Tampa appreciate balanced quality. They understand that artistic endeavors match neatly with the relaxed lifestyle that comes from living in such a beautiful part of the country.

Accordingly, Tampa residents support a number of cultural organizations, including the Tampa Theatre. This historic landmark hosts hundreds of events for thousands of visitors each year. The grand movie palace, built in 1926, proudly transports audiences to a Mediterranean courtyard underneath a sea of stars where fortunate guests can enjoy specialty films, classic movies, and concerts. One of the things that makes the Tampa Theatre truly unique is the grand pipe organ, which is played before most films.

Accompaniment to silent films is provided by Rosa Rio, a 106-year-old Tampa resident whose career began in the silent film era. In the 1930s and '40s she was dubbed "Queen of the Soaps," having provided organ accompaniment for several classic radio shows. Rosa worked with many Hollywood legends, including Lucille Ball, Orson Welles, and Art Carney. She created and recorded scores for over 365 silent films for the Video Yesteryears collection.

The Tampa Theatre is also one of many venues that support Tampa's regular film festivals in celebration of local and international artists. Most notably, the International Film Festival hosts seminars and gala events in coordination with cutting-edge film screenings. The Gasparilla Film Festival aims to be the largest festival in the Tampa/St. Petersburg area and treats thousands of viewers to international films. The Tampa International Gay & Lesbian Film Festival features compelling films and related events designed to entertain a diverse audience, bringing in more than 14,500 attendees. Guests can also celebrate Jewish culture at the Tampa Bay Jewish Film Festival; enjoy the Festival of the Moving Image's collection of theater, music, and dance offerings; or support the Independents' Film Festival brought to the public by the Education Channel.

Tampa is building an international reputation for producing imaginative works by world artists, and its residents are dedicated to advancing their products through fresh and innovative exhibitions. The city also has earned well-deserved recognition for producing art-focused educational programs that seek to reach the broadest audience possible. As a result, Tampa now hosts numerous private galleries, temporary art shows, and prestigious museums.

The city is especially proud of the Tampa Museum of Art, which houses a fine collection of art treasures and antiquities, and the Florida Museum of Photographic Arts has excelled in promoting the photographer's vision as a vital and central feature in modern life and culture. Tampa offers creative works in every section of town.

The generous and forward-thinking citizens of the Tampa Bay area support one of the best community radio stations in the country. The nonprofit, noncommercial community radio station WMNF began 28 years ago when a group of dedicated volunteers went door to door asking for donations for the fledgling station. The station presents eclectic music, arts, drama, and independent news and public affairs. Because of its commitment to artists, even those not on the top 40 lists, WMNF is responsible for bringing a wide variety of acts to the area.

Tampa's music scene has never been more exciting or accessible. The city's diverse offerings welcome the established and the newly discovered. All tastes are accommodated in a variety of venues. The most recent addition is the Ford Amphitheater at the Florida State Fairgrounds. This venue hosts top-name entertainers before audiences of nearly 20,000. The St. Pete Times Forum and the Sun Dome also draw outstanding musical talent, thrilling sporting events, and cultural festivals.

Smaller venues are equally accessible. Numerous clubs, restaurants, and cafes host a variety of musicians in Ybor City, Channelside, and South Tampa. The city also capitalizes on its fair weather by hosting outdoor concerts downtown, art festivals, and sponsored events in the park. Tampa's music scene is constantly reaching out to new audiences, whether it is jazz at the Blue Martini or Americana at the Key West–style Skipper's Smokehouse. Tampa is also home to the Florida Orchestra, one of the leading professional symphony orchestras in the state, with 80 professional musicians performing more than 150 concerts annually.

While visiting the music venues in Tampa, guests should stop by the Tampa Bay Performing Arts Center (TBPAC) and the Patel Conservatory. This facility is located on a picturesque nine-acre site along the east bank of the Hillsborough River. The Center is the largest performing arts center south of the Kennedy Center and is nationally respected for producing grand opera. TBPAC welcomes more than 600,000 patrons as guests to nearly 4,000 concerts, performances, and events each year. In total more than 10 million attendees have enjoyed its numerous world-class events, including one of the nation's leading Broadway series.

The University of Tampa, University of South Florida, and Hillsborough Community College also produce everything from comedy to the classics, cutting-edge drama, musicals, and family plays. Adding to Tampa's offerings is Ybor City's Tampa Improv. This comedy theater and restaurant brings top-name acts to Tampa, including cast members from Saturday Night Live and Hollywood performers like Wanda Sykes, Bob Saget, Cedric the Entertainer, and Judy Tenuta.

A great number of Tampa's residents participate in the arts, as audience members or as creators. And a growing number recognize the cultural vitality that embraces Tampa's thriving arts districts. Indeed, the City of Tampa is committed to promoting Tampa as a City of the Arts. During her first term, Mayor Pam Iorio envisioned a city that would celebrate the works of artists, writers, performers, film makers, and all forms of fine and commercial arts professionals. The city collectively seeks to provide opportunities for residents and visitors to enjoy a wide array of creative pursuits while encouraging the growth of creative businesses.

The people of Tampa recognize the importance of both the nonprofit arts and the commercial arts to a city. The artist community is drawn to the city's economic and artistic opportunities, diversity, and quality of life. Cultural tourism has flourished as a broad spectrum of national and international visitors have come to experience Tampa's authentic cultural, historic, and arts assets. The City of Tampa supports many programs that honor artistic expression through city-funded events and the Public Arts Program. The city's Public Art Office promotes the involvement of artists in projects throughout Tampa to enhance the physical environment and celebrate its character and identity.

Creative contributions have made a dramatic impact on the local economy. Tampa is not only a place to maximize one's cultural consumption but a place to enjoy the financial fruits of artistic labor. The arts bring in $402.2 million annually from 5.5 million visitors who enjoy local nonprofits and cultural institutions. Not only do these facilities add to Tampa's quality of life, but they also provide 7,000 jobs and a $147 million payroll.

Tampa is proud of its thriving arts districts and for good reason. Residents enjoy a wide range of galleries, music venues, plays, film festivals, and a thriving public arts program. Tampa's interests in the arts as a city is not only practically useful but esthetically significant because it demonstrates that the taxpayer and the ticket-buyer equally appreciate the value of art and culture to our community.

The arts enhance our quality of life, and they are a key player in the economic development of our city.

Mayor Pam Iorio

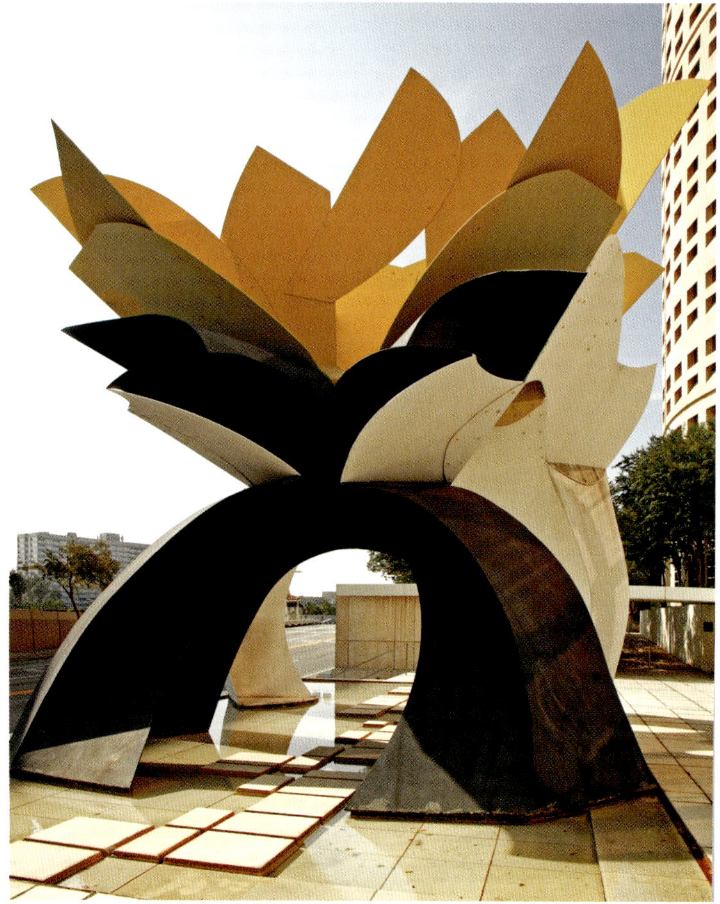

George Sugarman, *Untitled*, 1992. Steel, 36 feet. Kennedy Boulevard and Ashley Drive. City of Tampa Public Art Program. This minimalist yellow, black, and white painted sculpture is positioned next to the Bank of America building. Sugarman's works are all "explosive" in nature, and this work is no exception. Photo by Ron Williams.

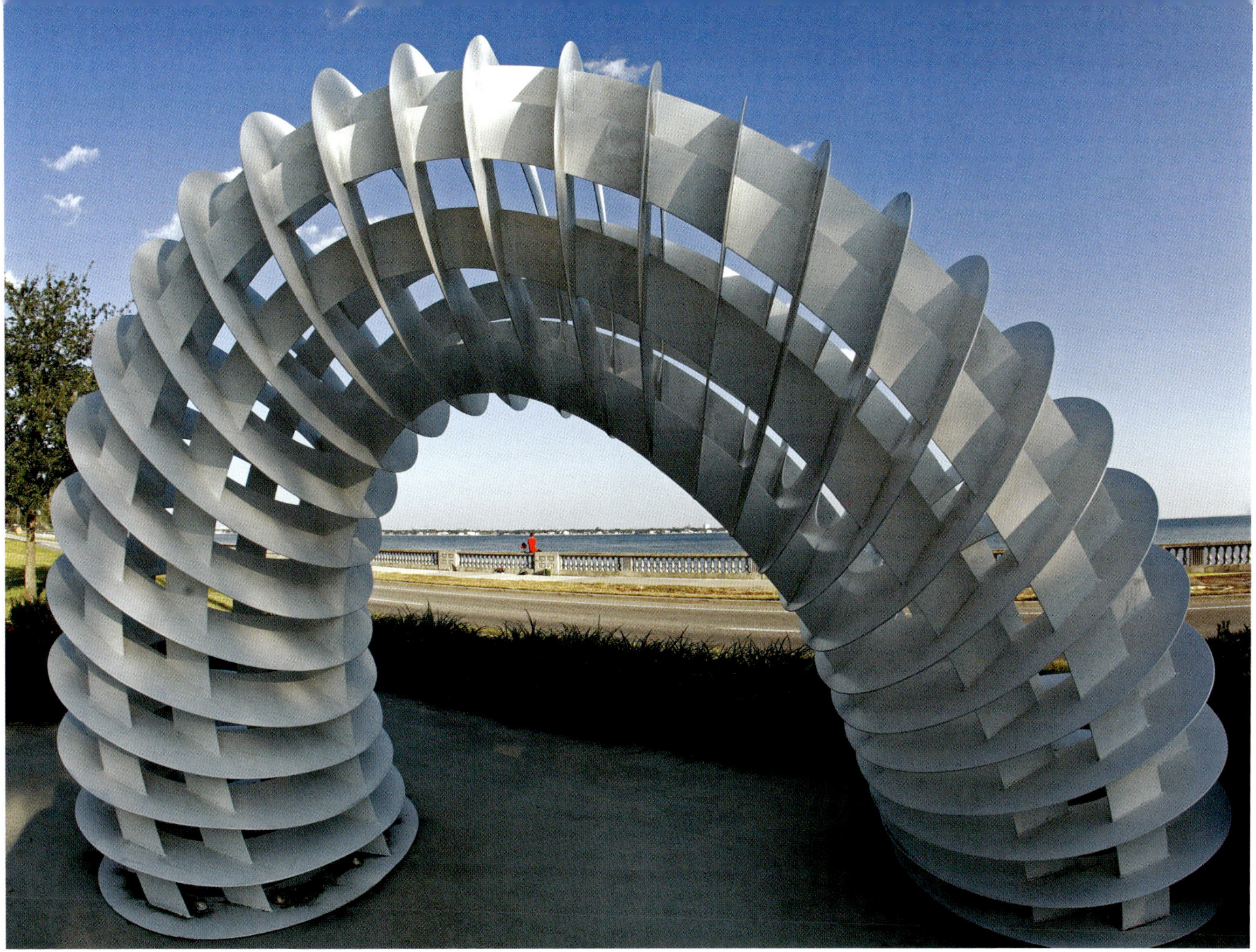

Mary Ann Unger, *Wave,* 1989. Steel, 10 × 15 × 6 feet. Bayshore Boulevard median just north of Bay to Bay Boulevard. City of Tampa Public Art Program. This artwork is reminiscent of the motion of a wave breaking onto the shore. The open arch form of the white wave evokes the form of a shell or the ribs of a boat's hull.
Photo by Ron Williams.

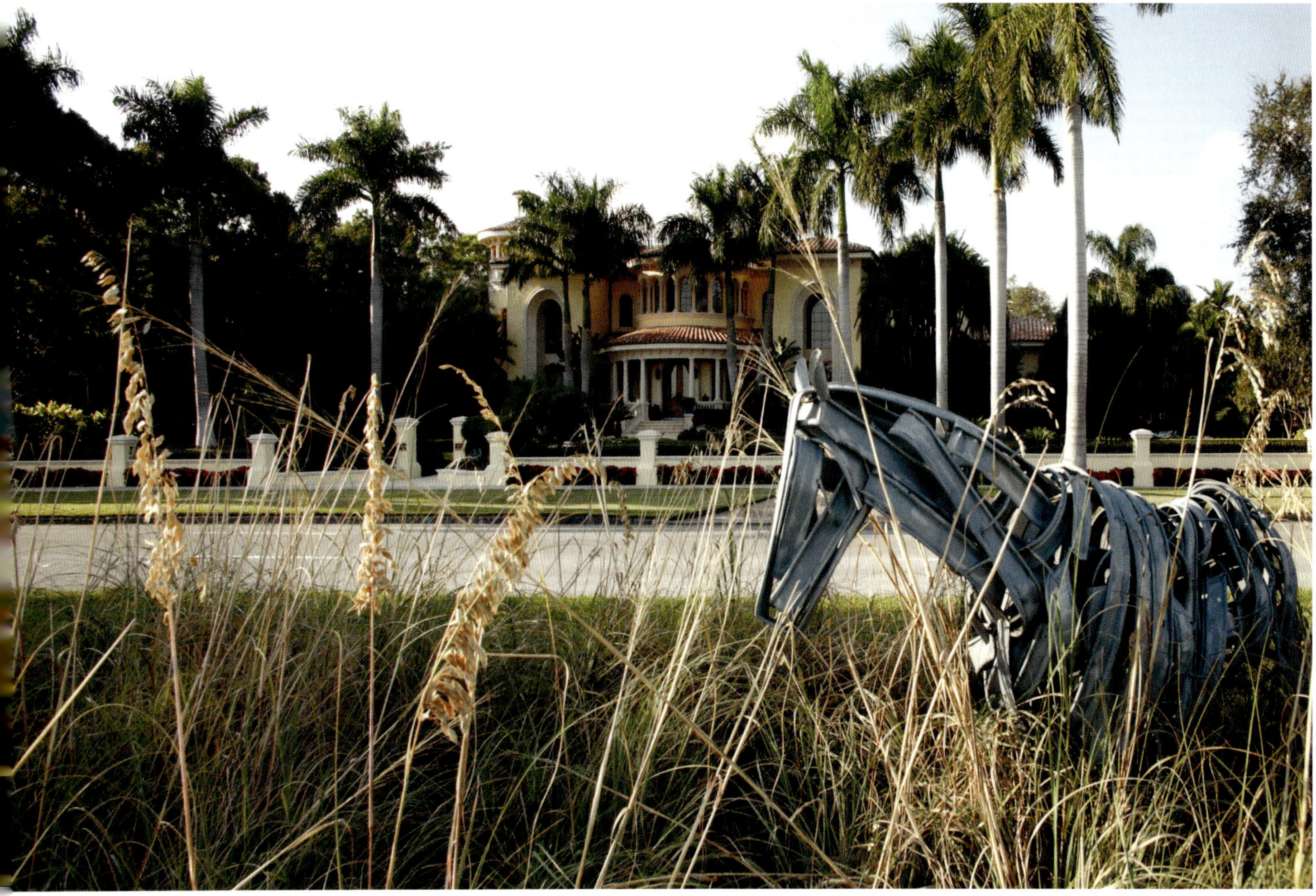

Bud Oleson, *Equanimity*. Metal. Bayshore Boulevard and Gunby. City of Tampa Public Art Program. Tampa's Public Art Program promotes the involvement of artists in projects throughout the city that enhance the physical environment and celebrate Tampa's character and identity.

Photo by Ron Williams.

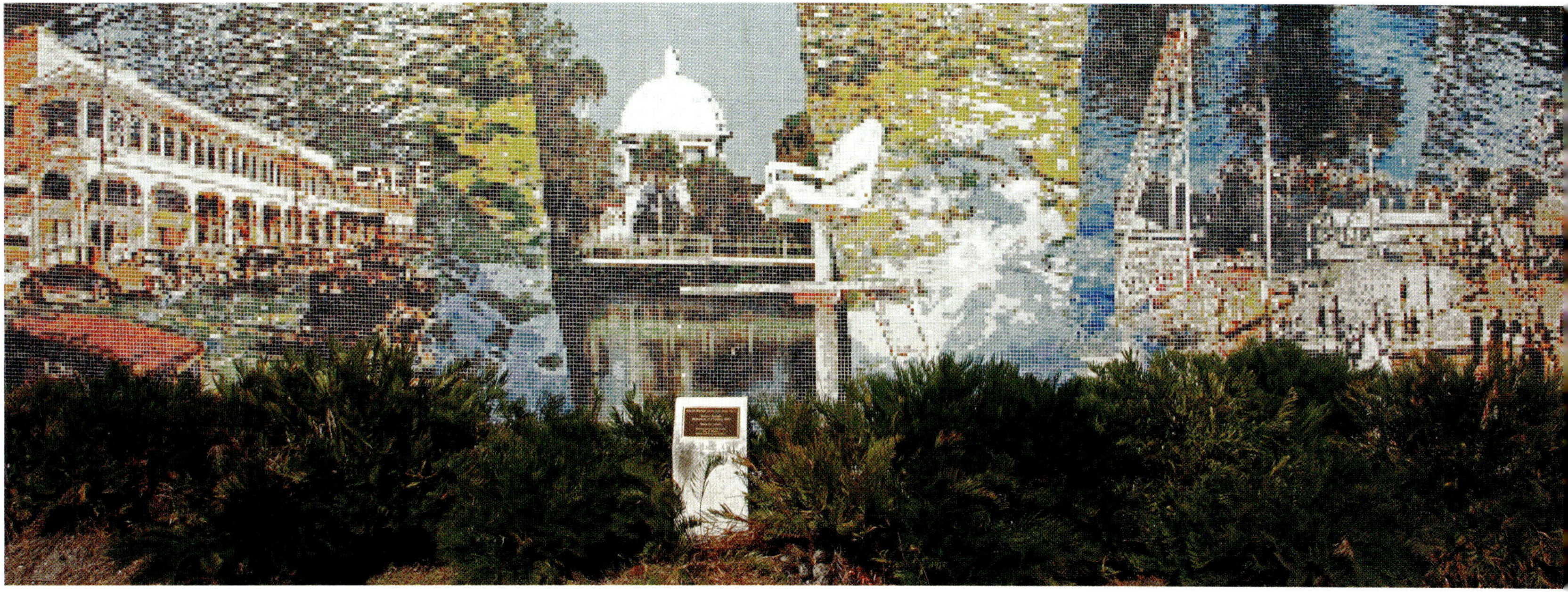

Bruce Marsh, *Sulphur Springs: Reflections of a Century*, 2000. Glass tile mosaic, 9 × 33 feet. Sulphur Springs Park. City of Tampa Public Art Program. This glass tile mosaic, depicting local historical images, is sited just off of the Hillsborough River.
Photo by Ron Williams.

Contemporary art challenges us. It broadens our horizons. It asks us to think beyond the limits of conventional wisdom.

Eli Broad

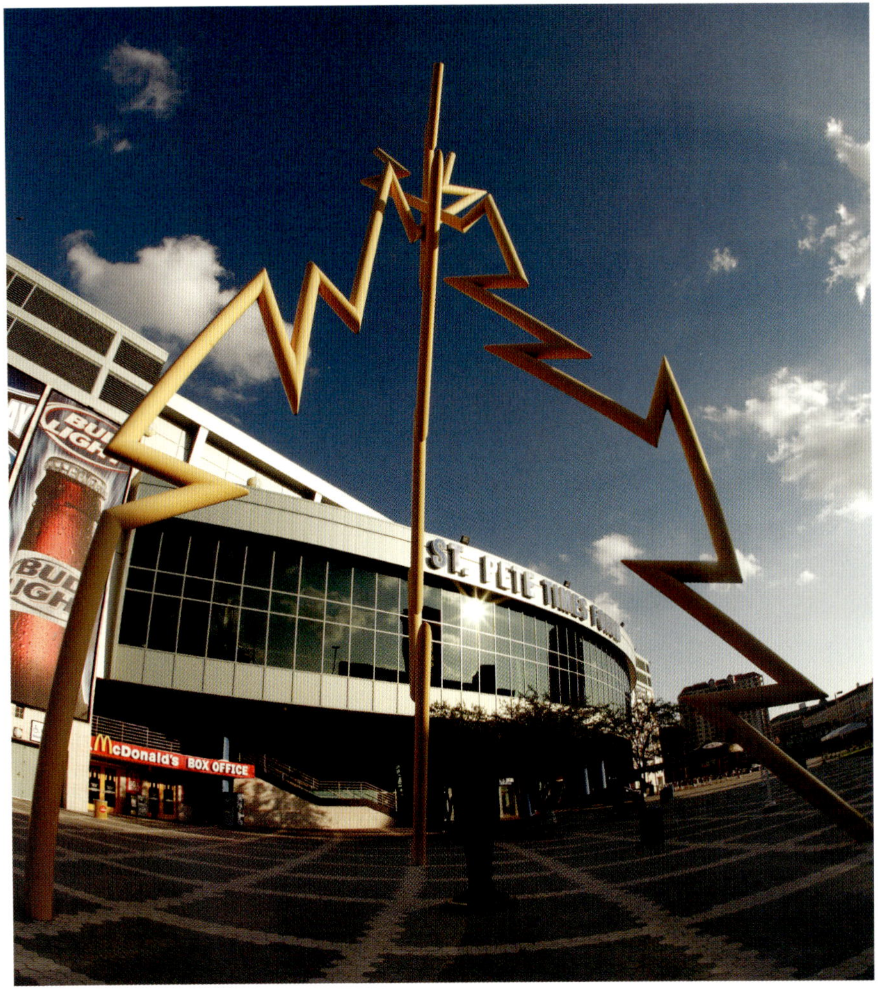

Jonathan Borofsky, *Lightning*, 1997. Steel, 75 × 38 × 38 feet. Ice Palace Plaza. City of Tampa Public Art Program. Borofsky's artwork consists of a nine-foot-high steel silhouette surrounded by three angled, yellow lightning bolts. The figure at the center of the sculpture is a human presence, which is not defined as either male or female. Viewers are meant to interact with the artwork and can walk through the central space created by the bolts themselves. Photo by Ron Williams.

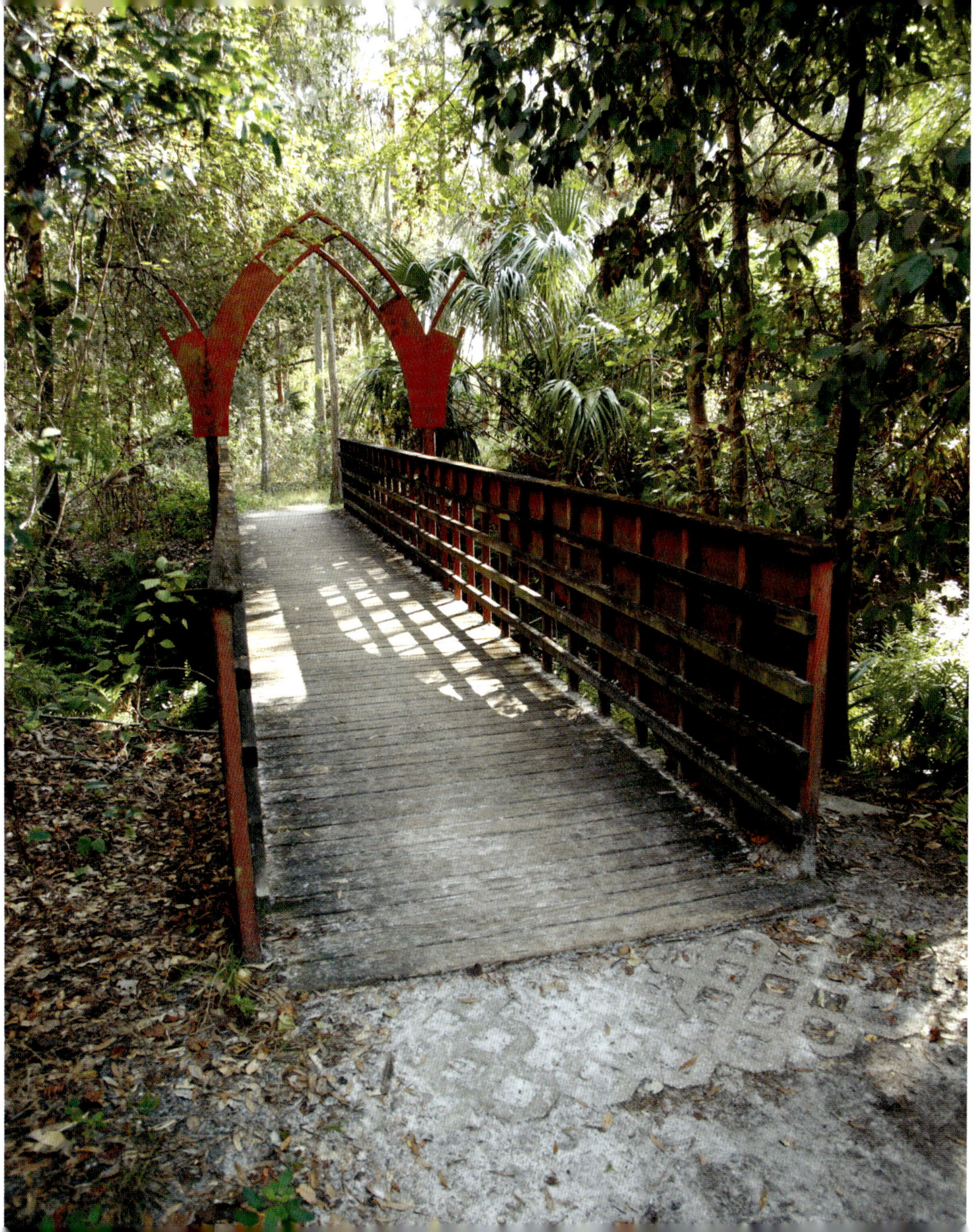

Robert Calvo, *Arcade*, 1990. Steel and wood. Two bridges, 5 × 35 feet. Al Lopez Park. City of Tampa Public Art Program. Calvo's artwork, a set of steel and wood pedestrian bridges within the grounds of Al Lopez Park, serves to emphasize a particular part of the park demarcated by two creeks. The bridges serve as portals or gateways for the pedestrians utilizing the site, evoking both a sense of place and the passage of time.
Photo by Ron Williams.

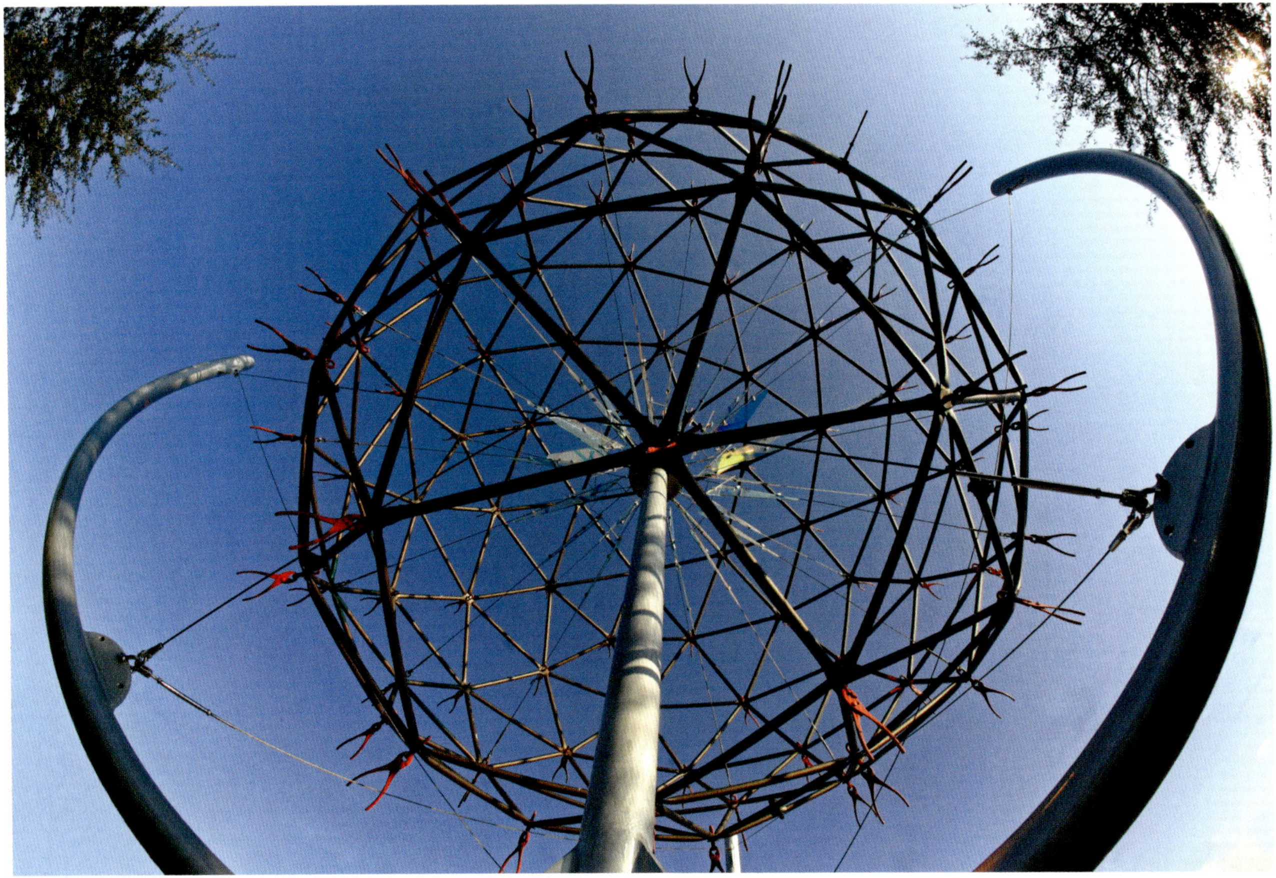

John Rogers, *Great Ball of Pliers*, 2003. Powder-coated galvanized steel, aluminum, safety-red pliers, diachronic glass, cables, 24 feet high and 14 feet in diameter. City of Tampa Public Art Program. *Great Ball of Pliers* is a three-frequency geodesic sphere constructed from 270 steel struts connected by 96 red safety pliers. The artist's objective was for the sculpture to be humorous, fun, and mysterious while implying deeper meanings.

Photo by Ron Williams.

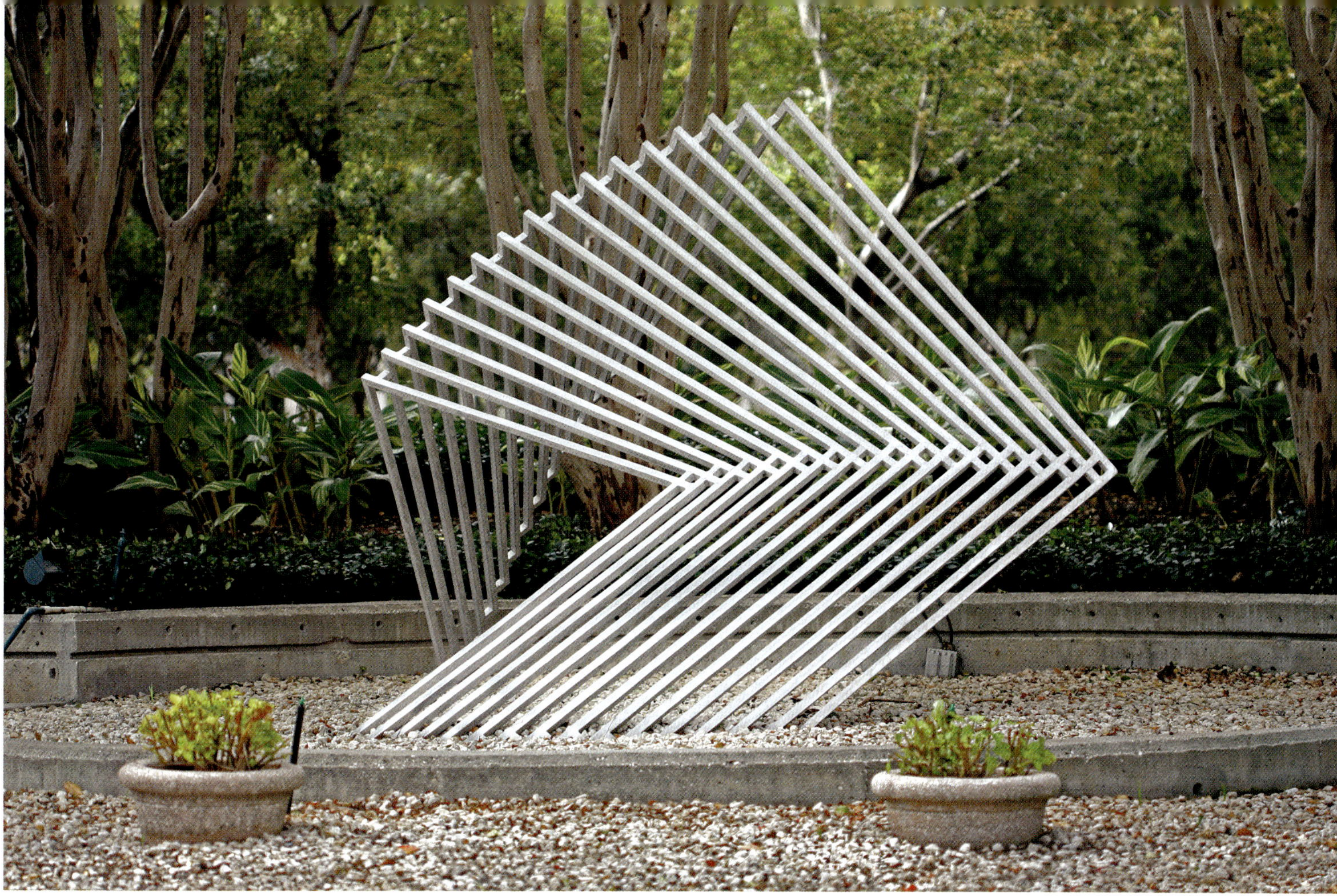

Linda Howard, *Zig Zag,* 1987. Aluminum, 8 × 8 × 10 feet. Tampa Performing Arts Center. City of Tampa Public Art Program. This brushed aluminum artwork is made up of geometric elements in repetition. Light reflecting on the patterns present on the aluminum is suggestive of energy. In Tampa's brilliant sunlight, this reflection serves to make the artwork almost transparent.
Photo by Ron Williams.

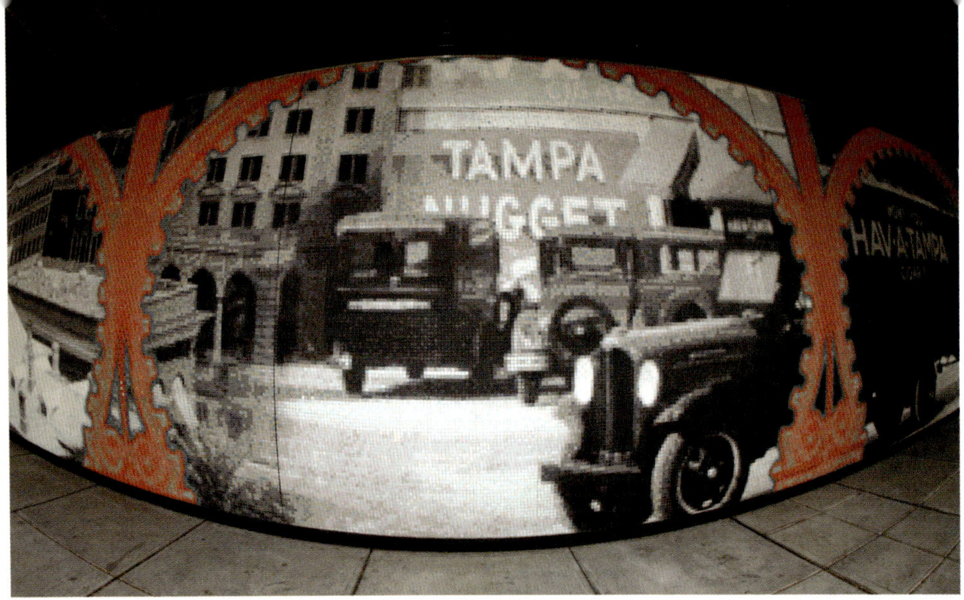

Mike Mandel, *Parking at the Courthouse*, 2000. Ceramic tile mural, 9.5 feet sloping to 15 × 145 feet. Tampa Police Department Parking Garage. City of Tampa Public Art Program. This mural is comprised of archival photographs which were digitized/pixelated and then translated into tile. Photo by Ron Williams.

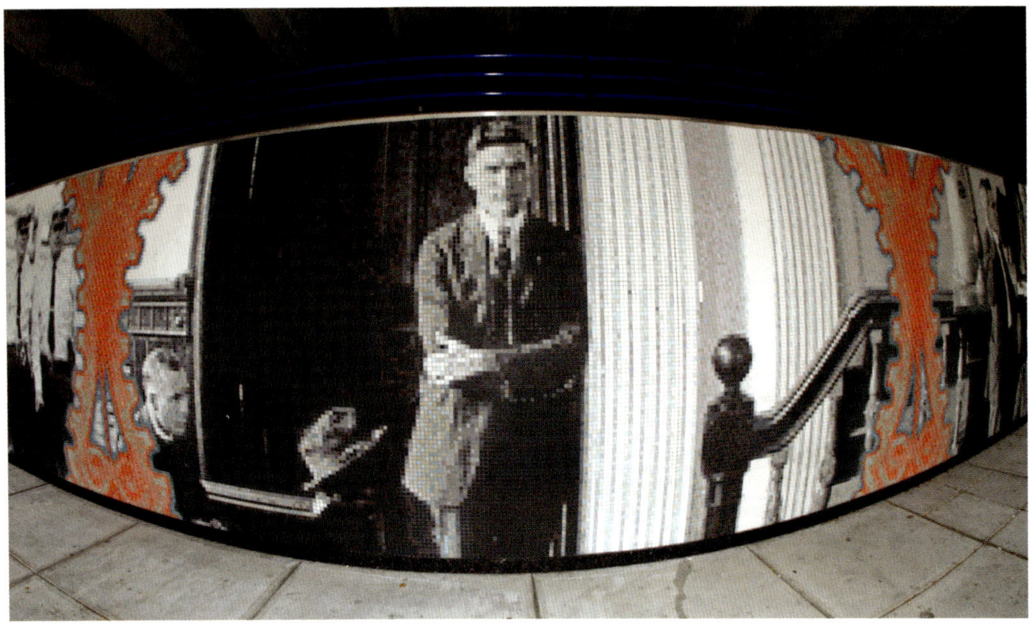

Art is man's expression of his joy in labor.

William Morris

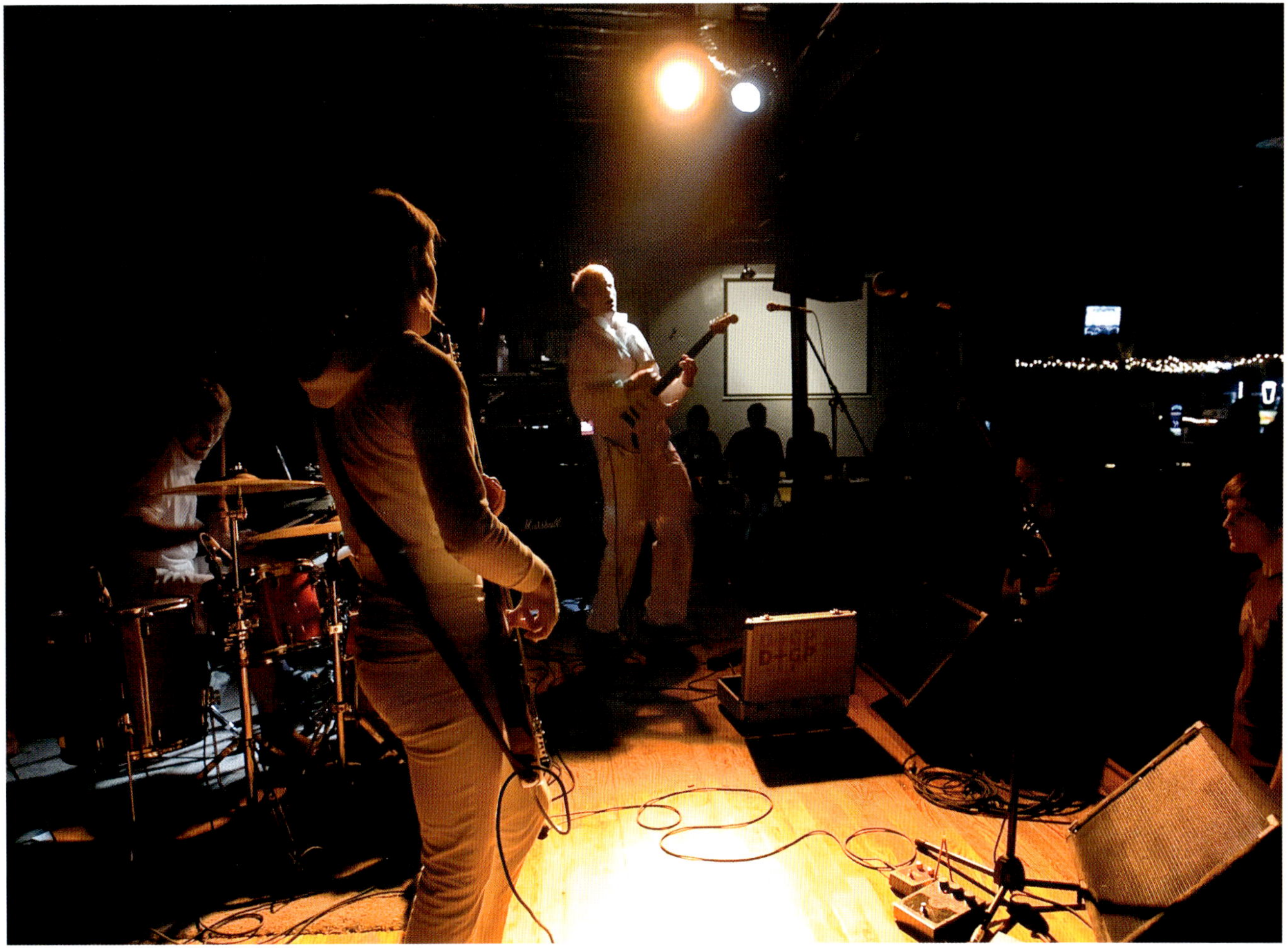

Dear and Glorious Physician, a local band from Gainesville, plays at the Crowbar in Ybor City.
Photo by Sean Birdsell.

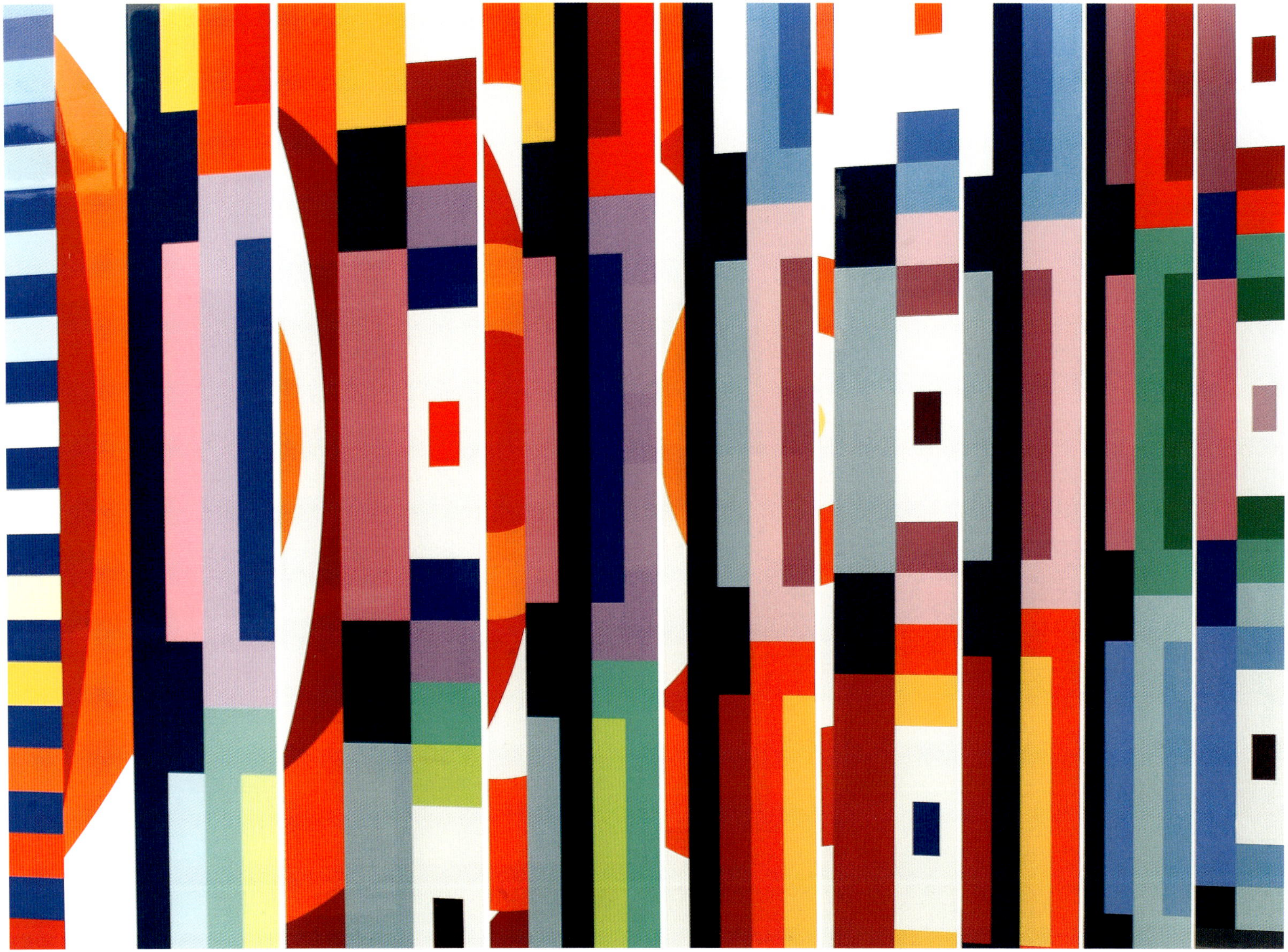

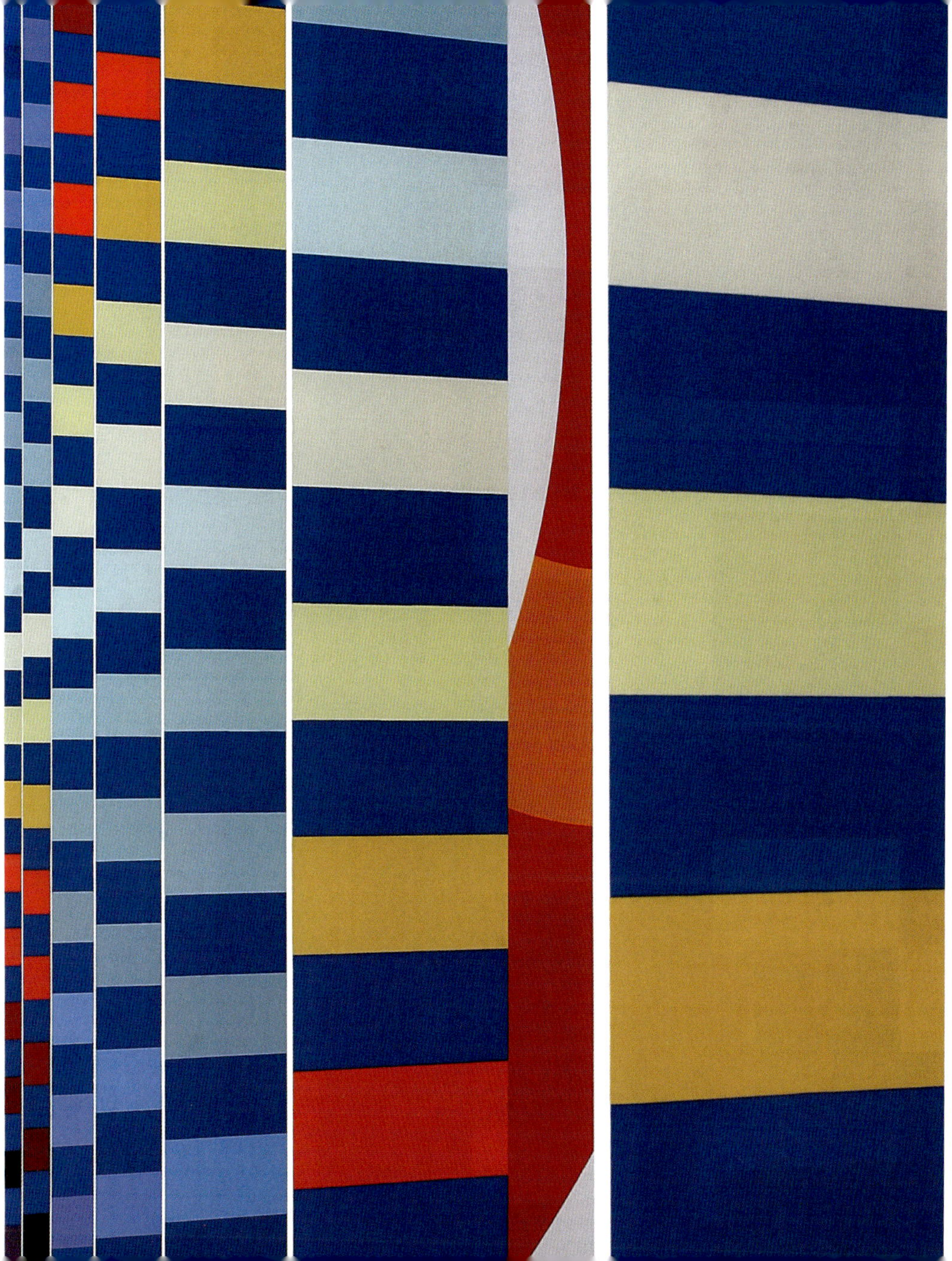

Yaacov Agam, *Visual Welcome*, 1995. Aluminum. Nine panels, 2 feet 2 inches × 10 feet each. Zack Street on the Hillsborough River. City of Tampa Public Art Program. This artwork, made from the type of aluminum used in aircraft production, consists of nine panels, set 30 inches apart. The panels are painted on both sides with Agam's characteristic kinetic patterns, which change and move as the viewer passes along the length of the sculpture.

Photo by Ron Williams.

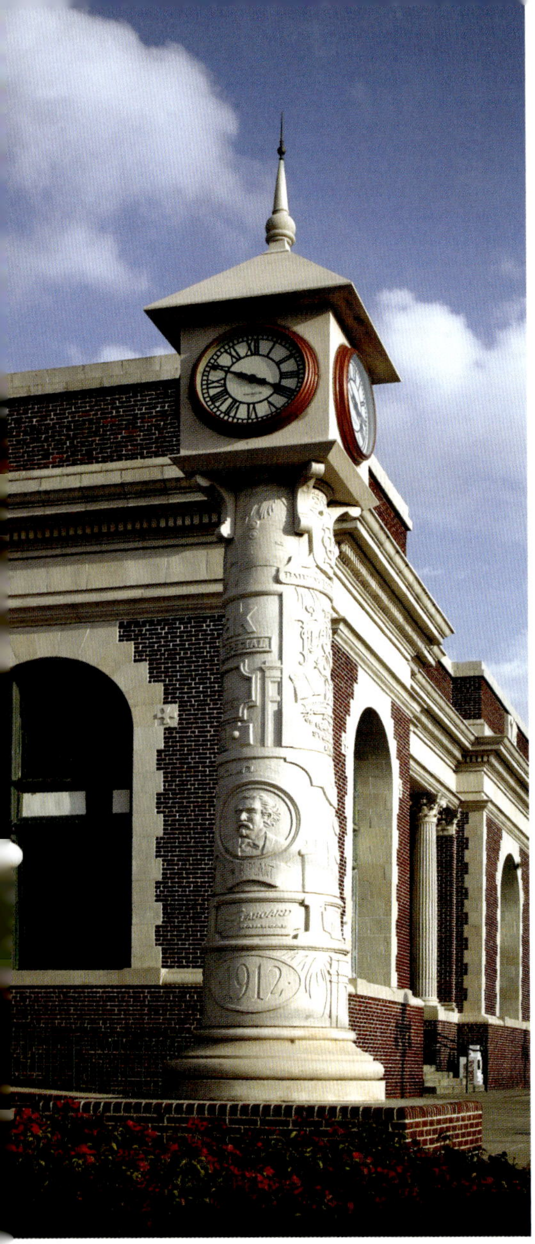

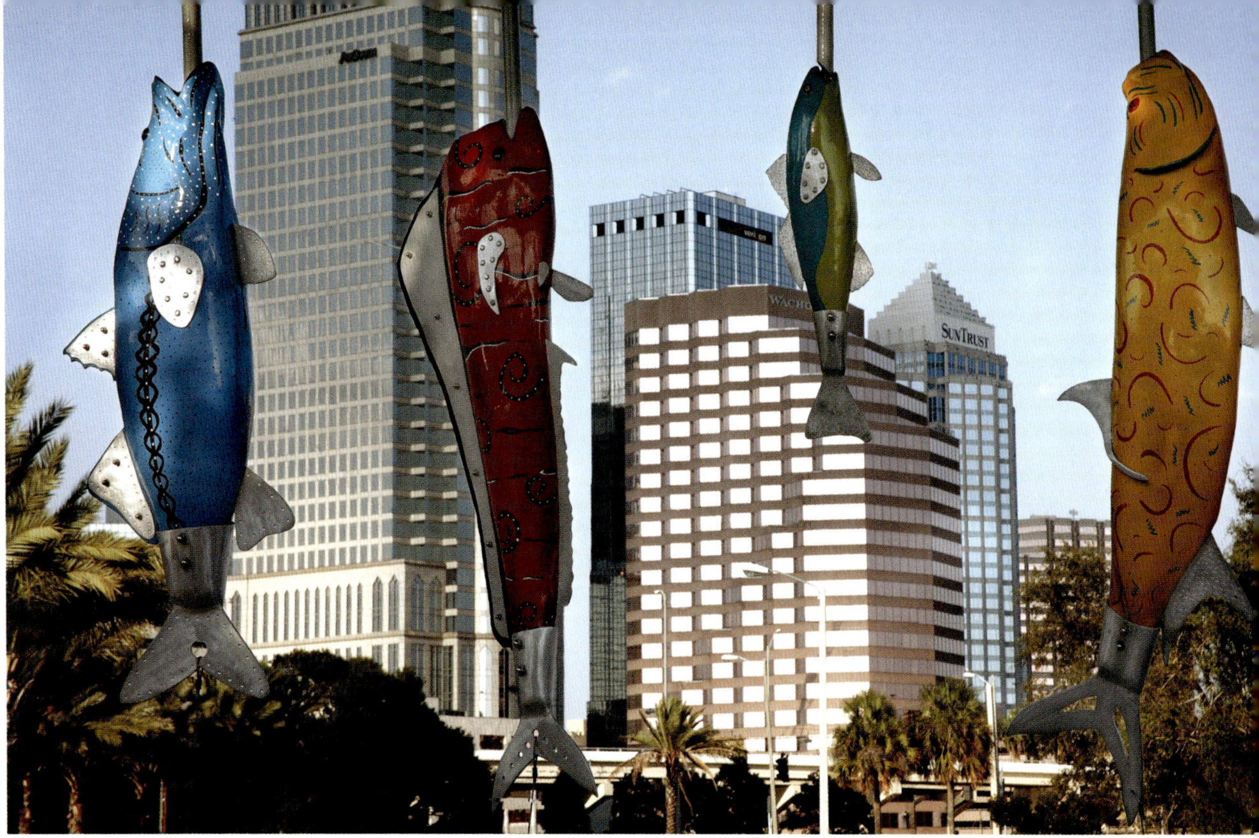

Lorraine Genovar, *Fish on Bayshore*, 1995. Fiberglass, 10 × 9 feet. Bayshore Boulevard. City of Tampa Public Art Program. Housed under an open structure formerly used by fishermen to display their prize-winning tarpon catches, Genovar's artwork consists of five fiberglass fish: a snook, a bull dolphin, a redfish, a tarpon, and a barracuda (not shown). These fish, which serve to blend old Tampa with new Tampa, are all indigenous to the state of Florida.

Photo by Ron Williams.

William Culbertson, *Centennial Clock Keep*, 2004. Tampa Union Station. City of Tampa Public Art Program. Built in 1912, Tampa Union Station is a landmark structure and is on the National Register of Historic Places. It is in the Italian Renaissance Revival style and has served as Tampa's primary cultural and economic gateway for many years. In the 1970s and '80s, the building fell into disrepair, but in 1998 it was restored to its original glory. The 5,236-square-foot, two-story red brick building is embellished with cast stone columns and a two-story opalescent glass window and terra cotta cornice. It currently houses the City of Tampa's neighborhood office, in addition to serving as a functioning train station.

Photo by Ron Williams.

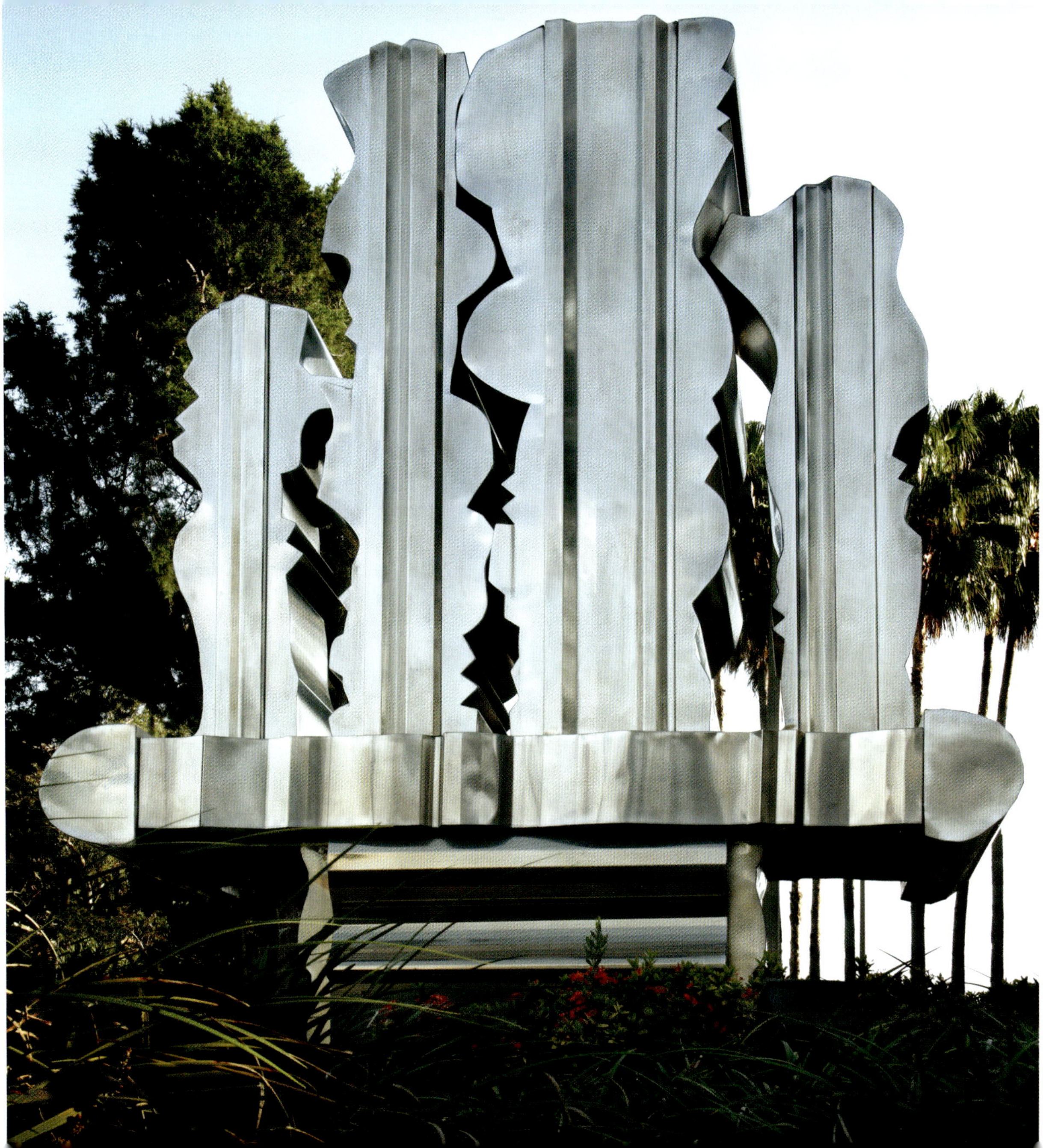

Geoffrey Naylor, *Family of Man*. Stainless steel. 13 × 8 × 4 feet. Bayshore Boulevard. City of Tampa Public Art Program. This minimalist stainless steel artwork depicts a man, a woman, and children.

Photo by Ron Williams.

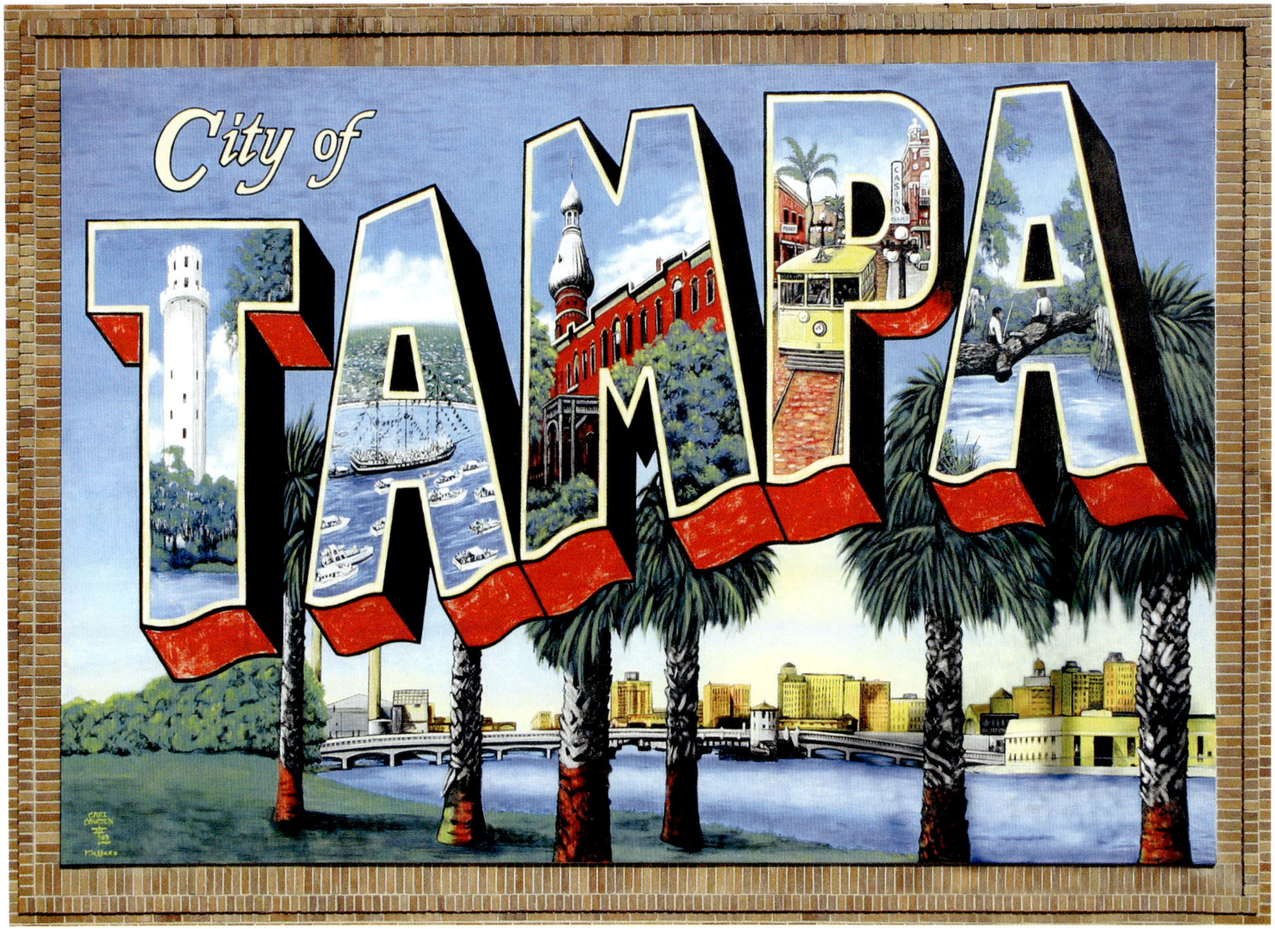

Carl Cowden, *Florida Avenue Mural*, 2003. Acrylic on stucco. 1102 North Florida Avenue. City of Tampa Public Art Program. Artist Carl Cowden's postcard-inspired mural merges images from the past and the present on this historic building.

Photo by Ron Williams.

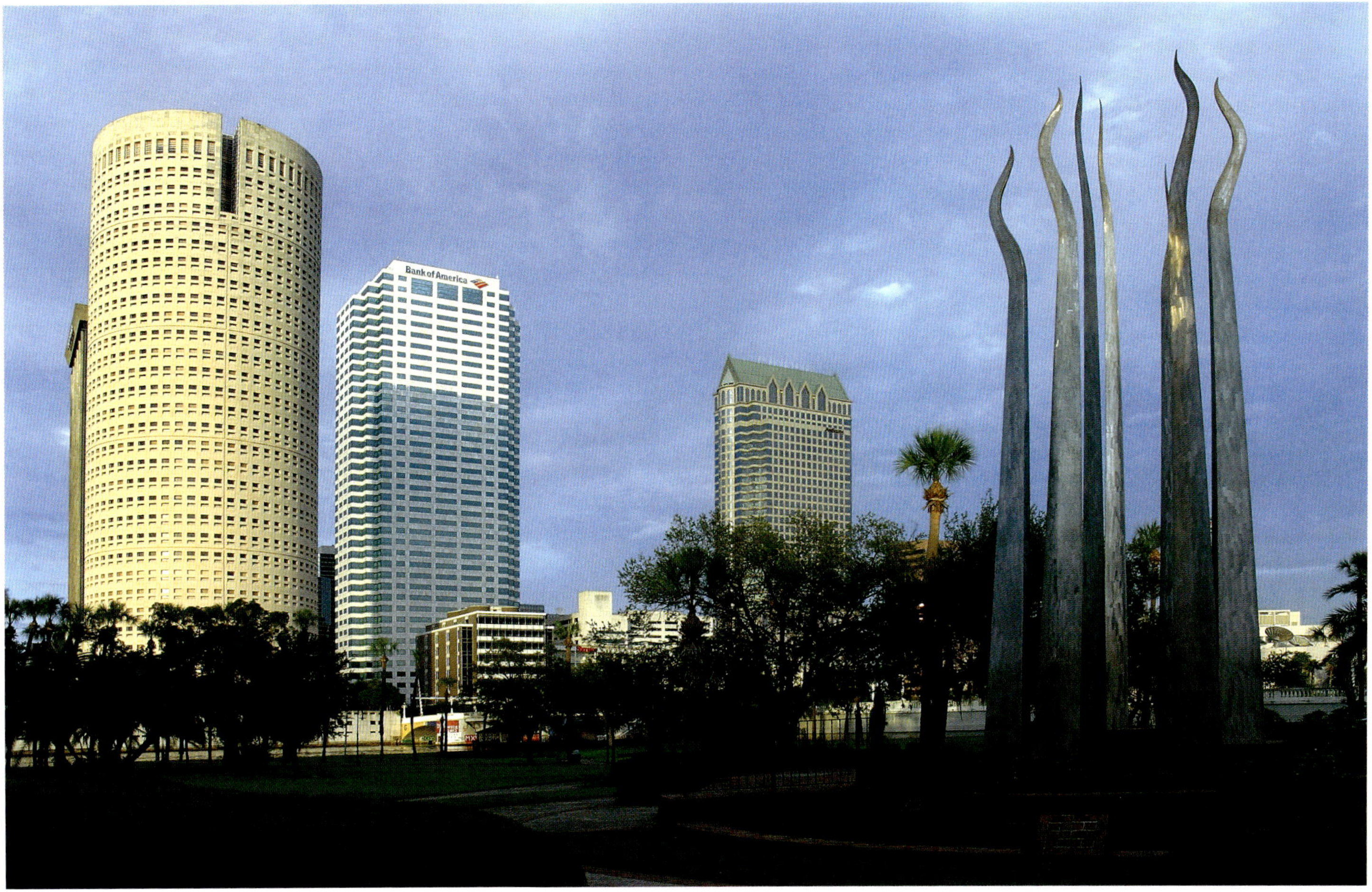

University of Tampa, *Sticks of Fire*. Early European explorers learned the word "Tampa" from Native Americans. Its meaning is speculative at best, though many claim it means "sticks of fire" in the language of the Calusa, a native Florida tribe.

Photo by Ron Williams.

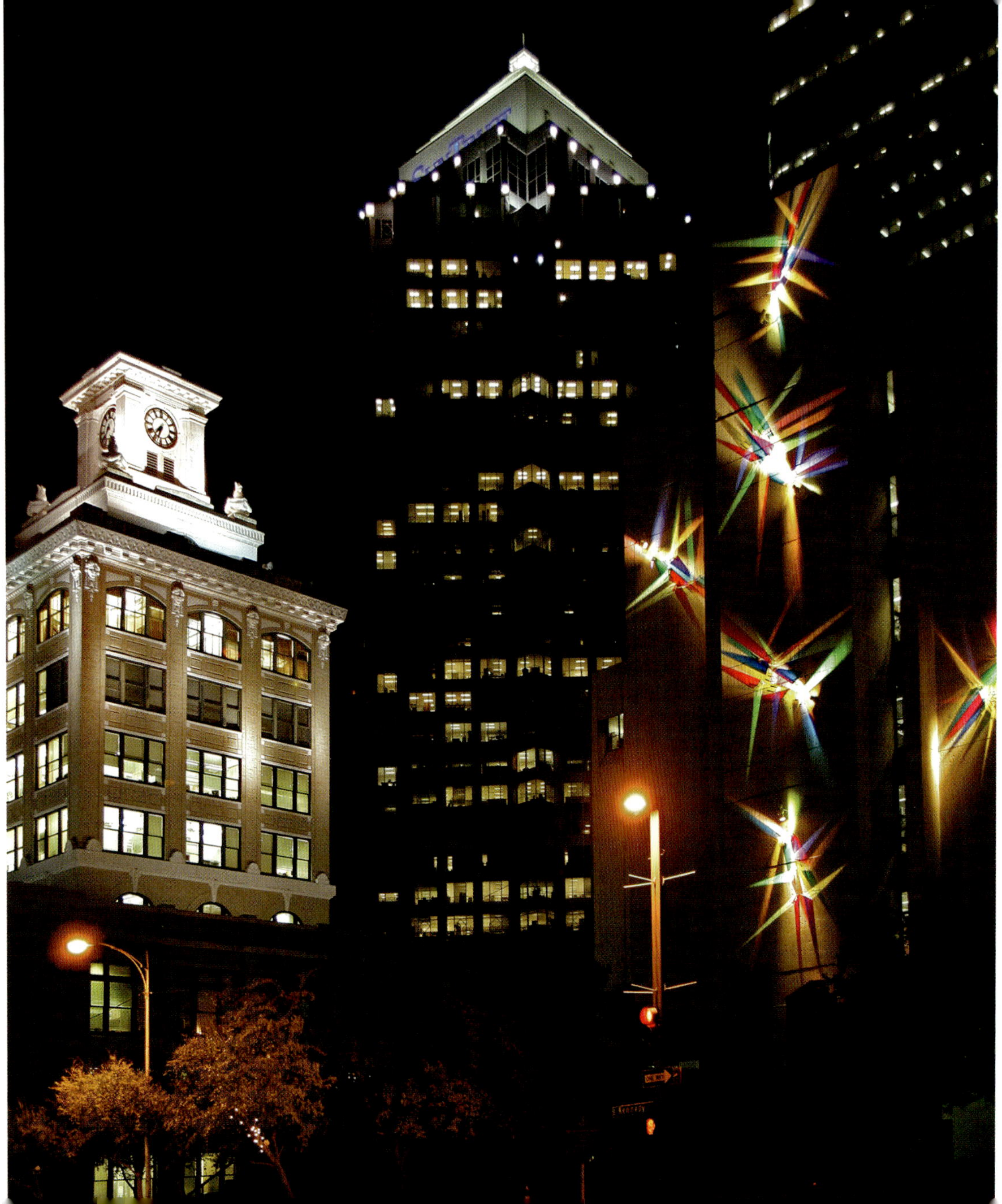

Stephen Knapp, *Luminous Affirmations*, 2005. Laminated safety glass, halogen lighting. Tampa Municipal Office Building. City of Tampa Public Art Program. According to Knapp, each piece has a presence that far exceeds its physical dimensions. At once both physical objects and illusions, they remind us that dreams, hopes, and aspirations are the center of art's ability to touch the human spirit. The lights ebb and flow, reflecting the dynamism of the city.
Photo by Ron Williams.

The residents of Tampa are extraordinarily proud of their theater, and news is spreading. *LIFE* magazine recently designated the Tampa Theatre as one of "America's 21 Wonders."
Photo by Ron Williams.

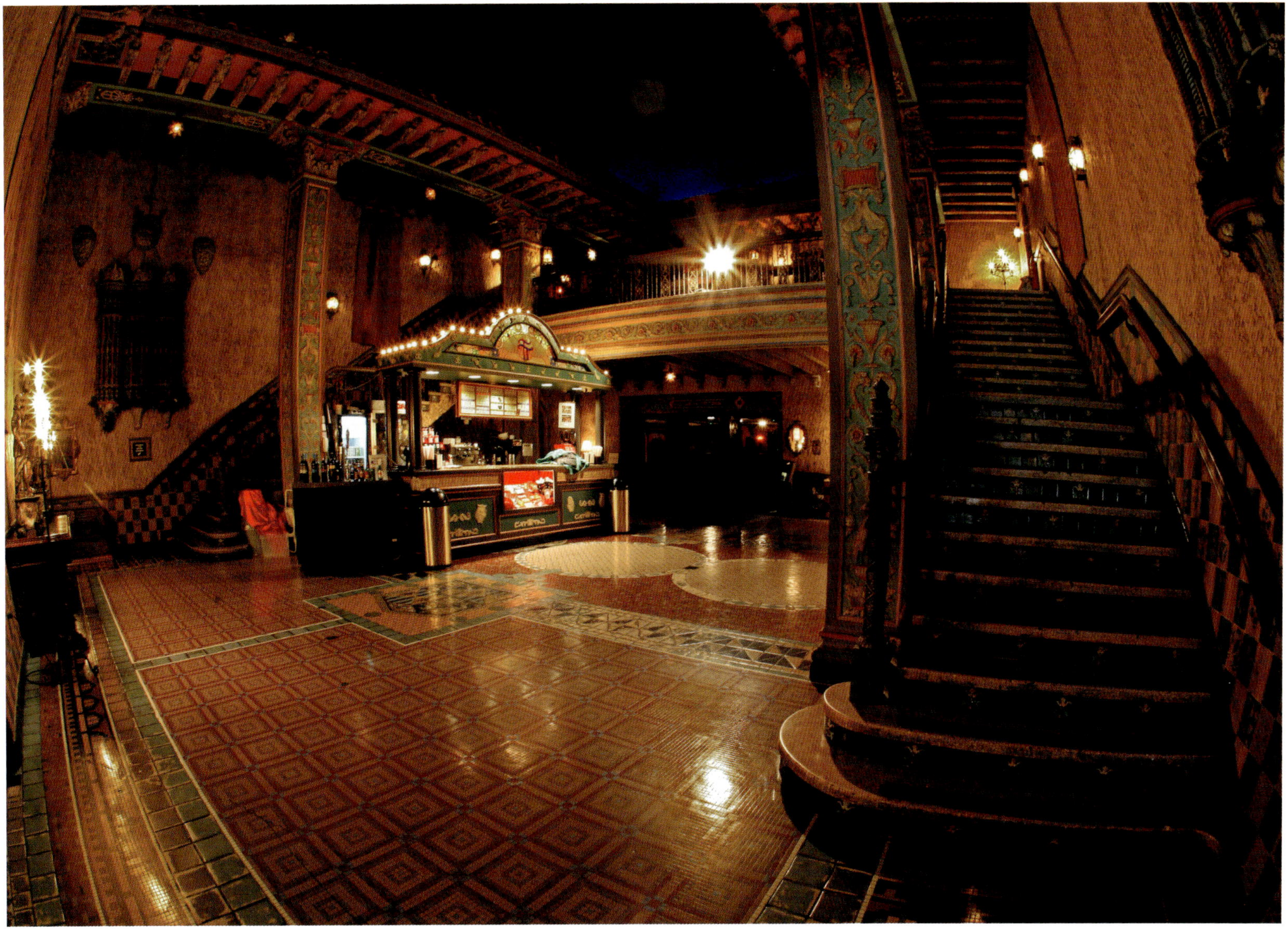

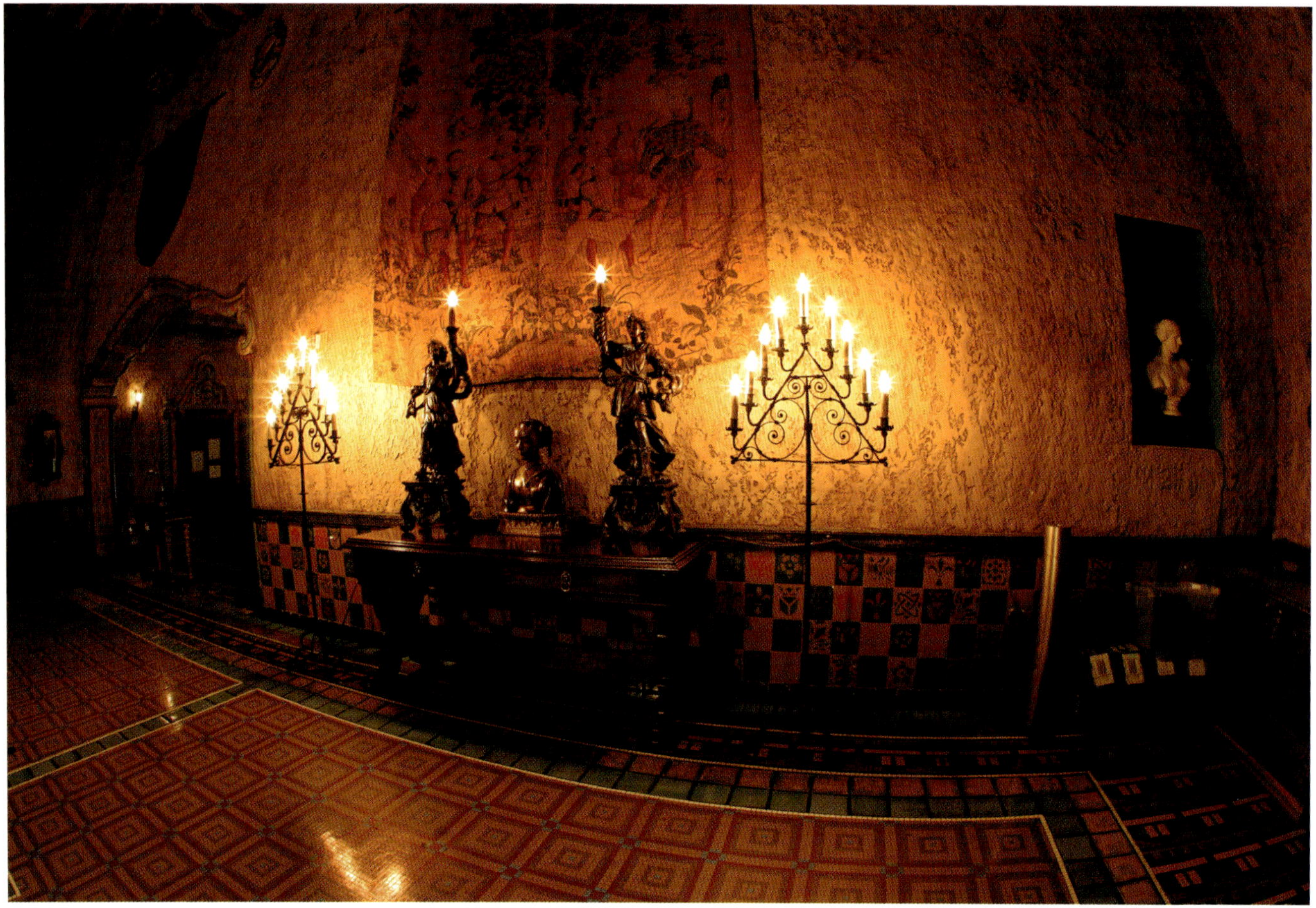

The Tampa Theatre has been a beloved community treasure since 1926. It is one of America's best-preserved examples of grand movie palace architecture.

Photo by Ron Williams.

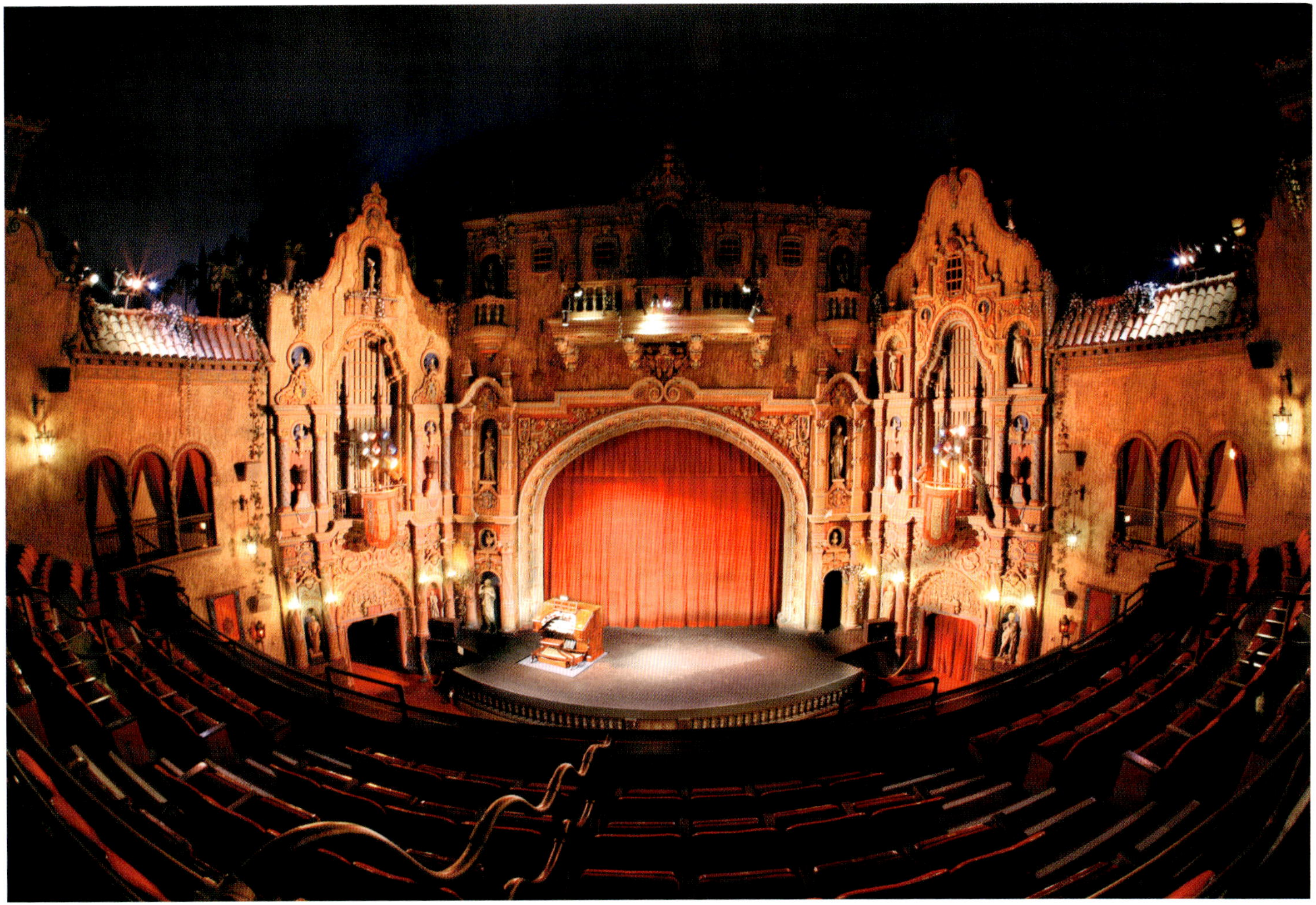

The Tampa Theatre hosts nearly 600 events annually, including films, concerts, special events, and tours.
Photo by Ron Williams.

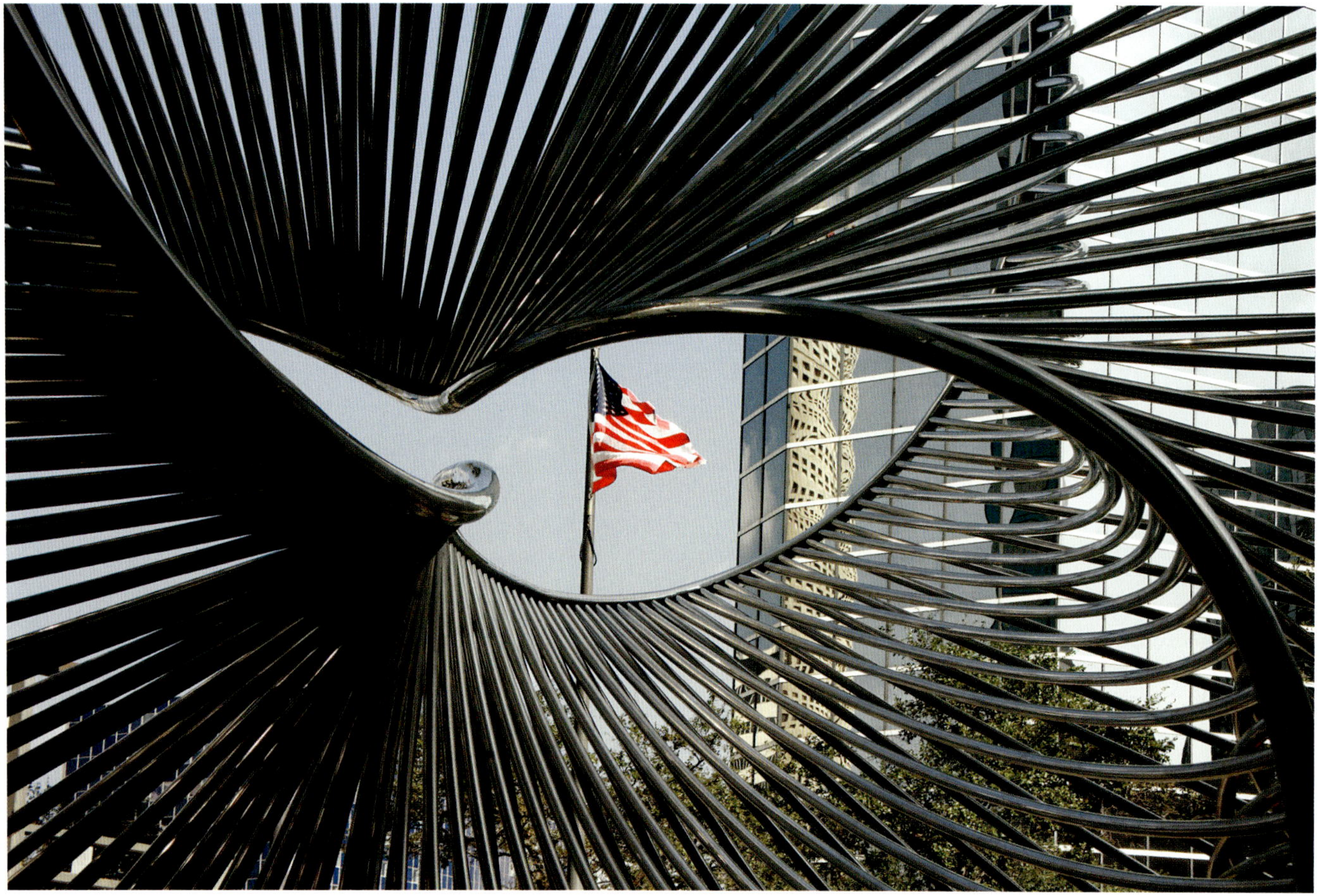

Charles Perry, *Solstice*, 1985. Stainless steel. 28 × 28 × 12 feet. 101 East Kennedy Boulevard. City of Tampa Public Art Program. Commissioned by Paramet Plaza Associates. This polished stainless steel sculpture (described by the artist as a "two-thirds twist triangular torus mobius") comprises 600 pieces, which were assembled at a remote location and moved to the current pool site. The sculpture appears to rest on the reflecting pool's surface. Perry's ribbed sculptures suggest precise spatial mathematics and share qualities with Gothic vaulting and modern turbines.

Photo by Ron Williams.

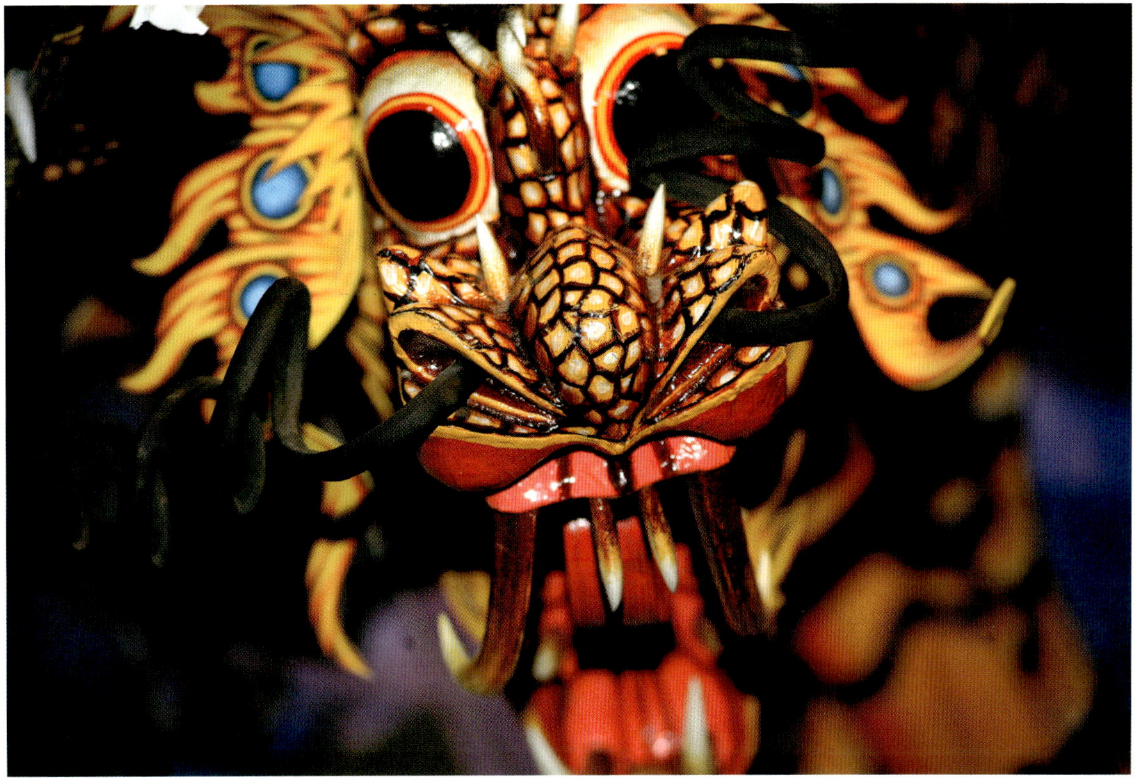

The Tampa Museum of Art presents Art After Dark. This special arm of the museum is dedicated to coordinating social parties, art auctions, and educational programs that promote emerging artists from around the bay. Tonight's feature is Anime.

Photo by Ron Williams.

All art constantly aspires towards the condition of music.

Walter Pater

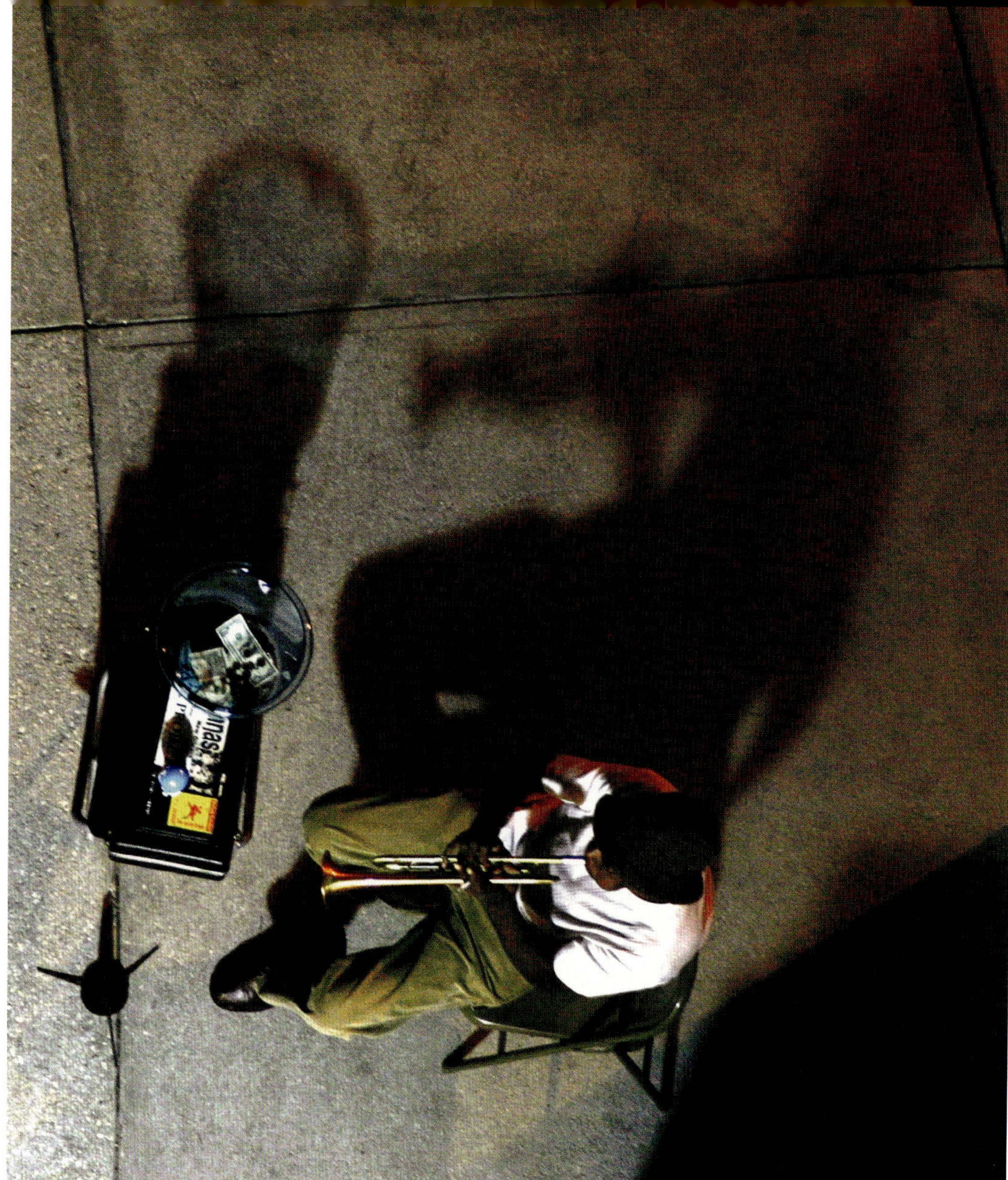

A trumpet player entertains passersby on a hot Friday night at Channelside.
Photo by Ron Williams.

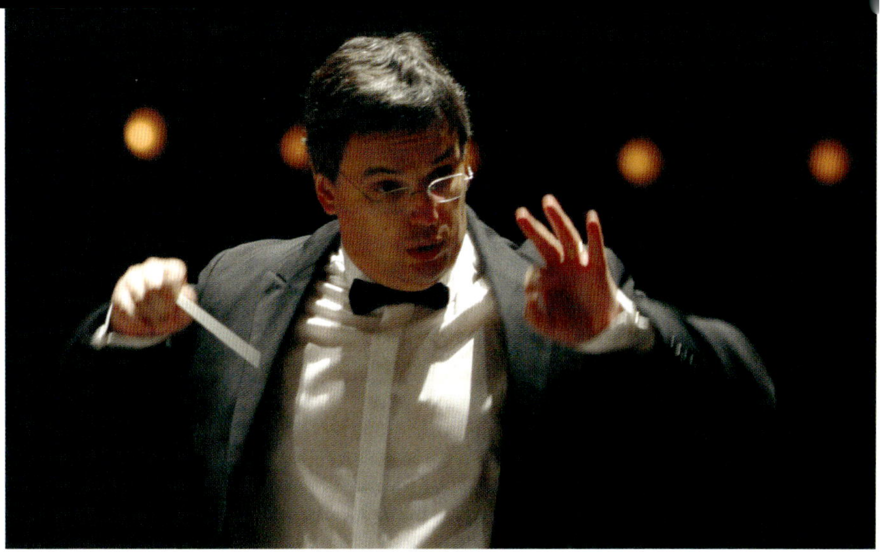

Music Director Stefan Sanderling conducts the Florida Orchestra, which is recognized as Tampa Bay's leading performing arts institution and one of the best regional orchestras in America. With 80 professional musicians, the orchestra performs more than 150 concerts annually in the tri-city area of Tampa, Clearwater, and St. Petersburg. Photos by Martin U.K. Lengemann.

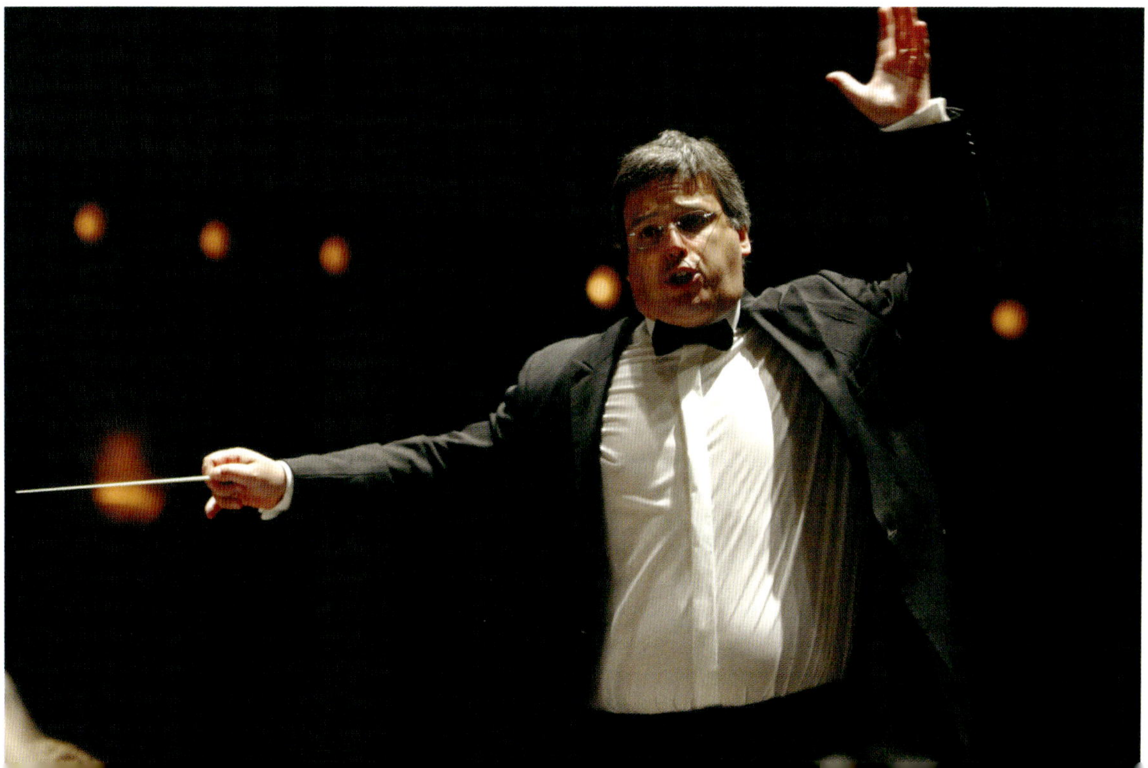

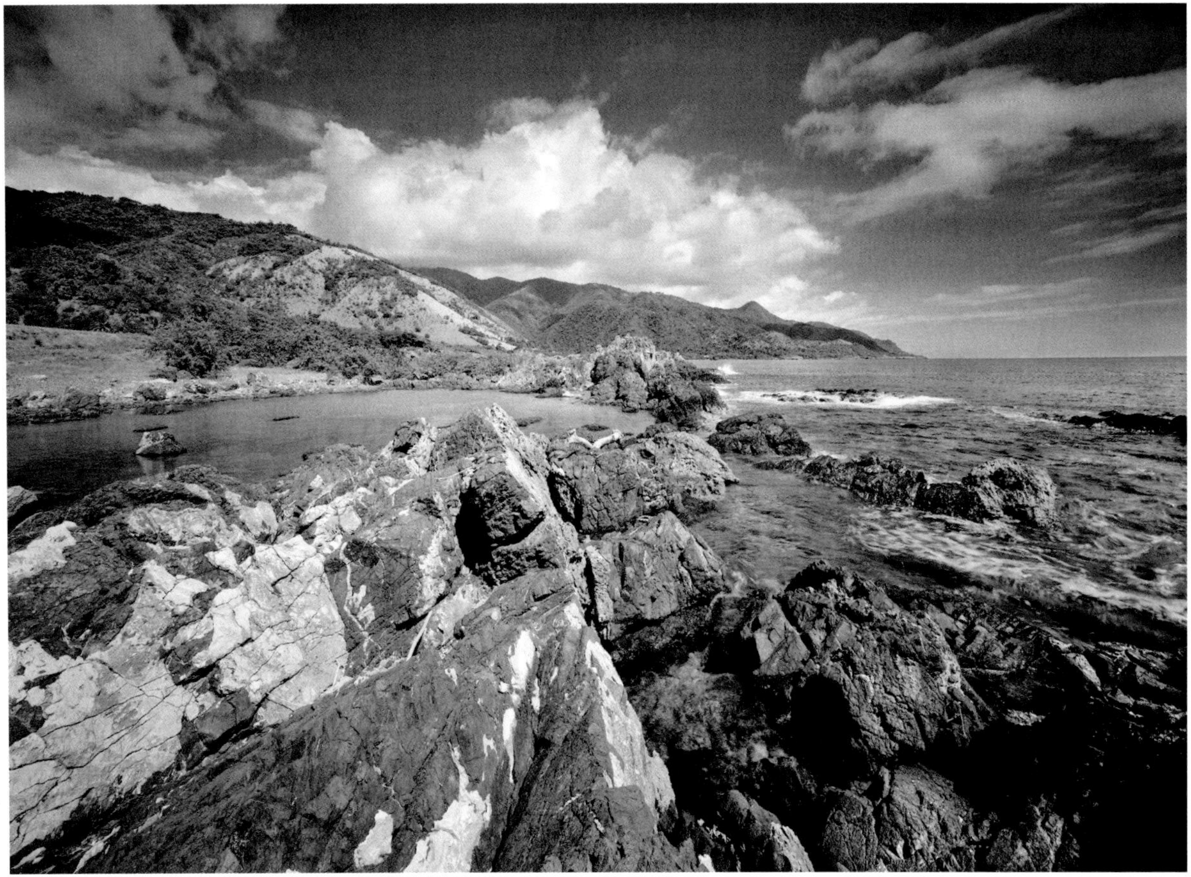

Clyde Butcher's "Via Escencia" in the Florida Museum of Photographic Arts (FMoPA) exhibition "Cuba." The museum exhibits all aspects of historic photography, contemporary photography–based artworks, and social documentary and photojournalism. FMoPA's aim is to explore all aspects of this versatile medium that is the mainstay of the visual vocabulary of the twentieth and twenty-first centuries. The museum also offers photography classes, lectures, and numerous events. Image provided with permission of the Florida Museum of Photographic Arts.

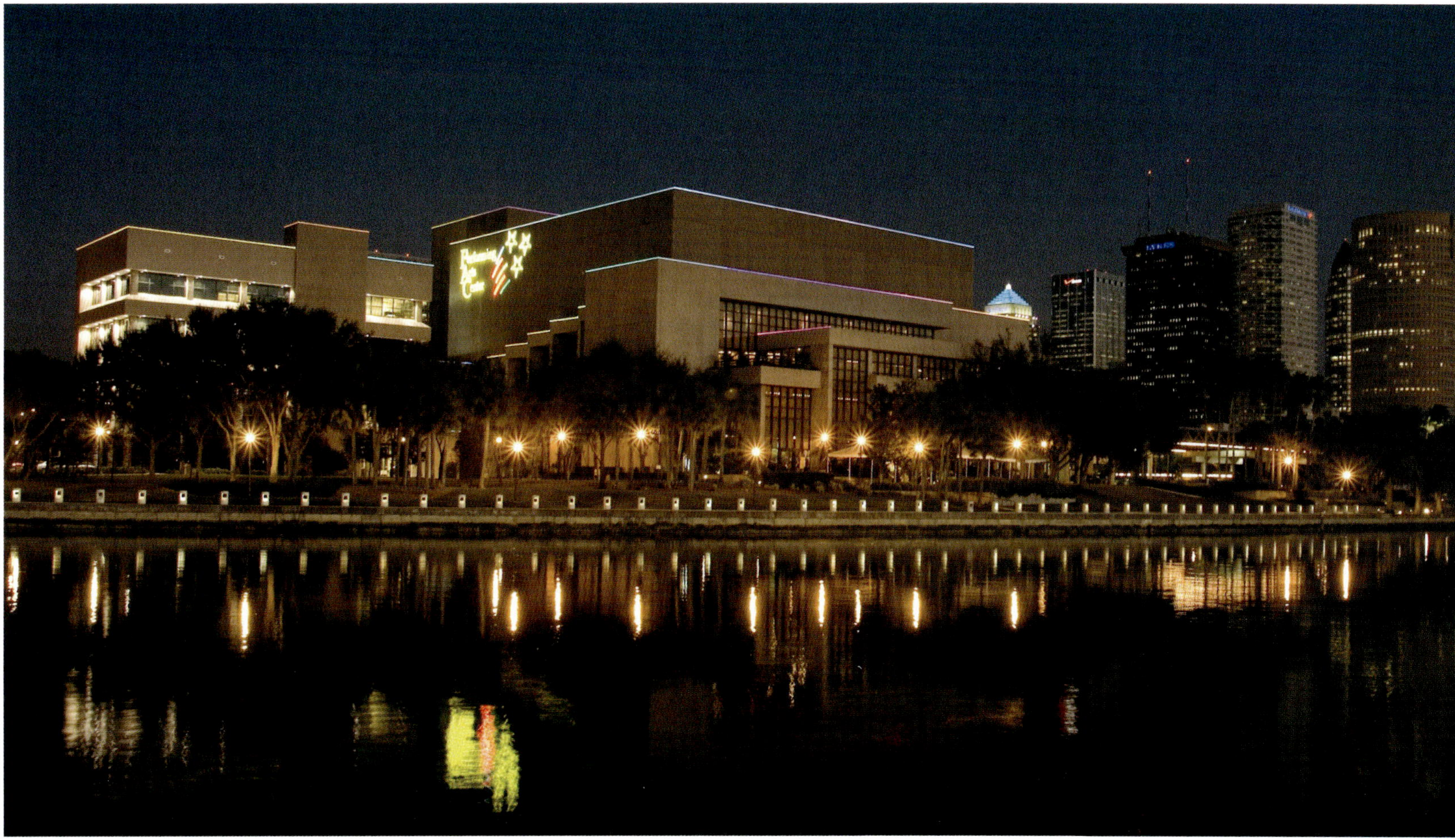

The Tampa Bay Performing Arts Center at dusk on the Hillsborough River, opened its doors in 1987. It hosts nearly 4,000 events per season and sponsors a school to teach theater through the Patel Conservatory.

Image provided with permission of the Tampa Bay Performing Arts Center.

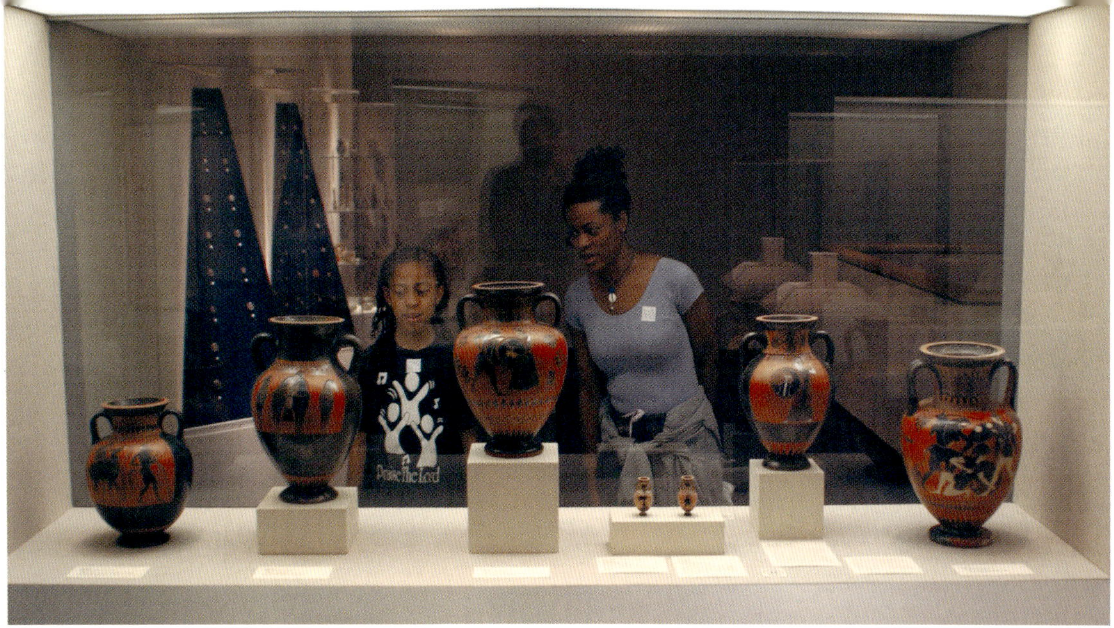

The Tampa Museum of Art provides a broad range of art-related experiences for visitors of all ages. Its collections include twentieth-century and contemporary art and a renowned collection of Greek and Roman antiquities. A changing special exhibitions program provides a mix of classical and contemporary shows.
Courtesy of Tampa's Downtown Partnership.

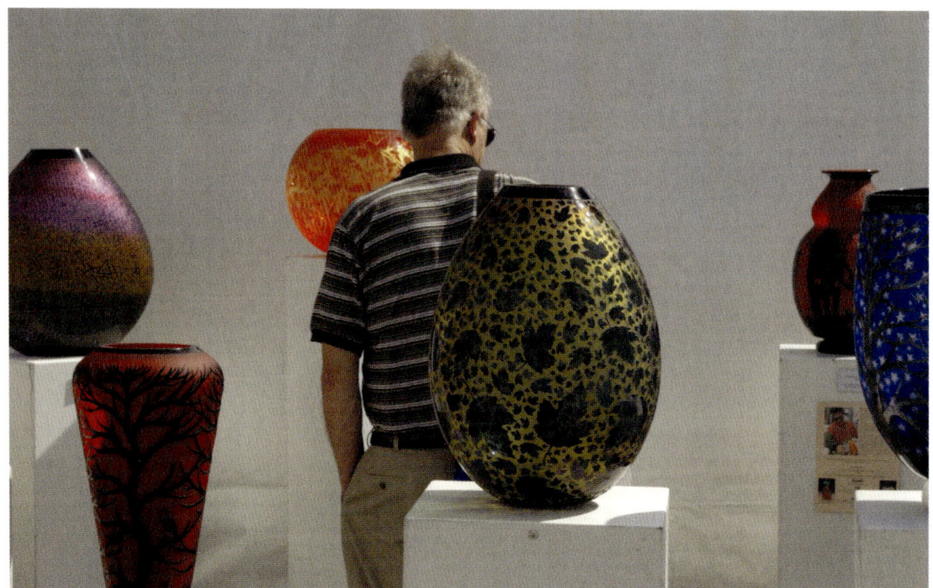

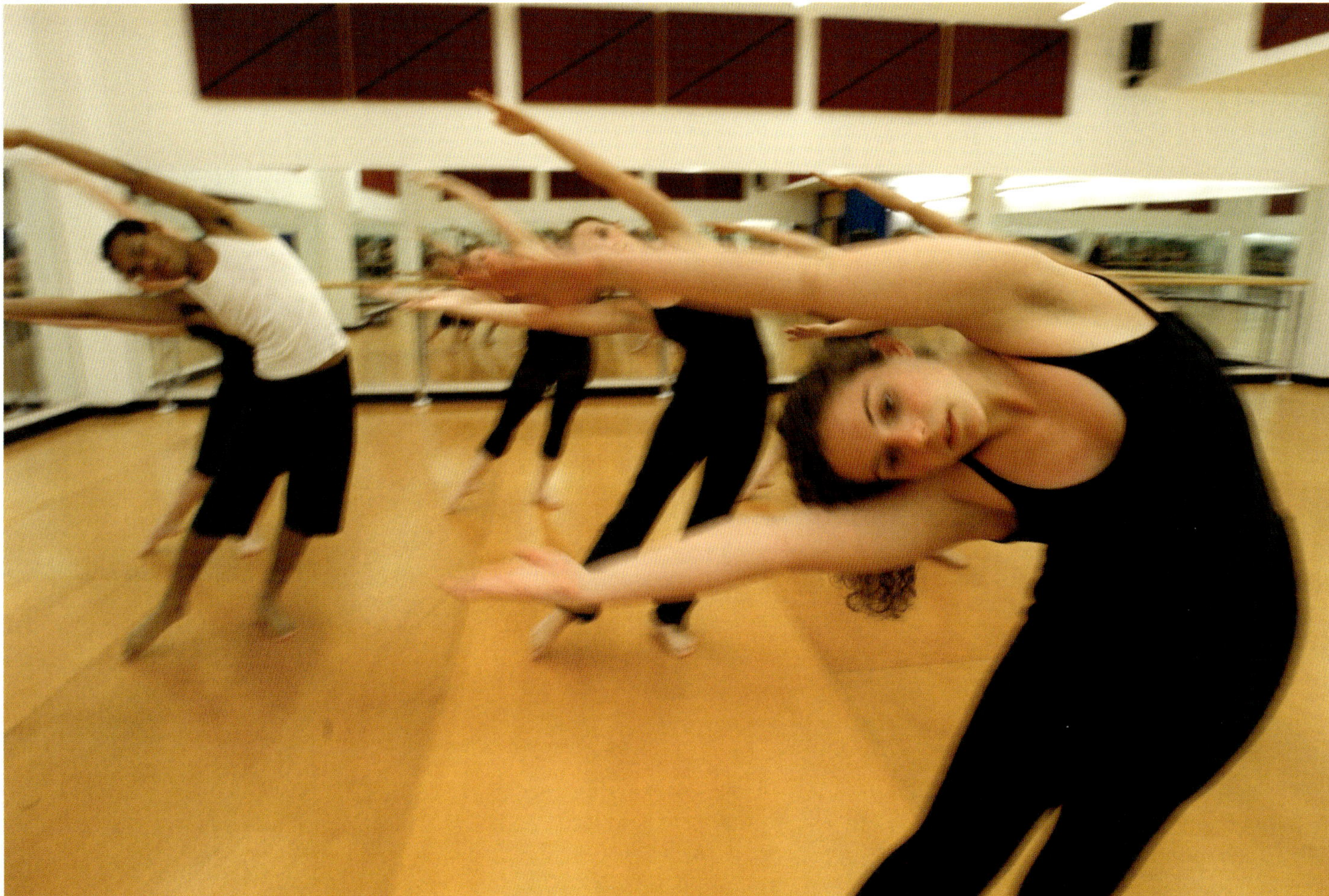

Dancers warm up at a rehearsal.
Courtesy of Tampa's Downtown Partnership.

City by the Sea

Tampa is well known for its Latin-inspired culture, warm weather, and gracious hospitality, yet nothing sets our city apart better than its beautiful waterfront. Tampa's port welcomes ships of all sizes. Home to small sailing vessels bobbing up and down on their lines and speedboats slipping in and out of narrow channels, this safe haven rests under a Florida-perfect sky. The bustling harbor welcomes an international parade of ships, and the busy harborfront is lined with shops, cafes, and stately palms. From on shore, residents and visitors enjoy breathtaking views of undersea life, fiery sunsets, and the occasional cruise ship crossing the horizon. With real estate developments dotting downtown harbor districts, cruise ships welcoming and delivering thousands of visitors per year, and private vessels setting sail on late summer evenings, it is easy to see why Tampa is truly a city by the sea.

Home to the largest port in Florida and the tenth-largest port in the Untied States, Tampa's waterfront has played an essential role in its development from a small fishing community to a world-class destination. The carefree waterside belies the hard work that goes into supporting this full-service port facility. Tampa's harbor contributes more than $15 billion to the local economy and has created 130,000 jobs for local residents, making it intensely vital to the residents of Tampa Bay.

Tampa's rich history and cultural diversity is wholly interconnected with the sea. Sea transport brought in immigrants from Latin America and the Caribbean who settled into distinct communities and pioneered trade networks across the shoaling waters. Above and below the surface, Tampa's harbor supports a wide array of wildlife from baby black skimmers and eastern brown pelican to manatees and bottlenose dolphins. From the water's edge anyone can catch a glimpse of smooth gray dolphins or be mesmerized by the fluttering of a stingray.

This same harbor is equally important to city visitors. Several major cruise lines depart from Tampa weekly, carrying millions of cruise passengers to destinations around the globe. By serving as an important gateway to the world, Tampa enjoys a delightful mix of international influences that is witnessed in the local art and music scenes.

The lively seaport has also shaped Tampa's downtown development in remarkable ways. Residential communities flourish by the water's edge, and family-friendly tourist attractions offer people of all ages the opportunity to enjoy moonlit dinners and daily cruises through beautiful indigo waters. With ongoing development of the 2.4-mile Riverwalk, locals have even more places to enjoy the view. The project features beautiful stretches of manicured parks, waterside restaurants, world-class museums, and renowned performing arts centers, making Tampa one of the most distinctive destinations in the United States. Floridians and their fortunate friends converge on seaside restaurants to watch some of the South's most spectacular sunsets and spot marine life playing along seawalls.

For many residents and visitors, no trip to Tampa's waterfront would be complete without touring the Florida Aquarium. Having already received more than 5 million guests, this attraction is rated one of the finest aquariums in the world. The facility hosts regular underwater shows, ecofriendly tours, aqua camps for children, and the once-in-a-lifetime chance to dive with sharks. Next door is the American Victory Mariners Memorial and Museum Ship, which offers daily tours of the historic ship and occasional sailings replete with dozens of reenactors firing blanks at World War II–era airplanes as they dive over the ship.

Not everyone needs to hop aboard a seagoing vessel to appreciate Tampa Bay;

the view from land is equally spectacular. Sailboats, sunsets, and aquatic life are a common backdrop to Tampa's famous Bayshore Boulevard. Known for being the world's longest continuous sidewalk, this pathway skirts the water and attracts hundreds of skaters, runners, and bikers enjoying the water's salty spray and the occasional dolphin clicking and squealing near the seawall. Near the westernmost end of Bayshore, one of Tampa's many fine parks—Ballast Point—allows visitors to wander to the end of a rustic pier that juts out over the water. But one needn't leave the car to enjoy the atmosphere: simply drive the four and a half miles from Gandy Boulevard to the Platt Street Bridge and enjoy fantastic views of Tampa Bay along with beautiful historic homes and modern condominiums.

Wrapping everything together is the Hillsborough River. This thoroughfare winds through quiet neighborhoods, along towering office parks and art centers, and past the waterfront convention center. The tranquil river offers an unsurpassed opportunity to see everything Tampa has to offer. Not surprisingly, America's top universities send varsity oarsmen to Tampa each spring to train in the warm tranquil waters that pass through the city and out to the sea. Weekend adventurers also enjoy Tampa's rivers and frequently refer to this area as canoe country.

For those who love the water, Tampa has everything: sailing, kayaking, cruising, power boating, or relaxing on the beach. Ben T. Beach, Davis Island Beach, or Picnic Island offer the perfect chance to read a book, ride wave runners, or take the dog for a run in his own private beach park.

Residents can wake up to beautiful water views from dozens of city skyscrapers or two island sanctuaries located near the downtown area. Harbour Island residents enjoy waterfront bistros, shopping, business centers, and world-class hotels. They can also use the in-town trolley for a quick commute to Tampa's urban art district.

Across the channel, locals from Davis Islands enjoy small-town amenities nestled into one main street filled with storefronts of every variety. They enjoy modern conveniences, restaurants, watering holes, and shops in true island comfort. Tucked away at the island's end is Peter O'Knight Airport and the Davis Island Yacht Club. This yacht club is home to one of the largest racing clubs in the Southeast, and for six months out of the year local yachts race the coastline every Thursday evening. Visitors have come to enjoy watching ships zoom across all four points of the compass under the setting summer sun.

Tampa's subtropical climate is perfect for enjoying concerts, outdoor film festivals, dining, dancing, and shopping right by the bay. All enjoy sitting underneath sunsets of flashing brilliant, burnt-red shards of color, feeling gentle trade winds, and watching ships weave across shoaling waters.

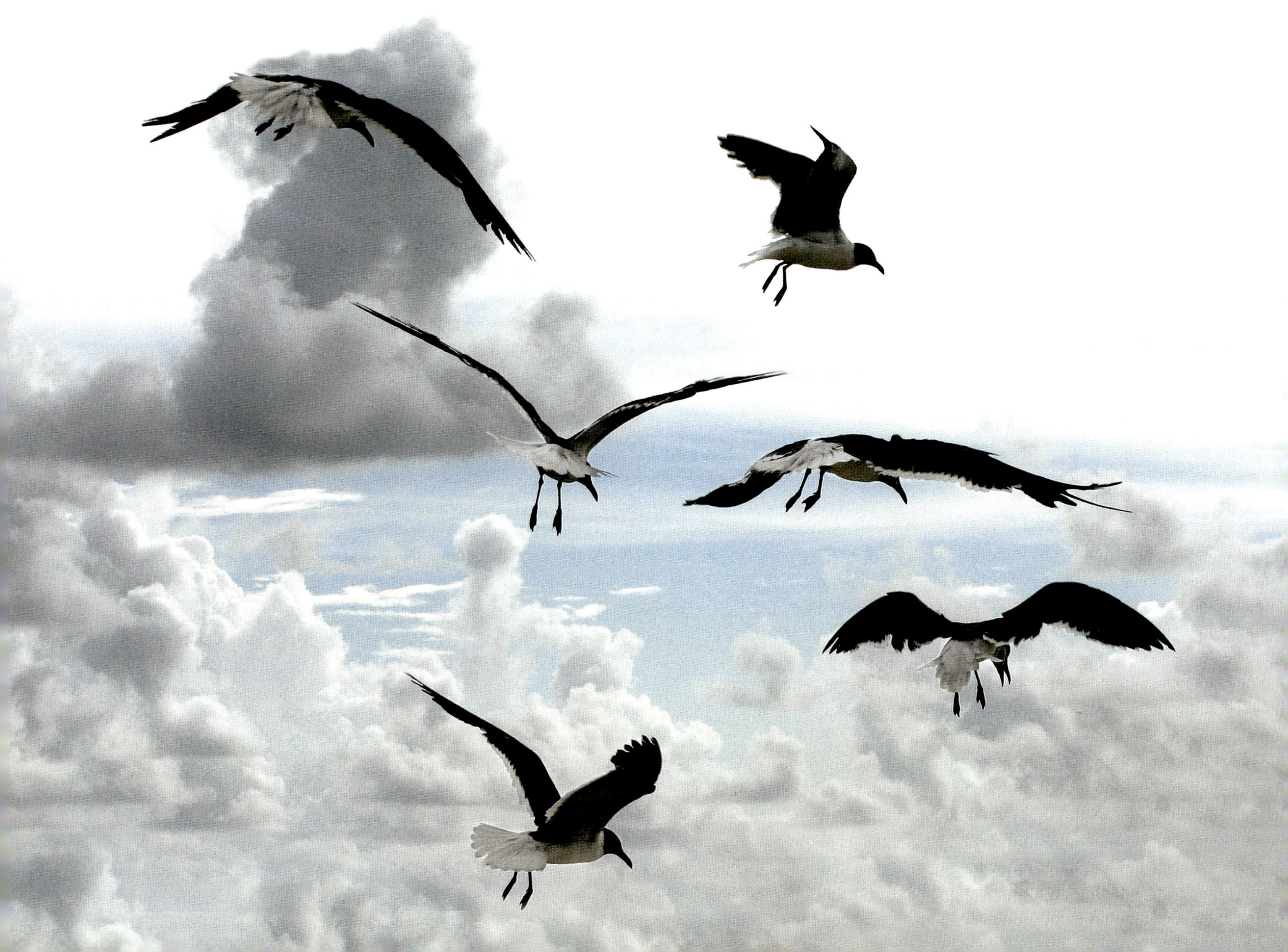

Tampa's sunsets are legendary, and local sailors enjoy a special view during Thursday night sailboat races. The friendly competitors regularly accept newcomers to help crew their ships.
Photo by Ron Williams.

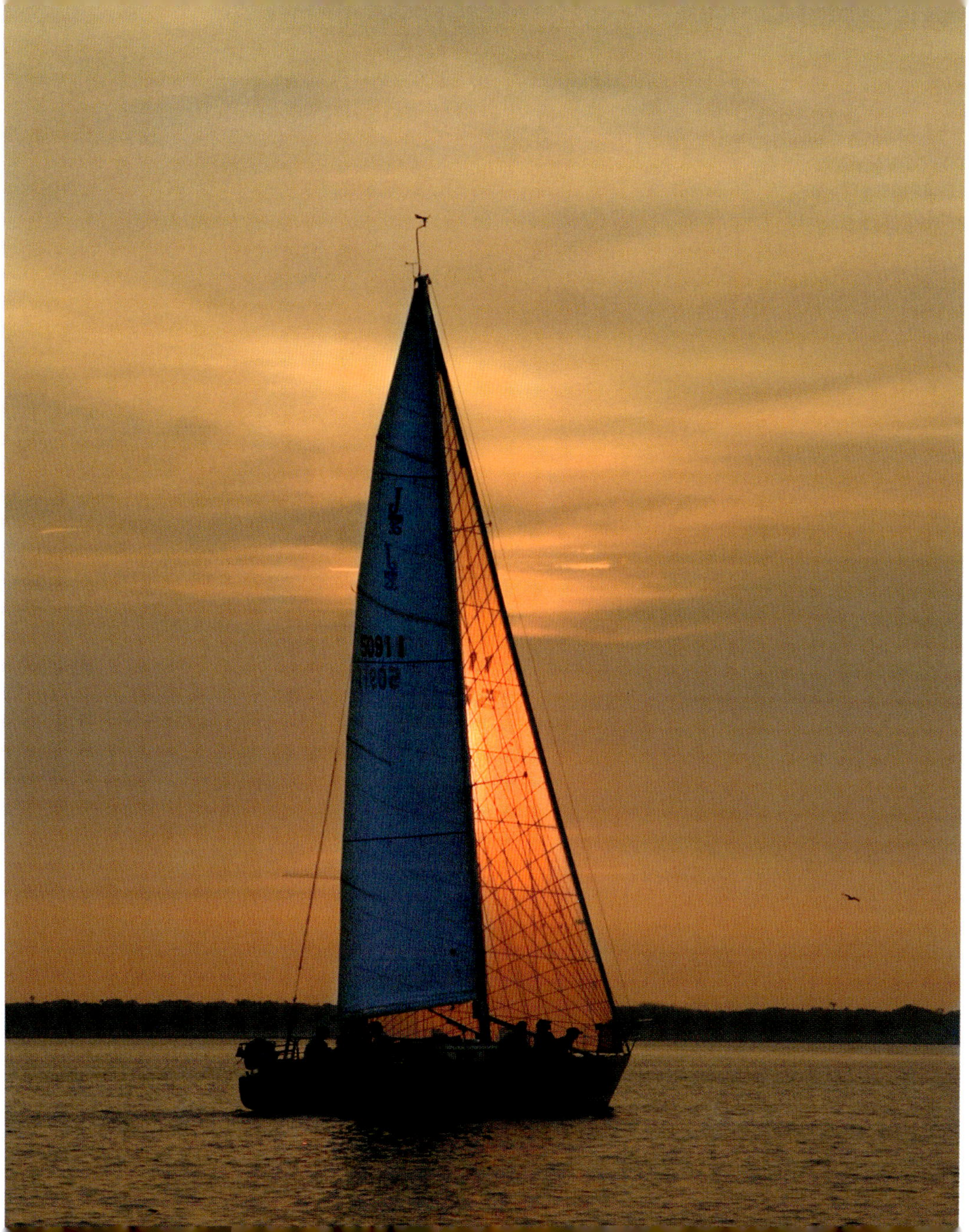

Seabirds take flight against the backdrop of Tampa's ever-changing clouds. Flocks of aquatic fowl are common sights along the waterfront.
Photo by Ron Williams.

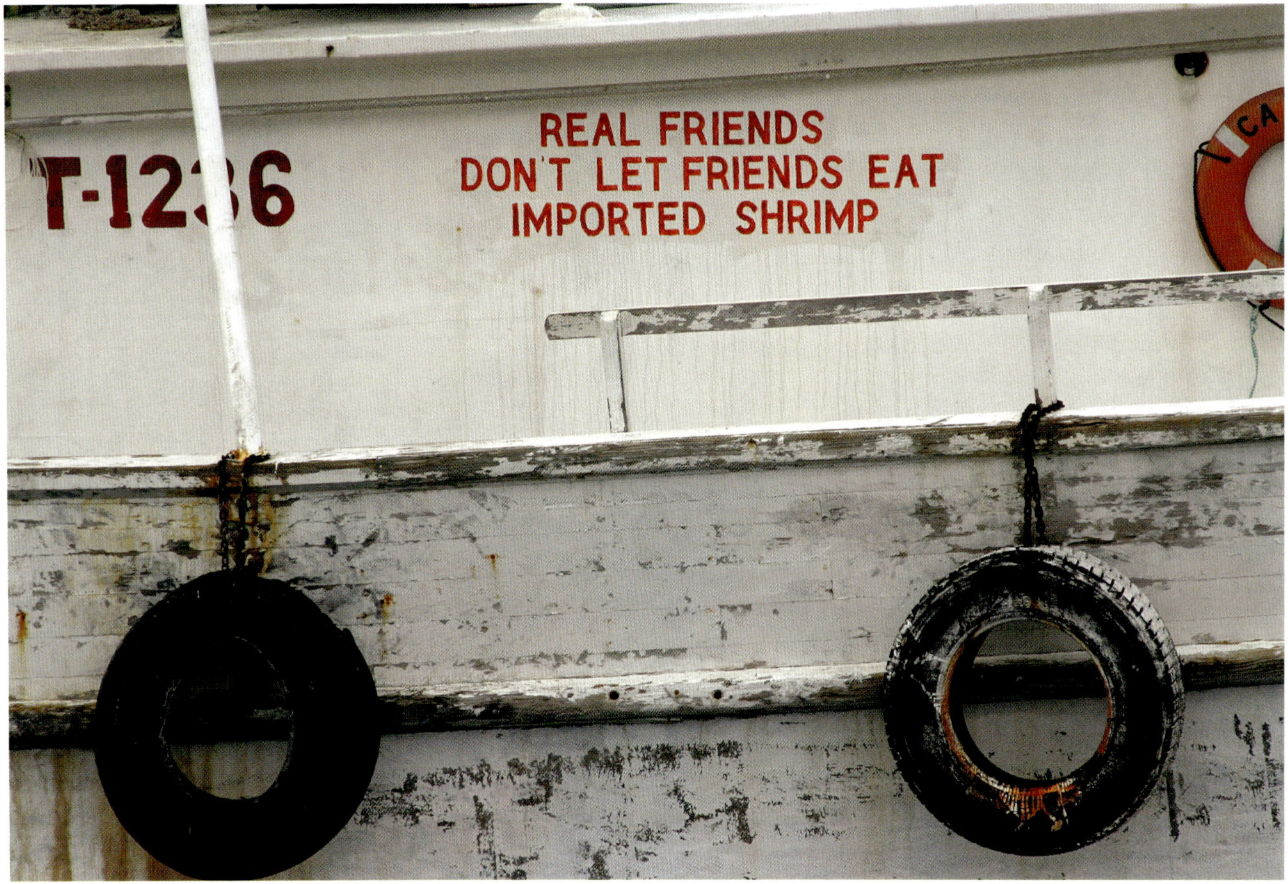

Recreational fishing makes a billion-dollar impact on the Sunshine State, and commercial seafood landings in Florida support nearly 10,000 jobs.

Photo by Ron Williams.

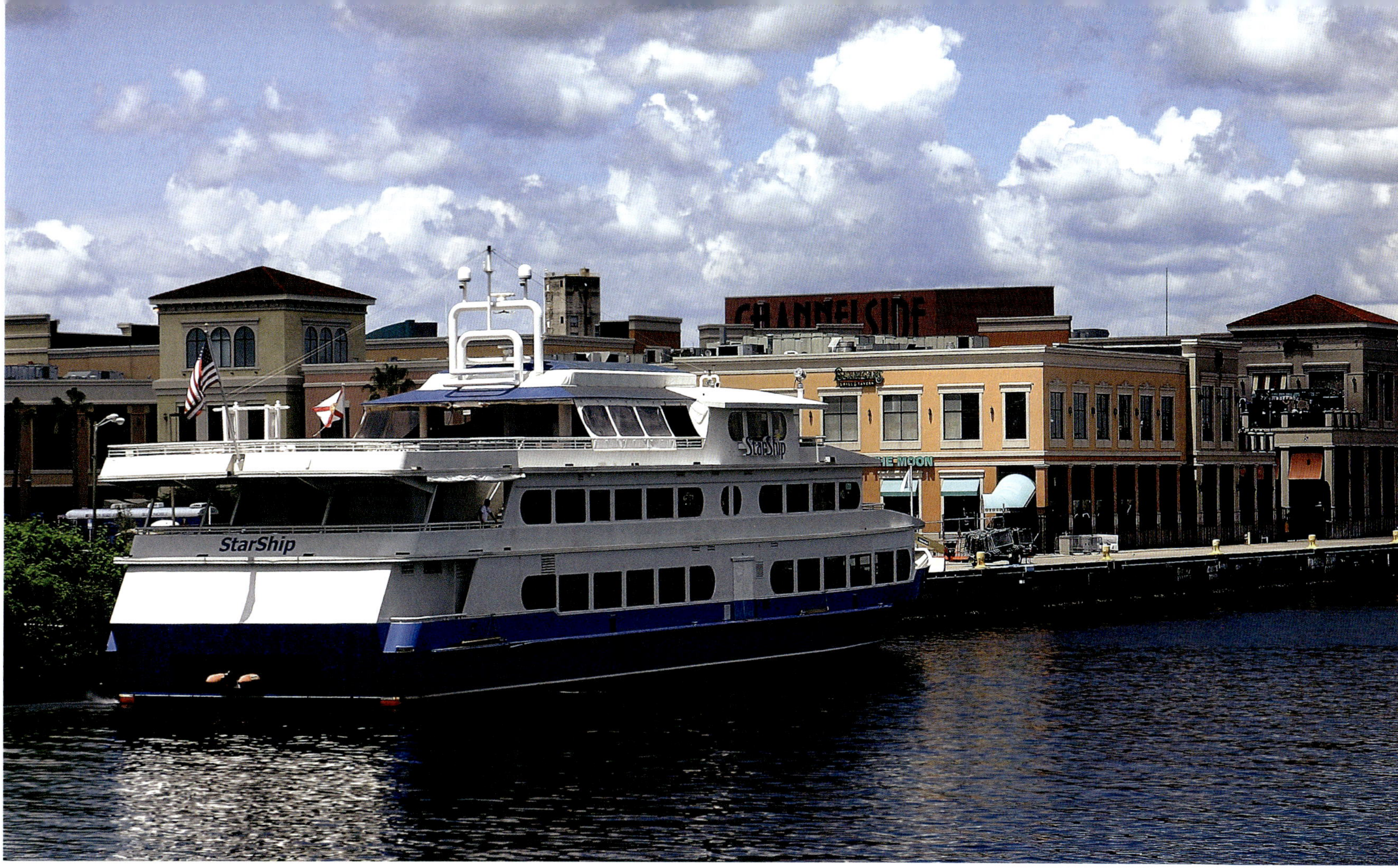

Yacht StarShip, an $8 million dining yacht based in downtown Tampa, is the first yacht in America to receive the coveted AAA three-diamond rating. It has also become Tampa Bay's number one dining yacht. Seventy-five percent of the passengers are locals, and over half are celebrating a special occasion.
Photo by Ron Williams.

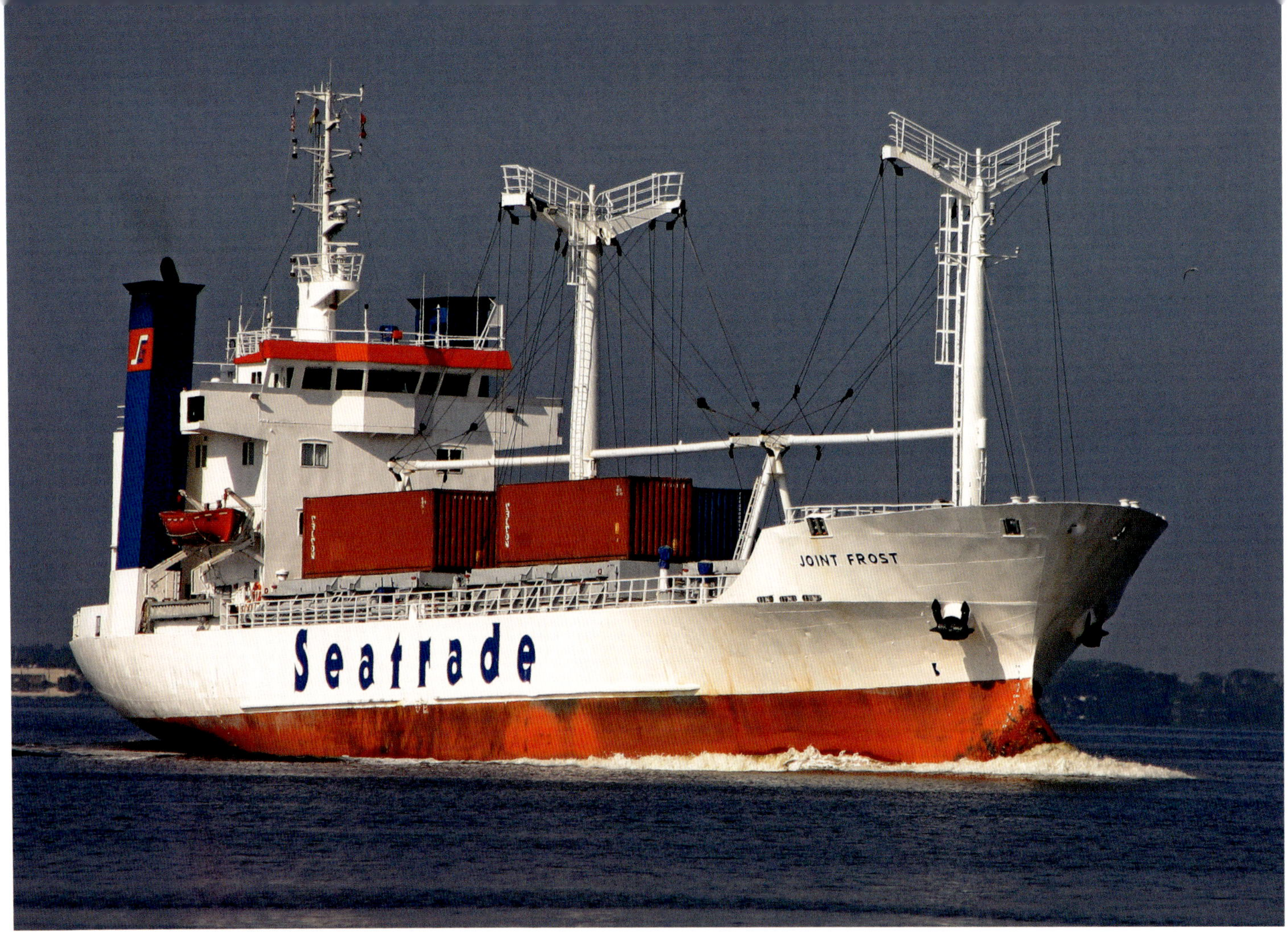

Tampa is by far the largest port in the state of Florida when measured by cargo tonnage throughput, handling approximately 50 million tons of cargo per year.
Photo by Ron Williams.

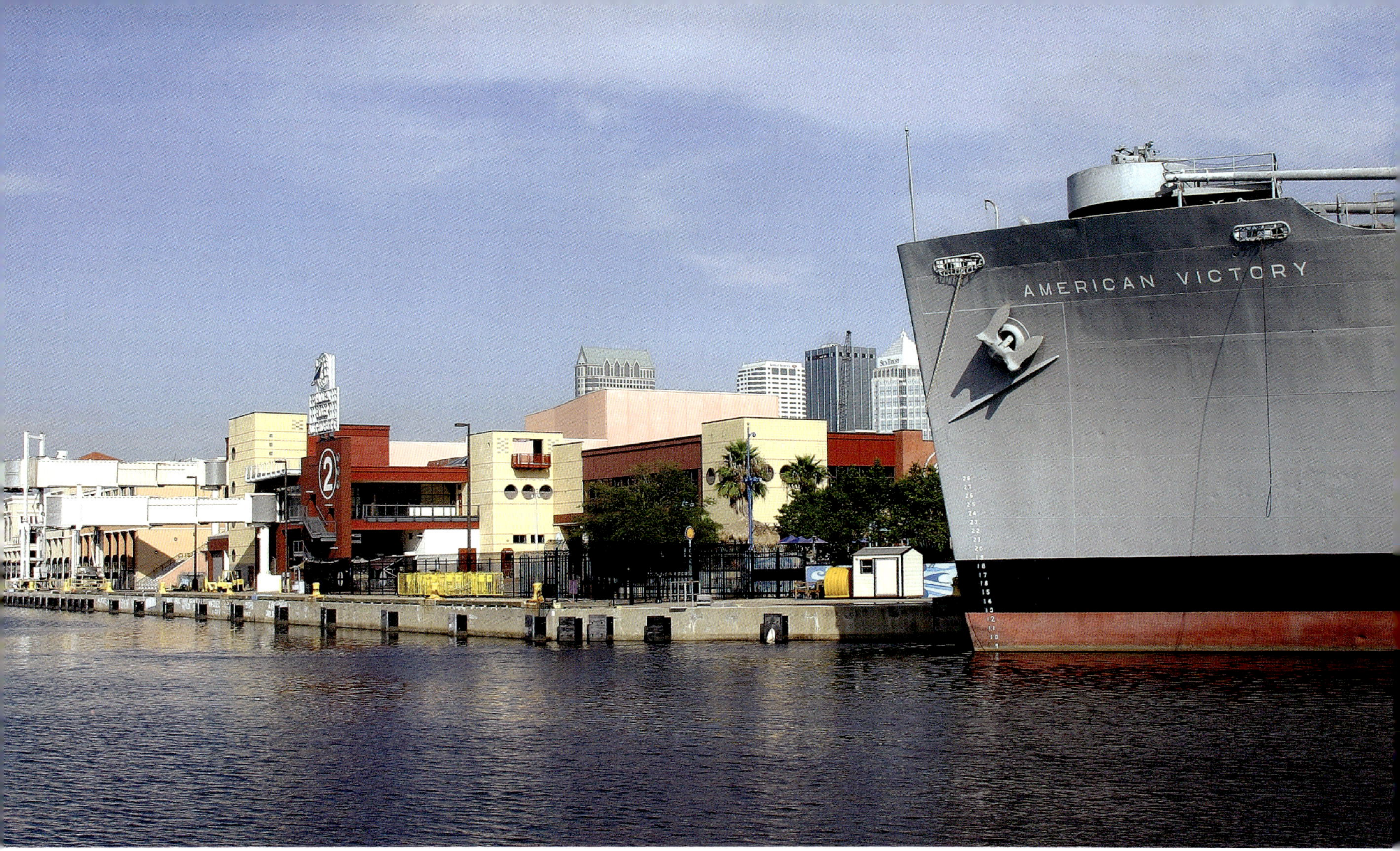

The SS *American Victory* docks beside Tampa's Channelside retail and entertainment district. Victory ships played a major role in winning World War II, transporting an estimated 85 percent of the troops, ammunition, and supplies to both the European and Pacific theaters.
Photo by Ron Williams.

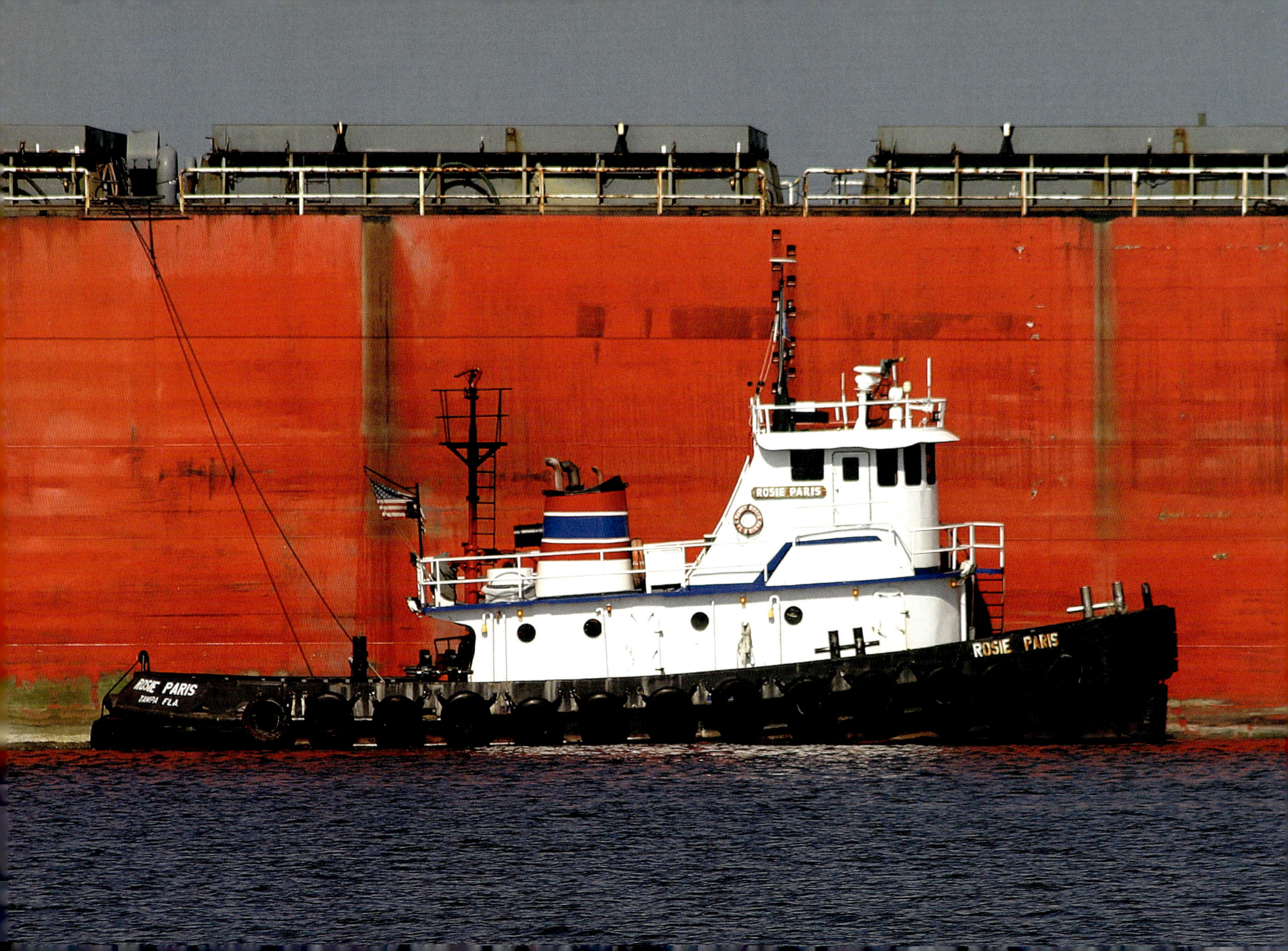
ROSIE PARIS
ROSIE PARIS
TAMPA FLA.
ROSIE PARIS

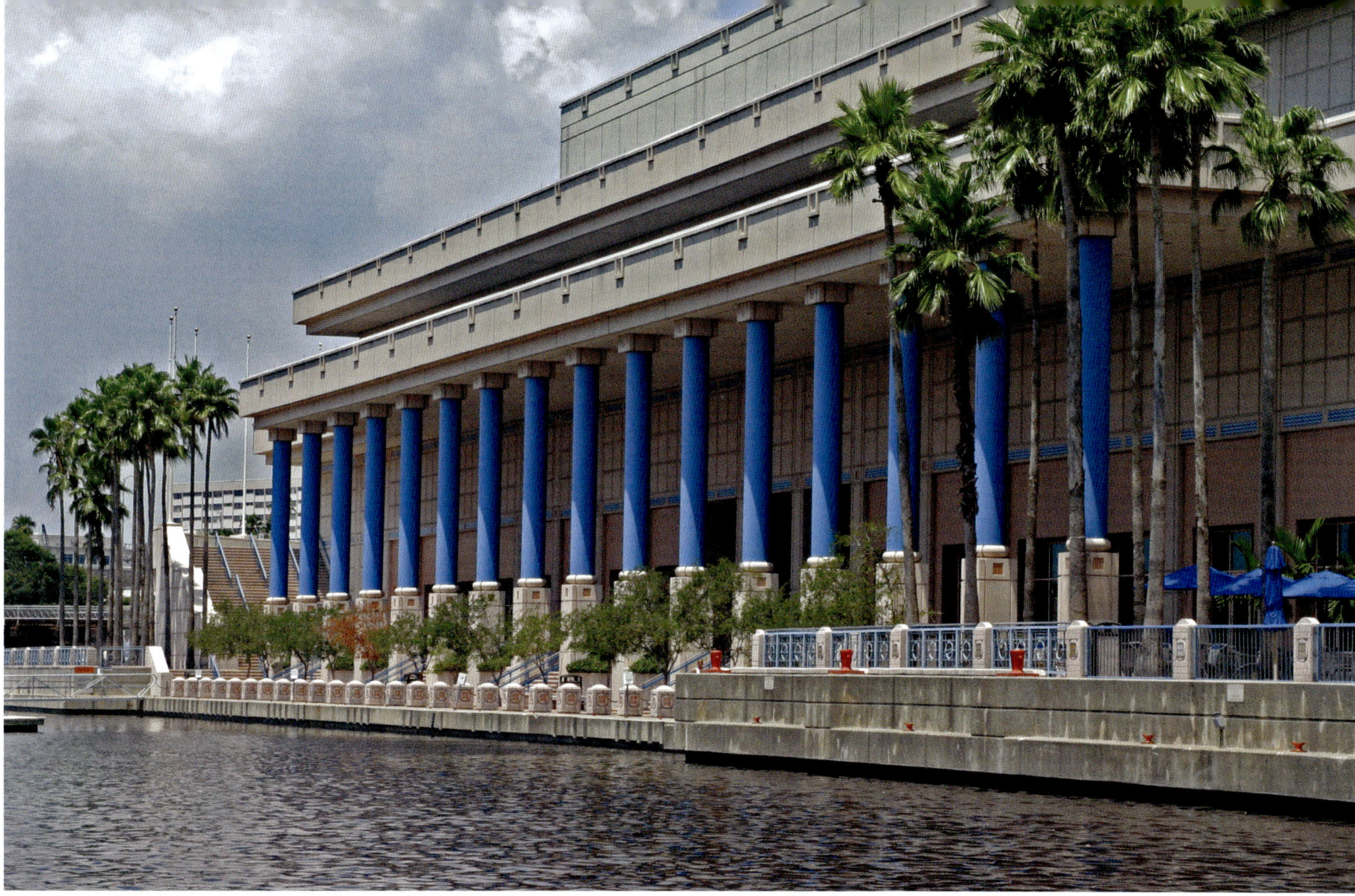

Tampa's Convention Center is nestled against the water's edge, a stone's throw from hotels, movie theaters, shops, restaurants, and clubs. The center hosts a variety of conventions, trade shows, and other special events year-round.

Photo by Ron Williams.

A little tugboat takes on a big load. The Port of Tampa is home to a vibrant and diverse traffic base. With nearly 7 million people within 100 miles of the port, this harbor keeps an active schedule.

Photo by Ron Williams.

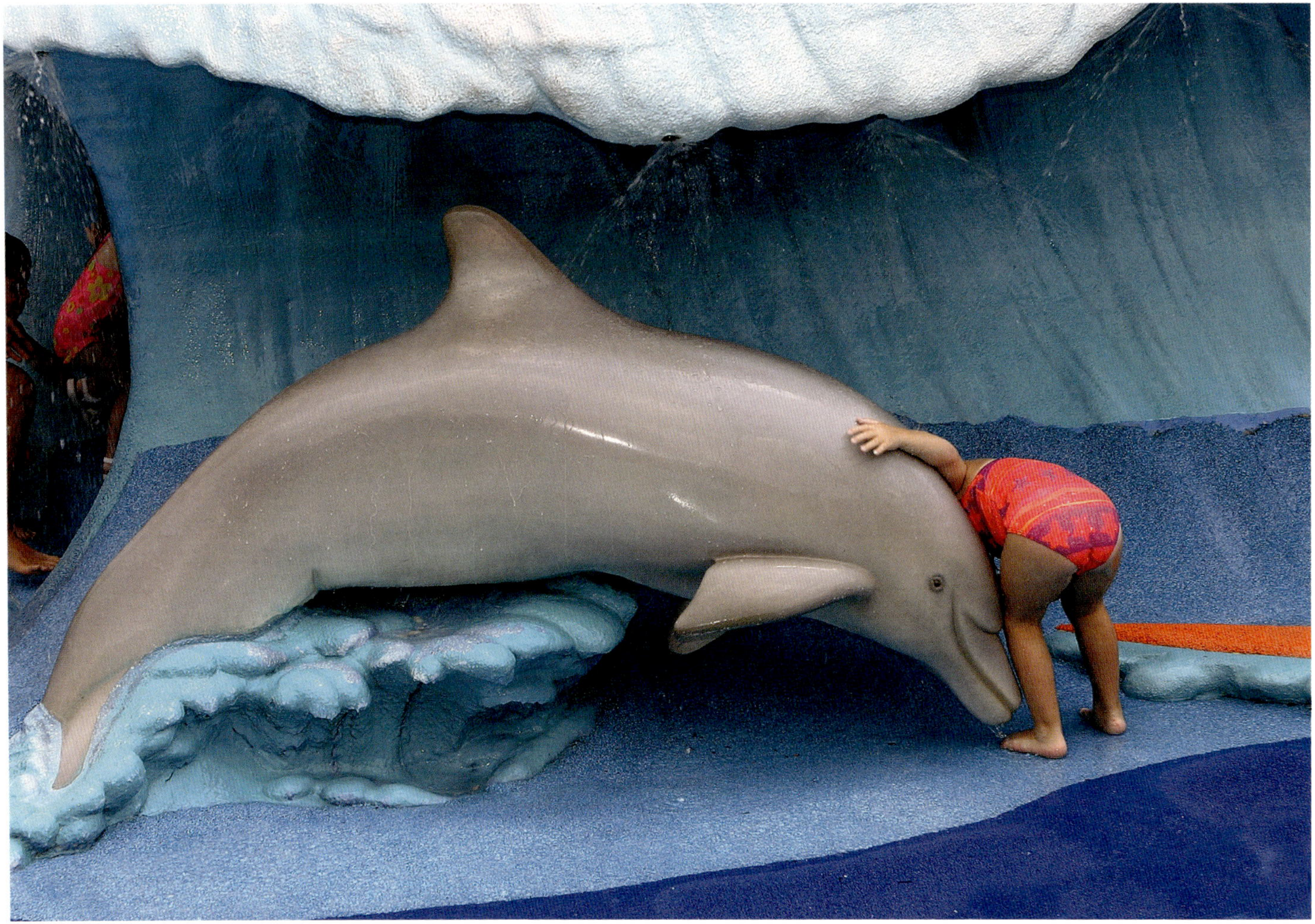

A child explores a replica dolphin at the Florida Aquarium, which is dedicated to public entertainment, education, and conservation. Its mission is to educate and inspire, and it is no wonder this destination is such a hit with the whole family.

Photo by Ron Williams.

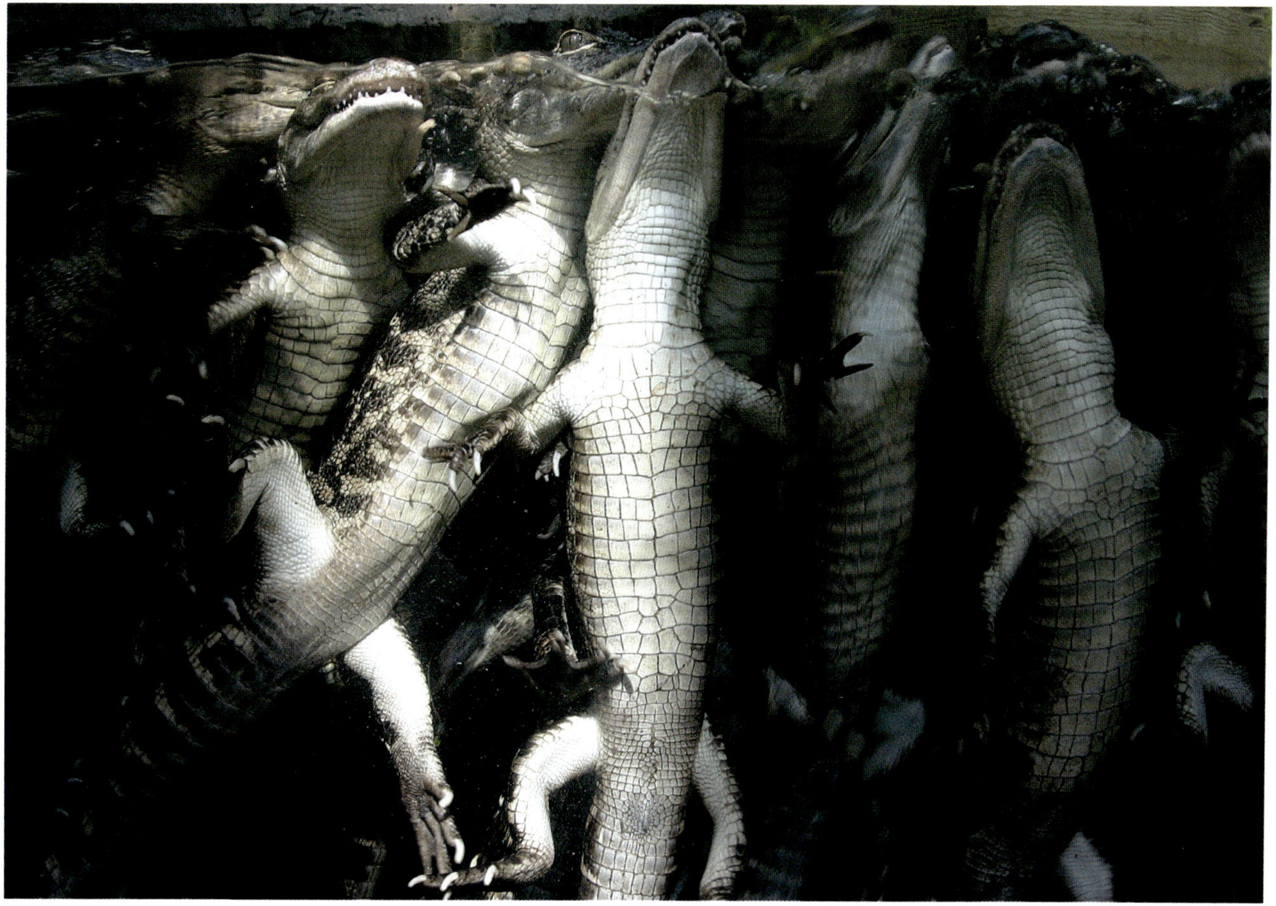

The Florida Aquarium is home to over 10,000 aquatic plants and animals from 1,340 species from Florida and all over the world. The cornerstone of the Channel District, the Aquarium serves as a significant example of Florida's commitment to preserving native landscapes, ecosystems, historical and archaeological sites, and ethnic and cultural traditions representative of the diverse geography and cultural life of our state.

Photo by Ron Williams.

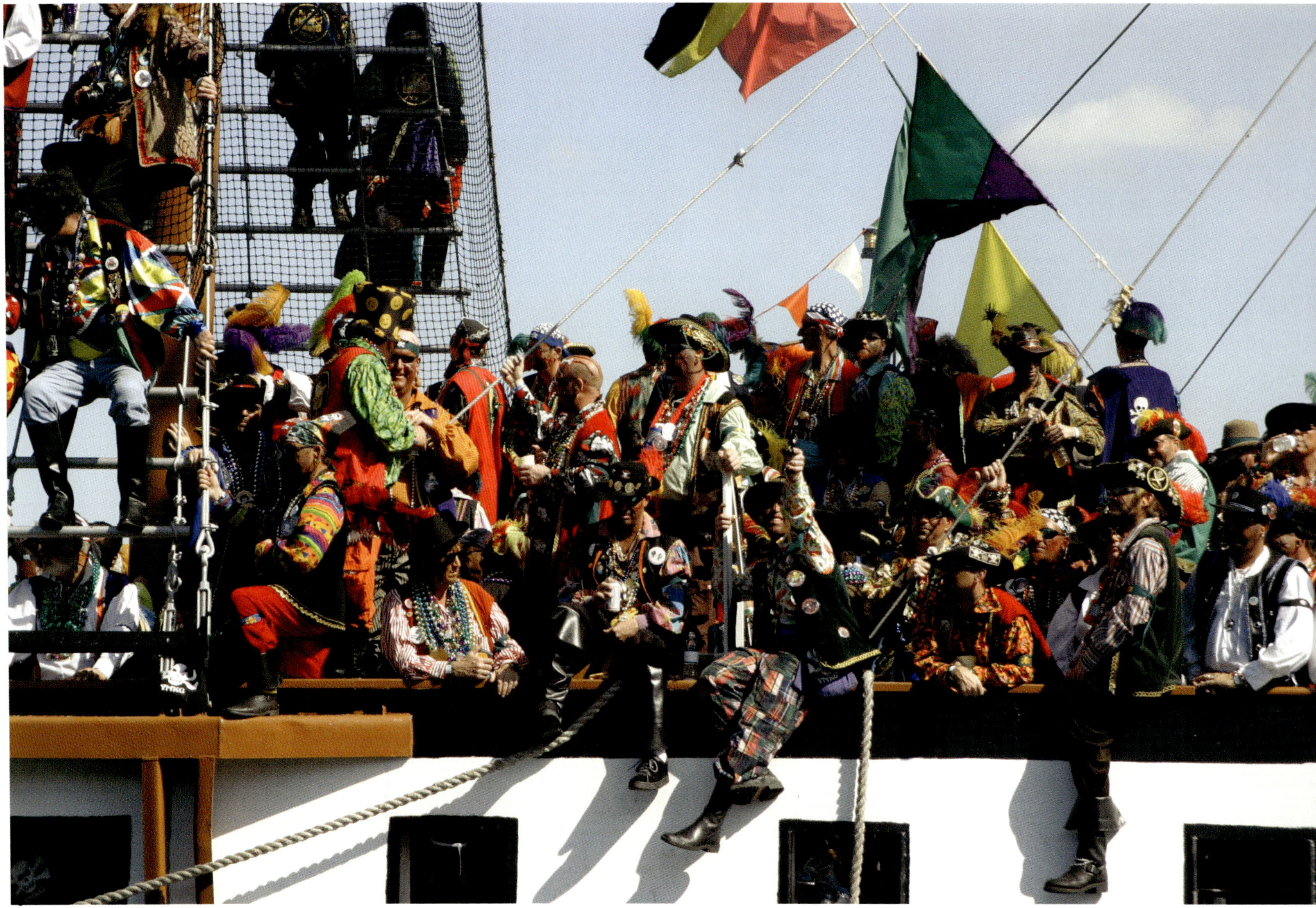

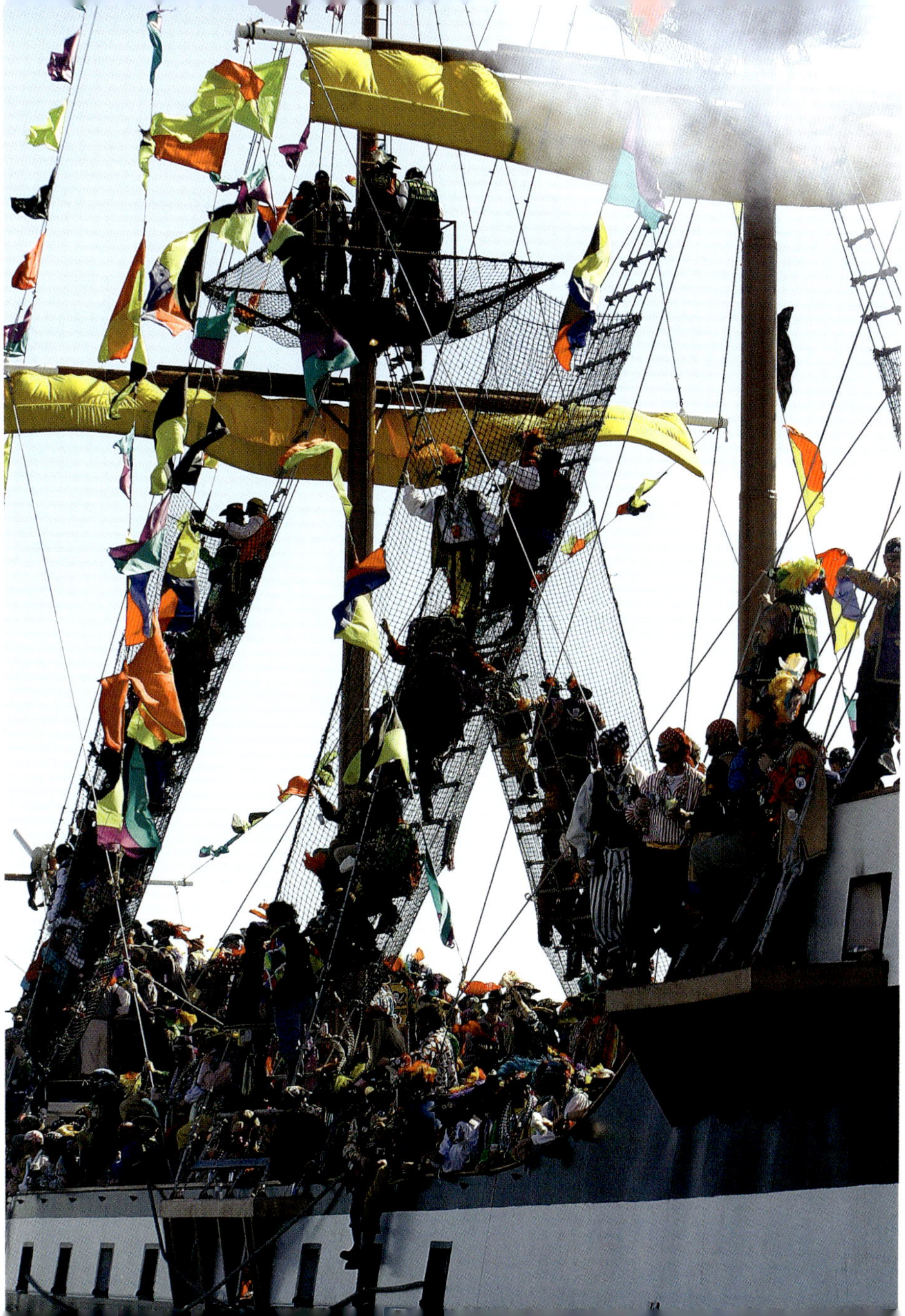

José Gaspar, also known as Gasparilla, reportedly raided the west coast of Florida during the late eighteenth and early nineteenth centuries as one of the "last of the Buccaneers." His legend is celebrated every year in Tampa with the Gasparilla Pirate Festival.

Photos by Ron Williams.

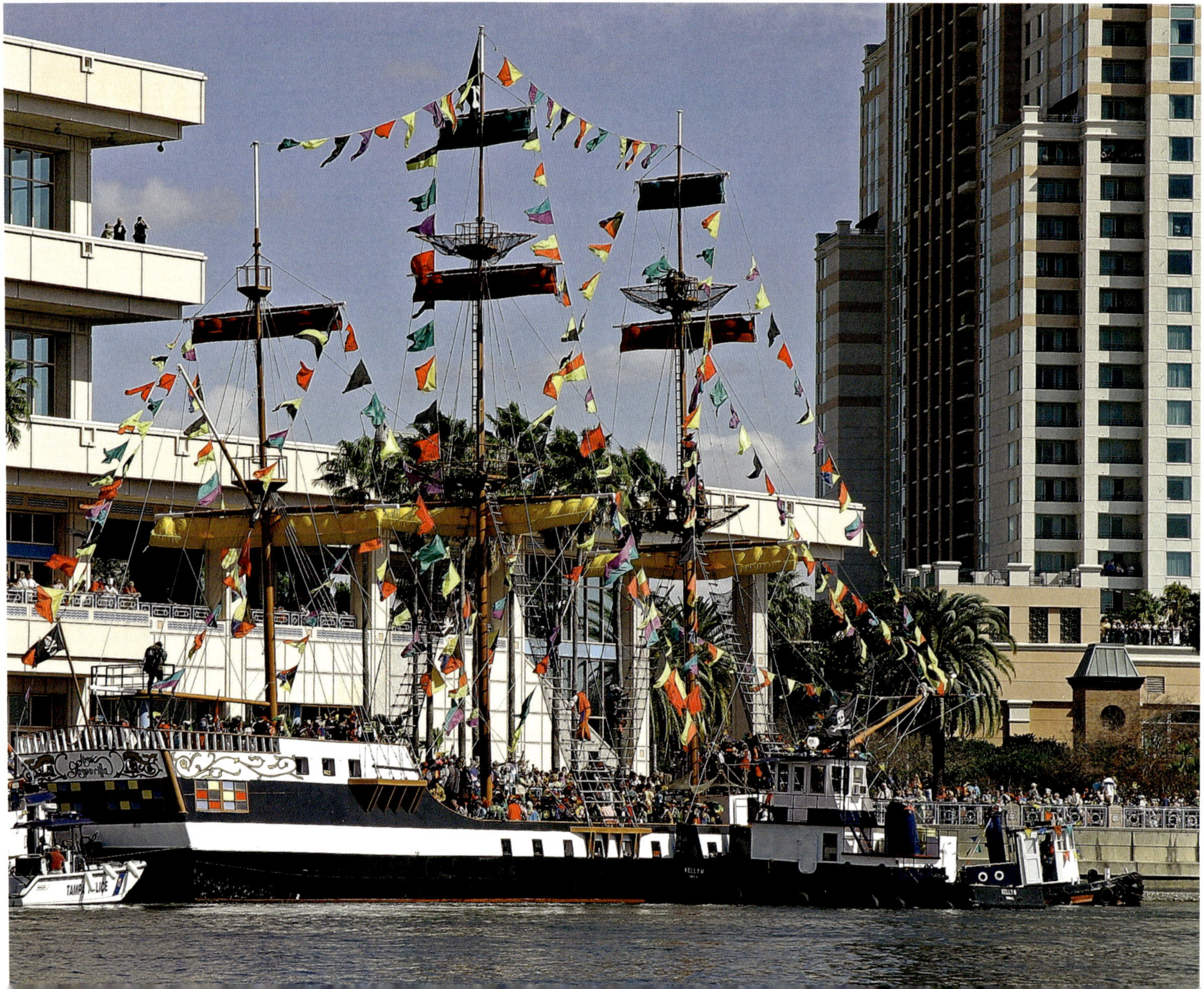

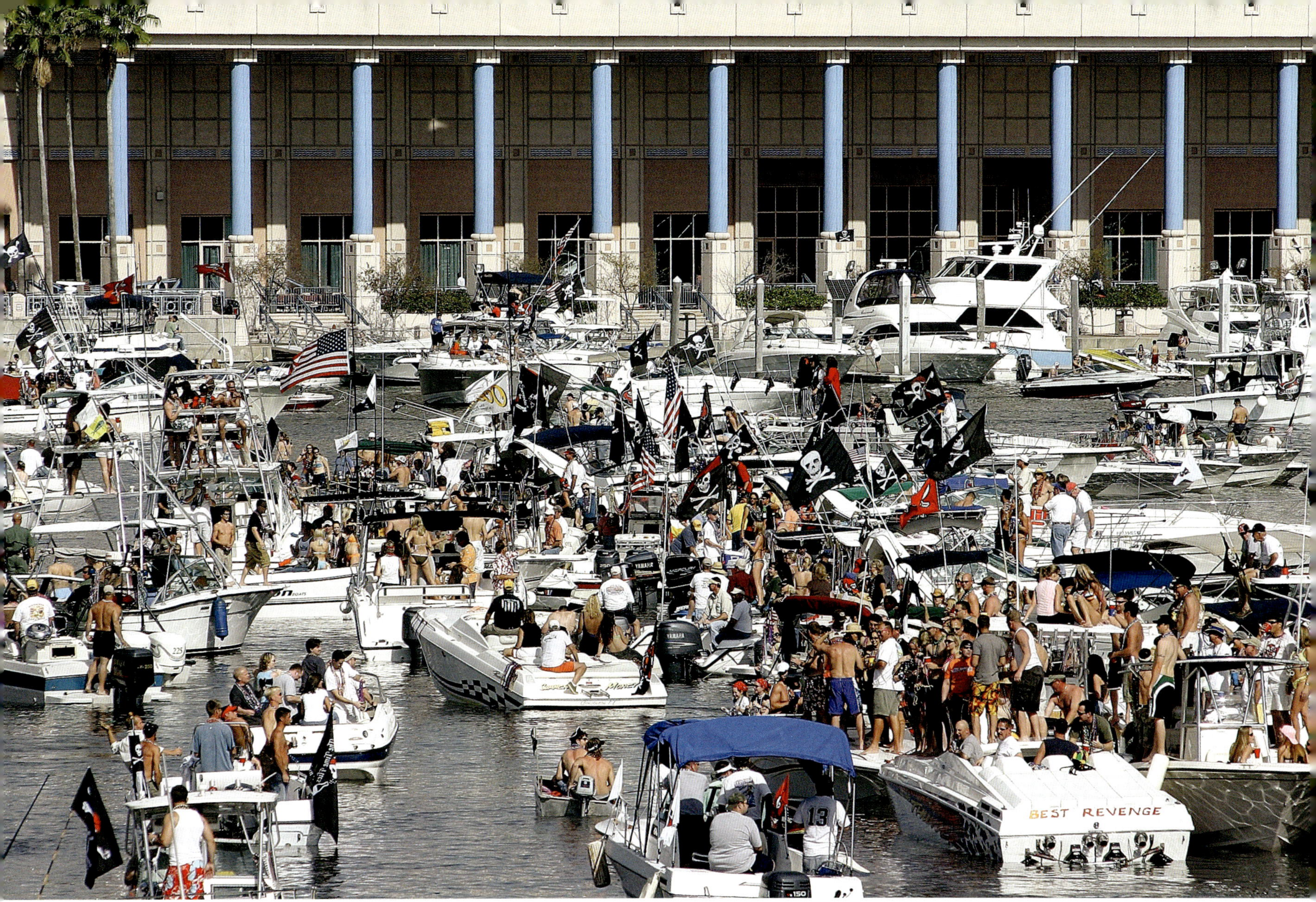
BEST REVENGE

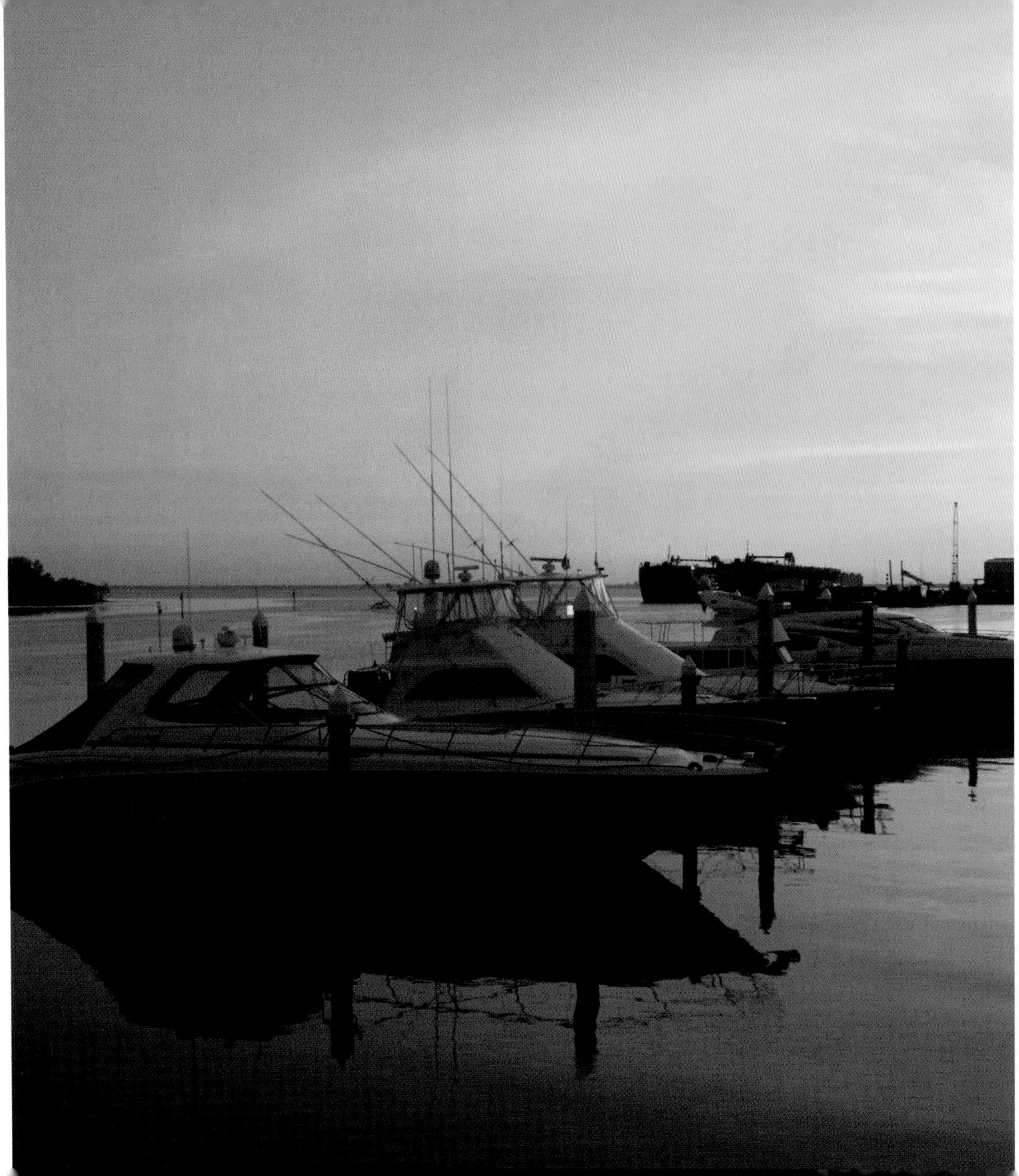

Golden sunsets are a common sight on Florida's west coast. Boaters have the added treat of pulling up alongside Tampa's many waterside restaurants to enjoy the view while dining on fresh seafood.
Photos by Ron Williams.

Eternity. It is the
sea mingled with the sun.

Arthur Rimbaud

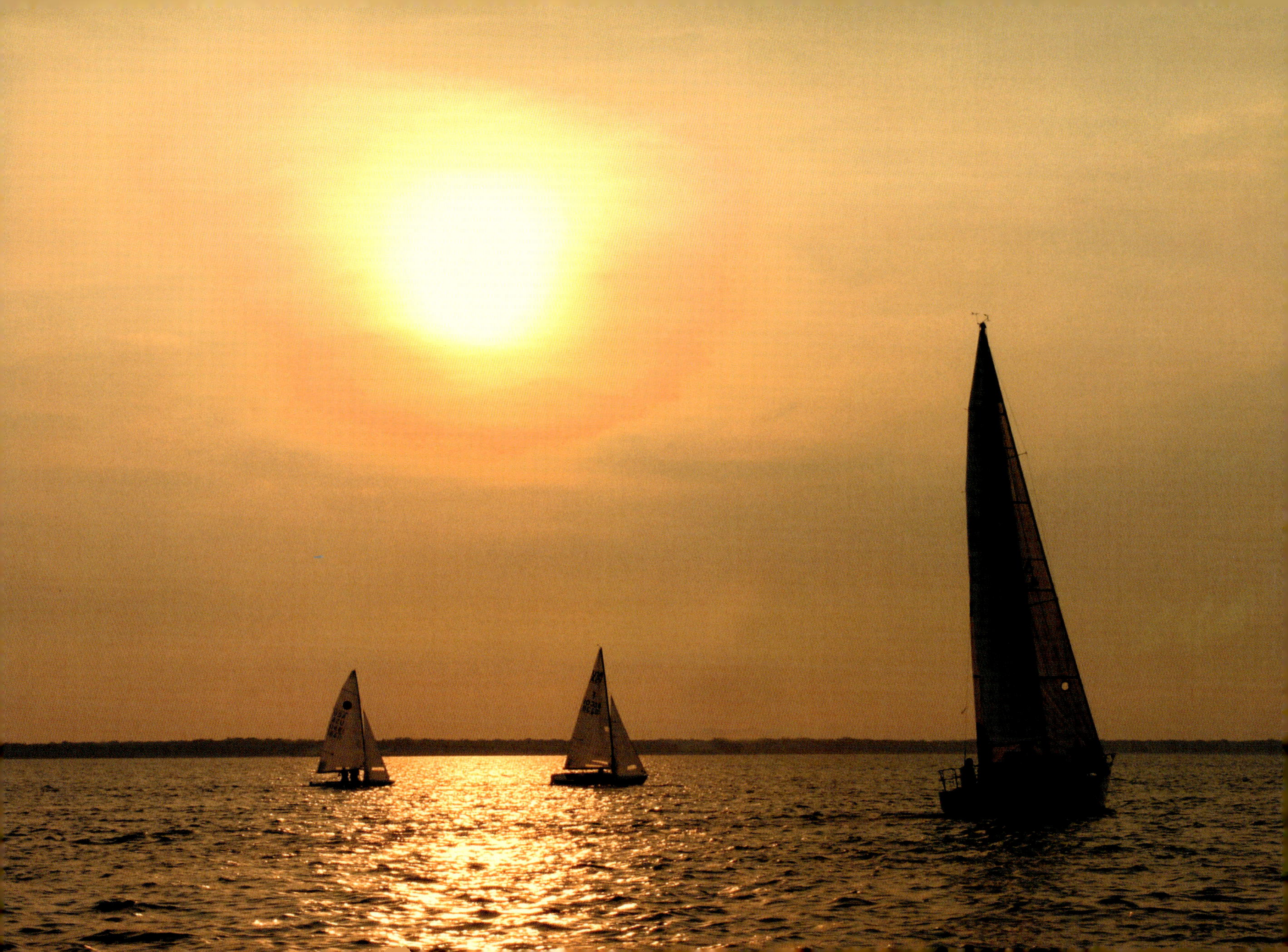

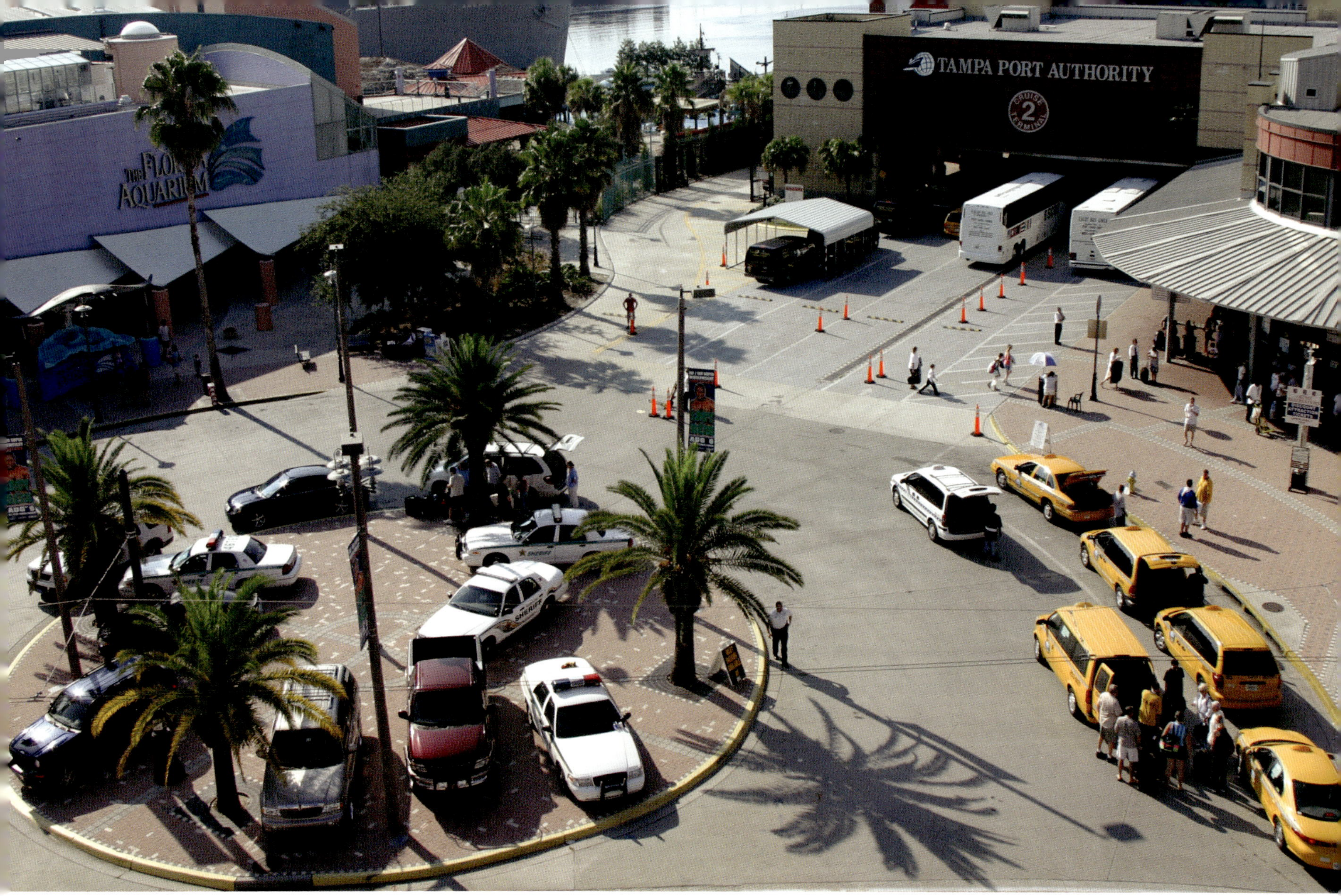
TAMPA PORT AUTHORITY
SHERIFF

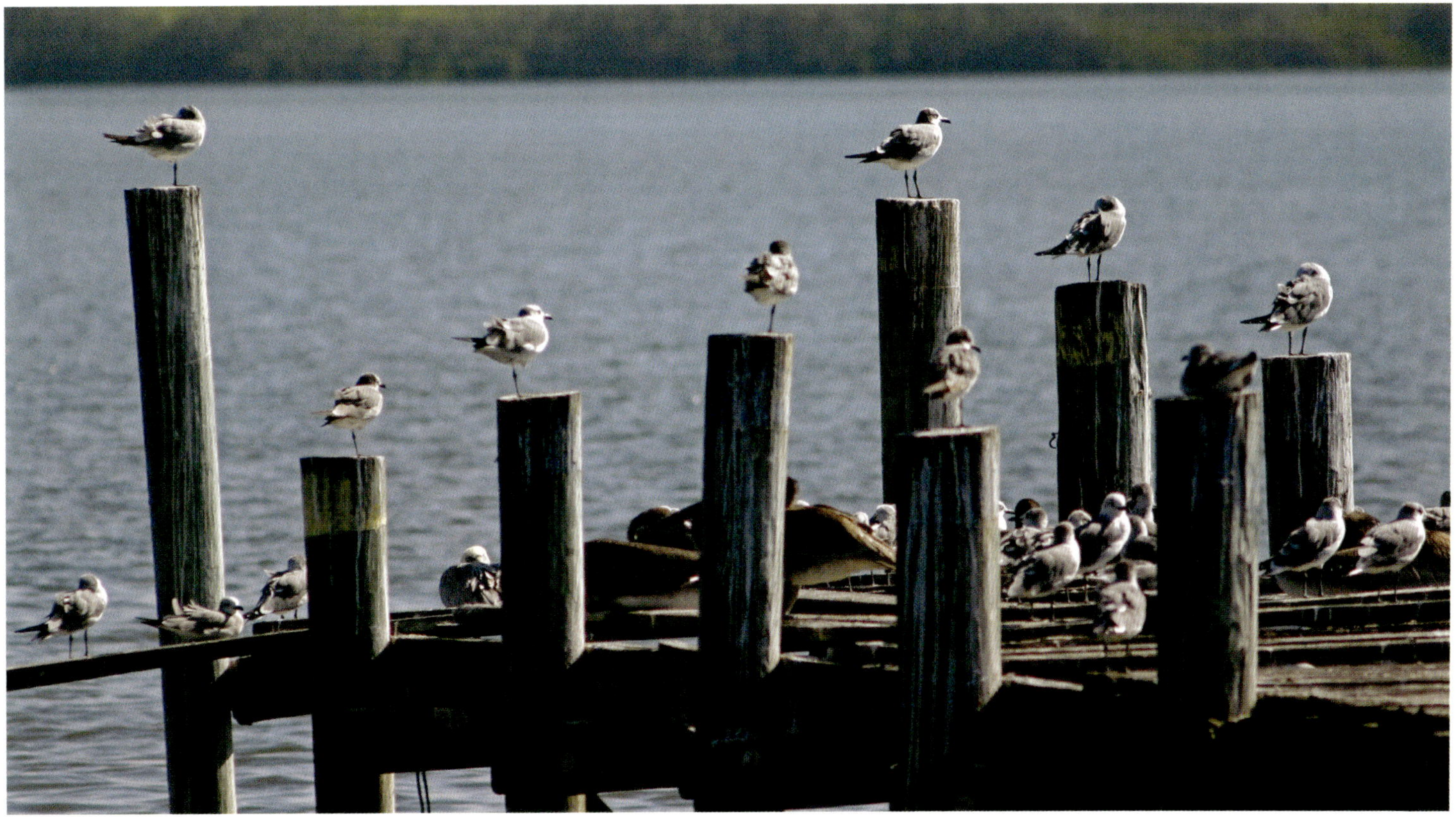

Seabirds rest in the afternoon sun on this Tampa dock.
Photo by Ron Williams.

Tampa's port bustles with activity as visitors prepare to depart for the high seas as guests of Holland America, Carnival Cruise Lines, and Royal Caribbean.
Photo by Ron Williams.

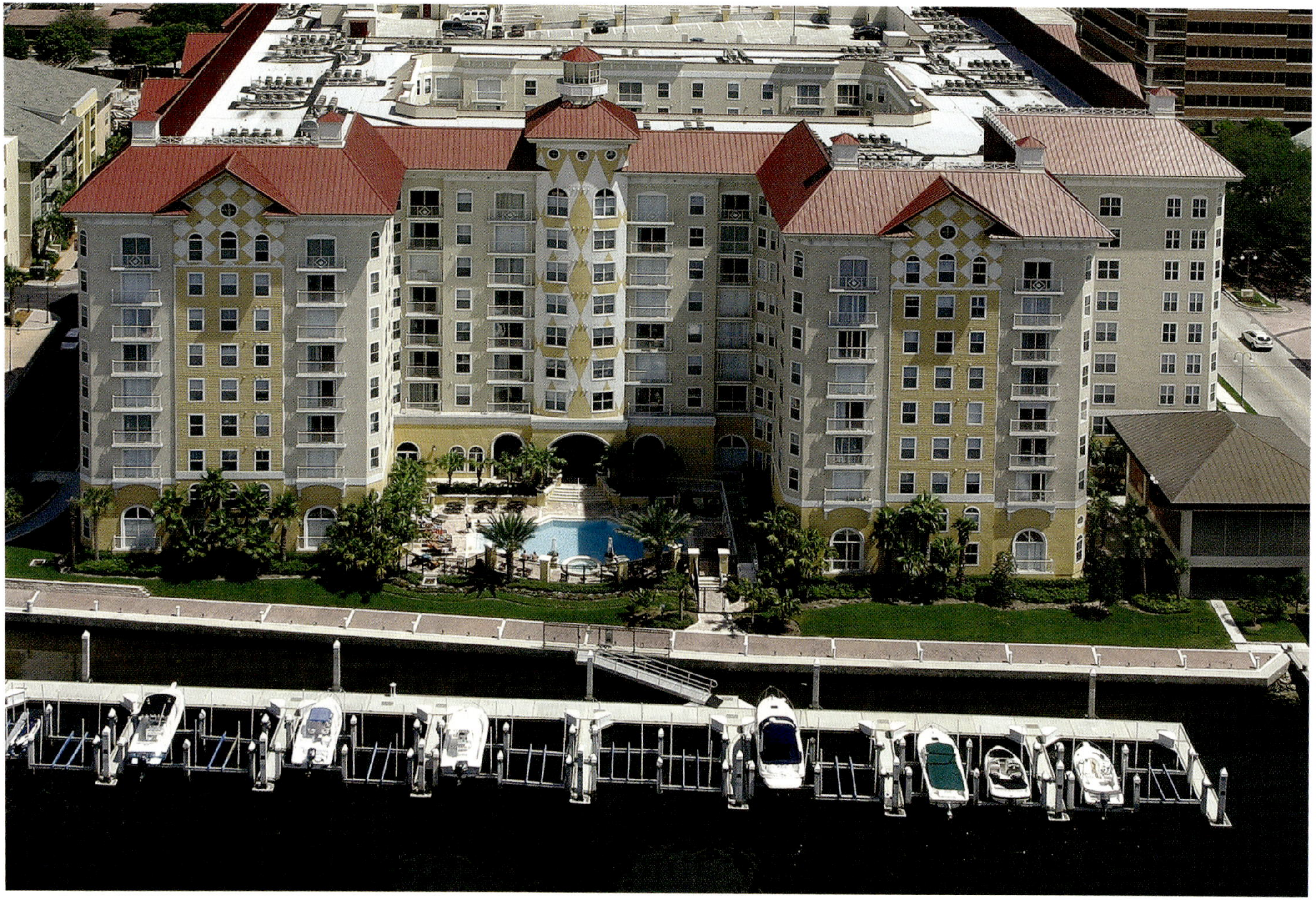

Harbour Island condominiums provide residential comfort and charm.
Photo by Ron Williams.

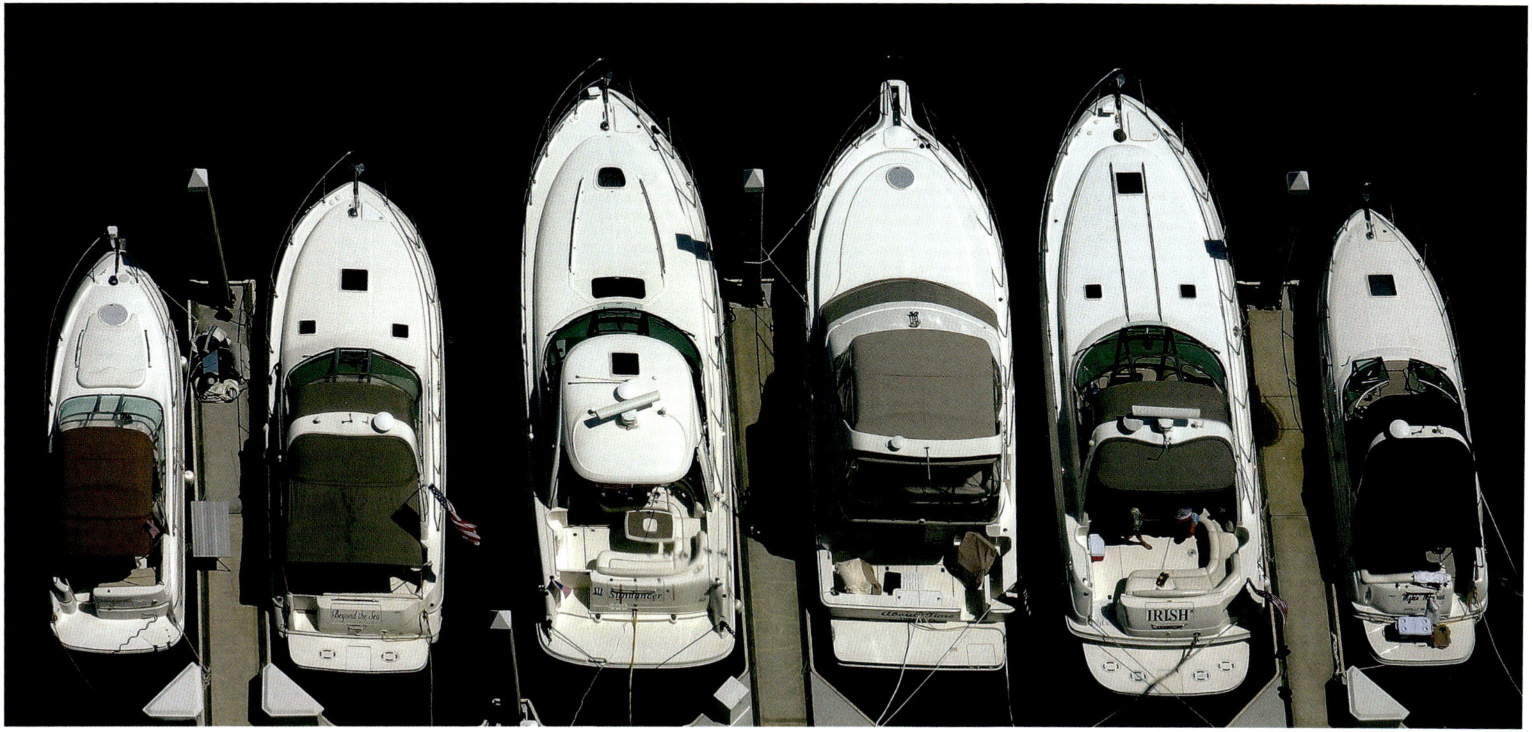

Boats stationed in a downtown Tampa dock are an alternative to driving to work.
Photo by Ron Williams.

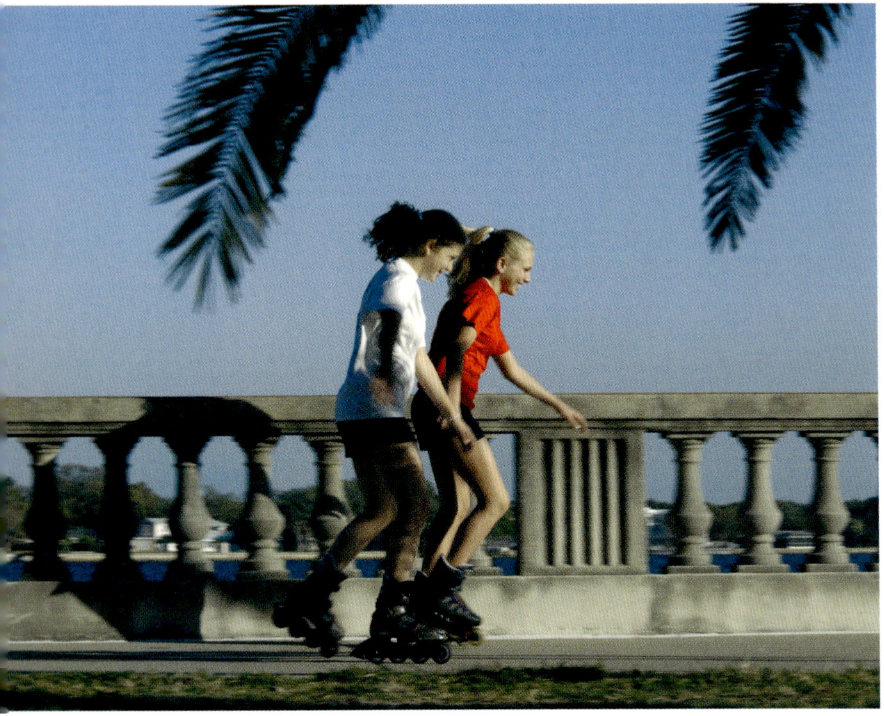

Two girls rollerblade down Bayshore Boulevard.
Courtesy of Tampa's Downtown Partnership.

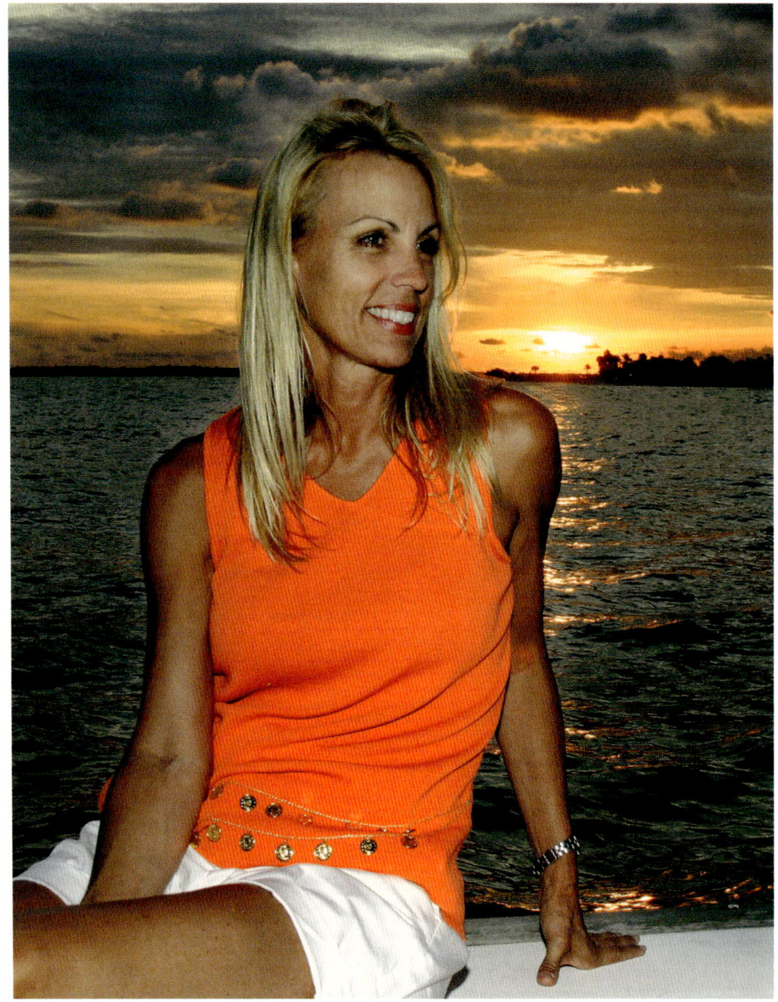

Davis Island Yacht Club draws boats out to sea on summer evenings for the Thursday night races. Resident Lori Woods enjoys the view.
Photo by Ron Williams.

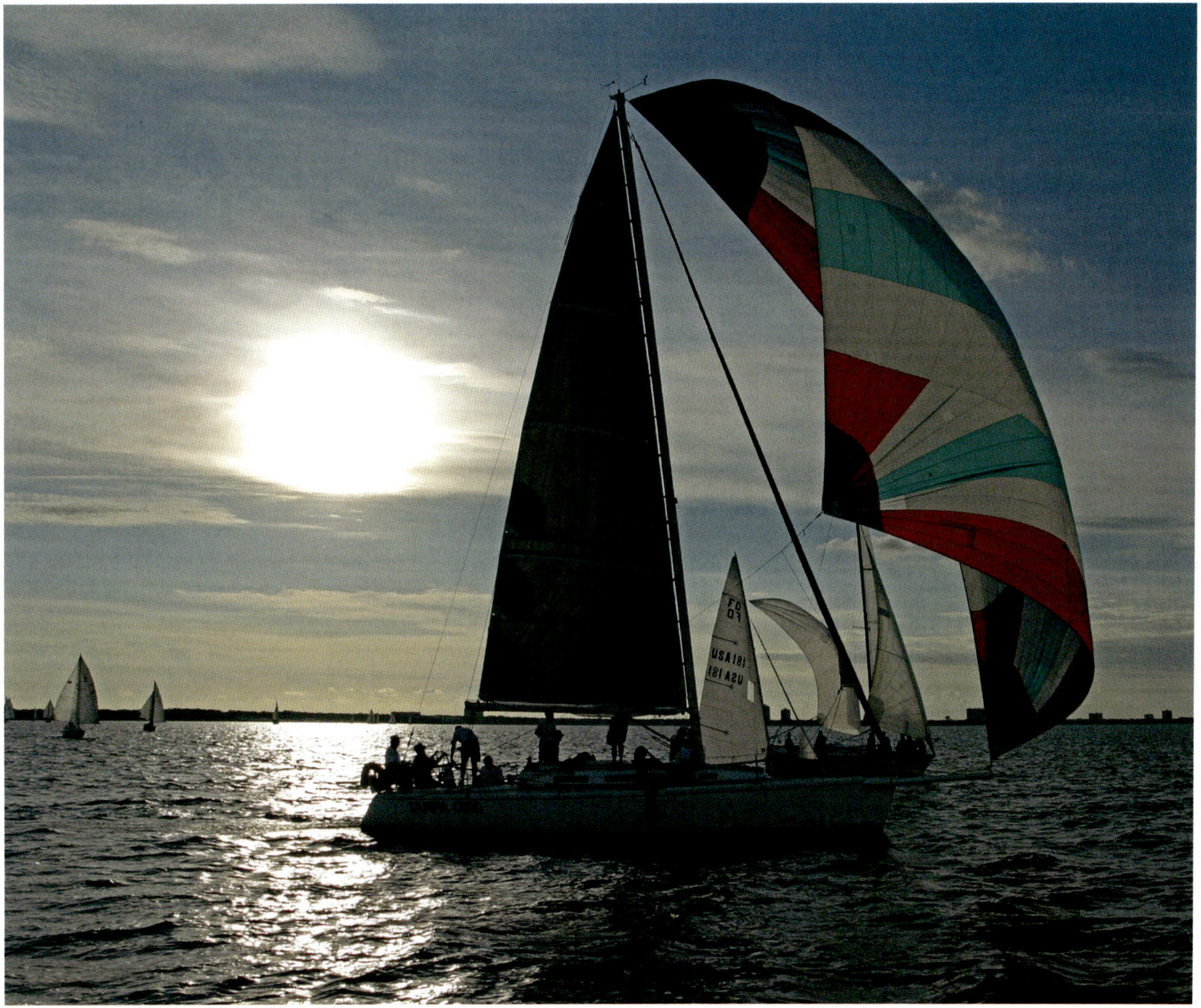

Sailing is a favorite pastime on Tampa Bay. The long summers and beautiful sunsets encourage active memberships at several local yacht clubs.
Photo by Ron Williams.

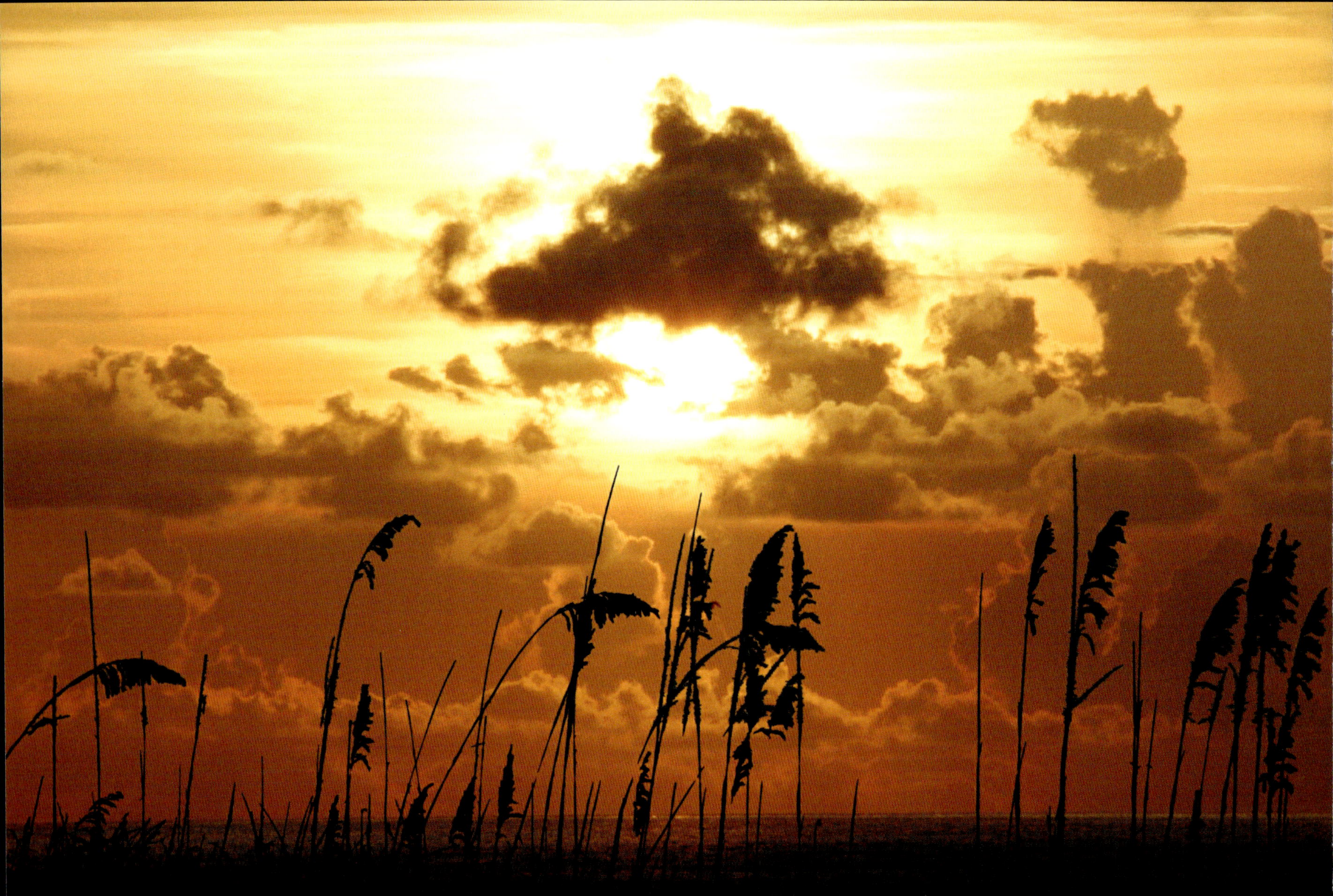

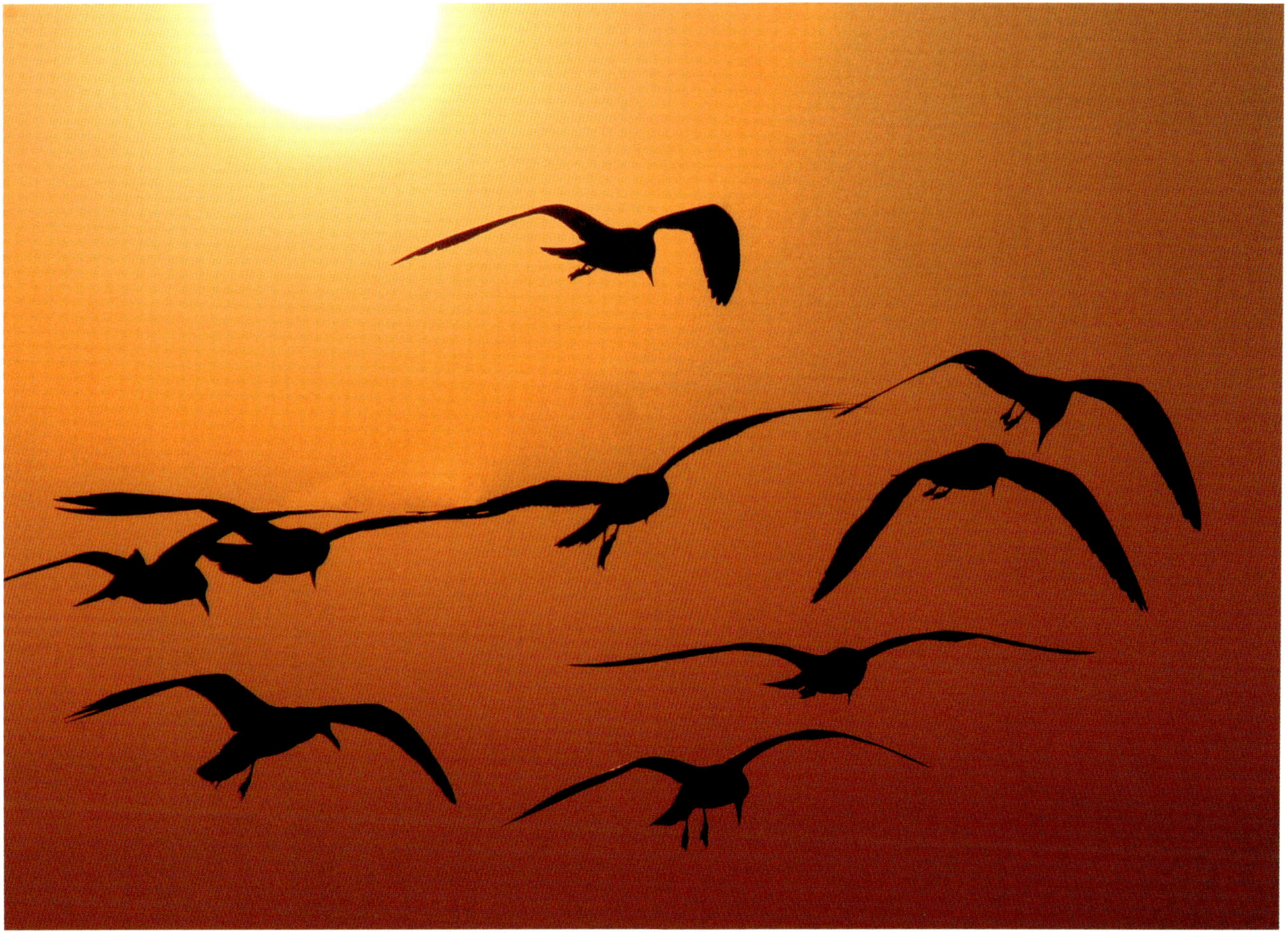

A small flock of birds silhouetted by an orange sunset.
Photo by Ron Williams.

Cypress Point Park is a relatively little-known treasure with a beautiful beach.
Photo by Ron Williams.

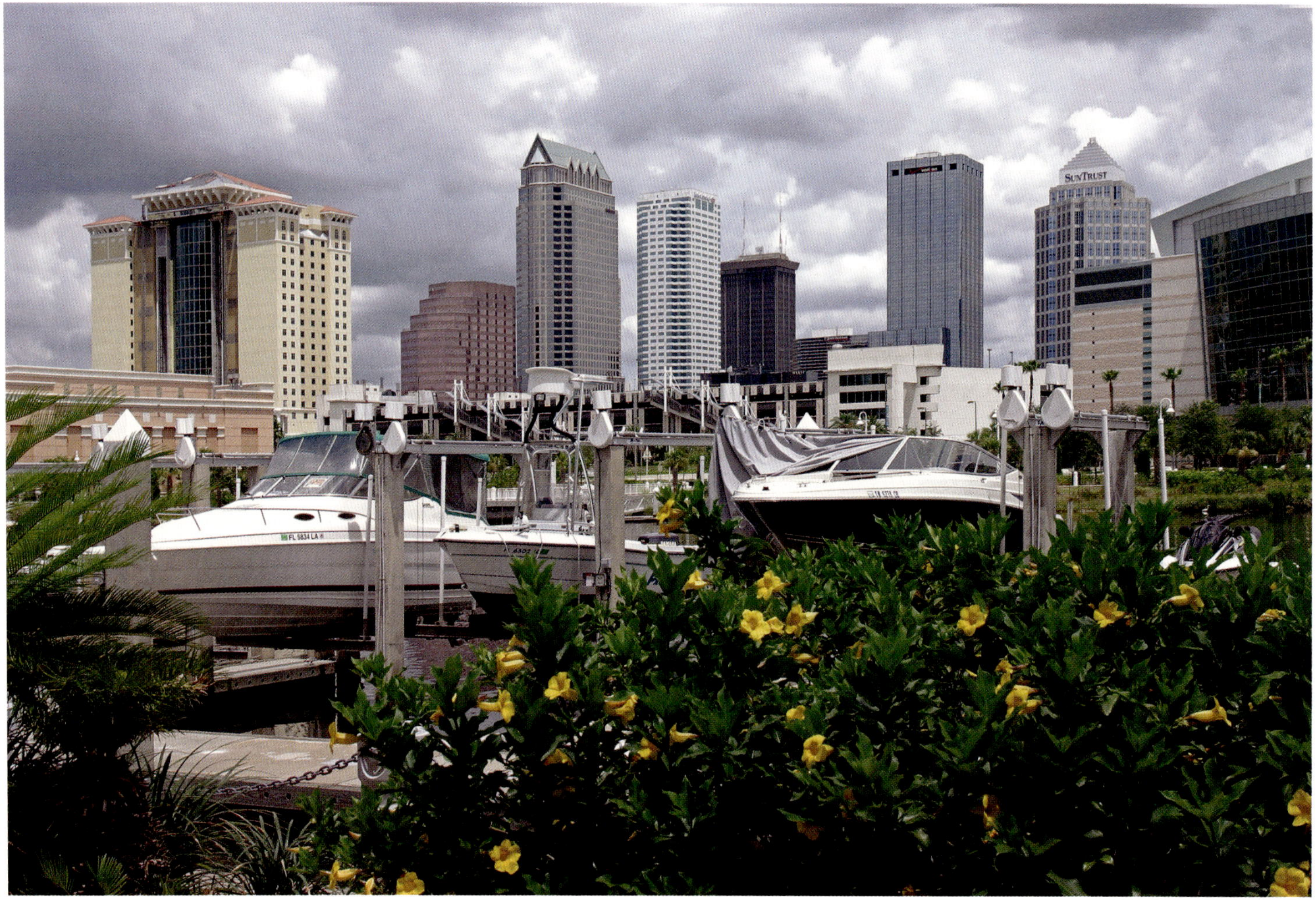

Docked boats in Tampa's downtown.
Photo by Ron Williams.

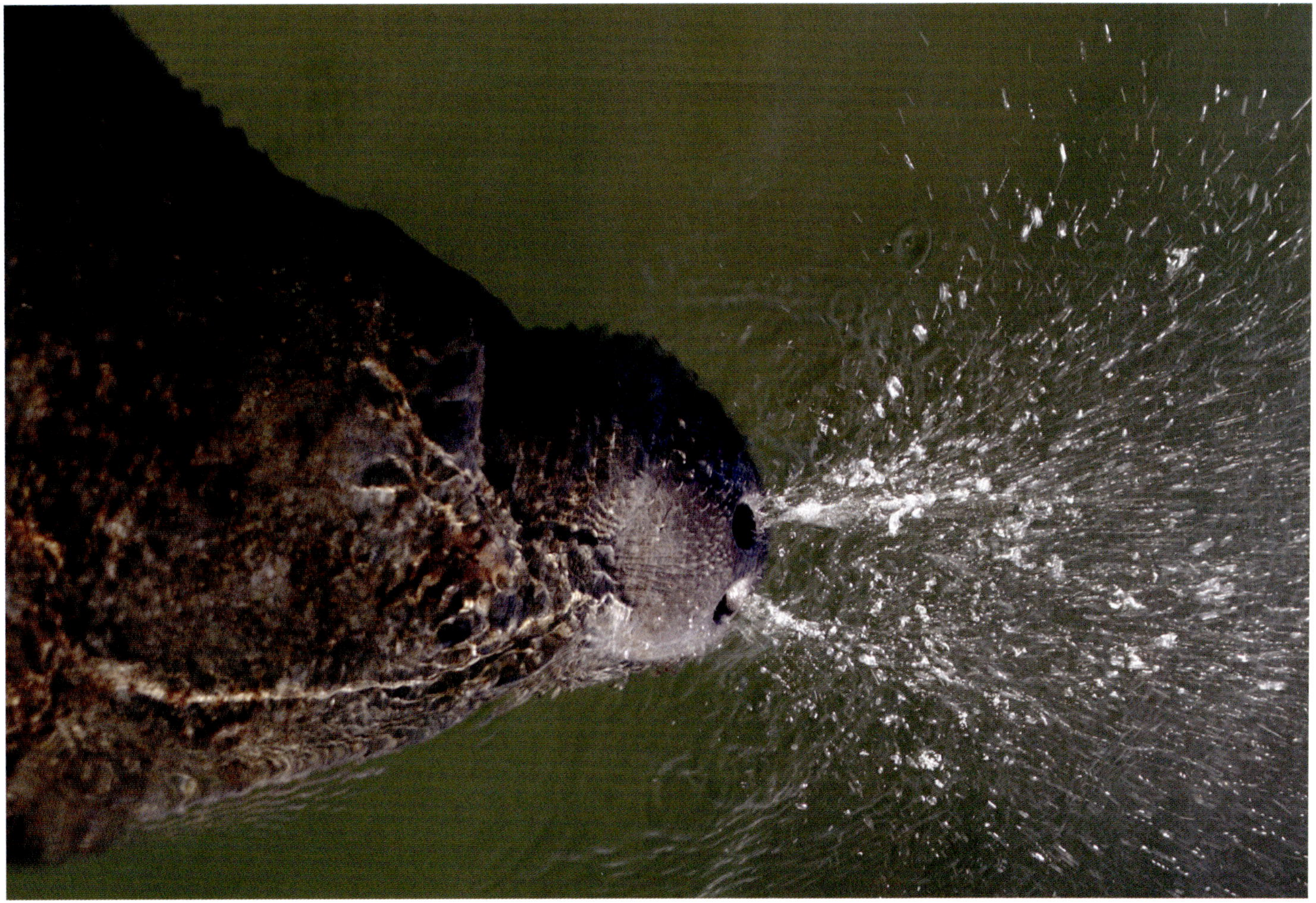

Tampa Bay is home to a growing manatee population that seeks out shallow, slow-moving rivers, estuaries, and saltwater bays. These environments are home to important food sources, including aquatic plants and sea grass. These large, slow, endangered animals can consume about 10–15 percent of their body weight in vegetation daily.
Photo by Ron Williams.

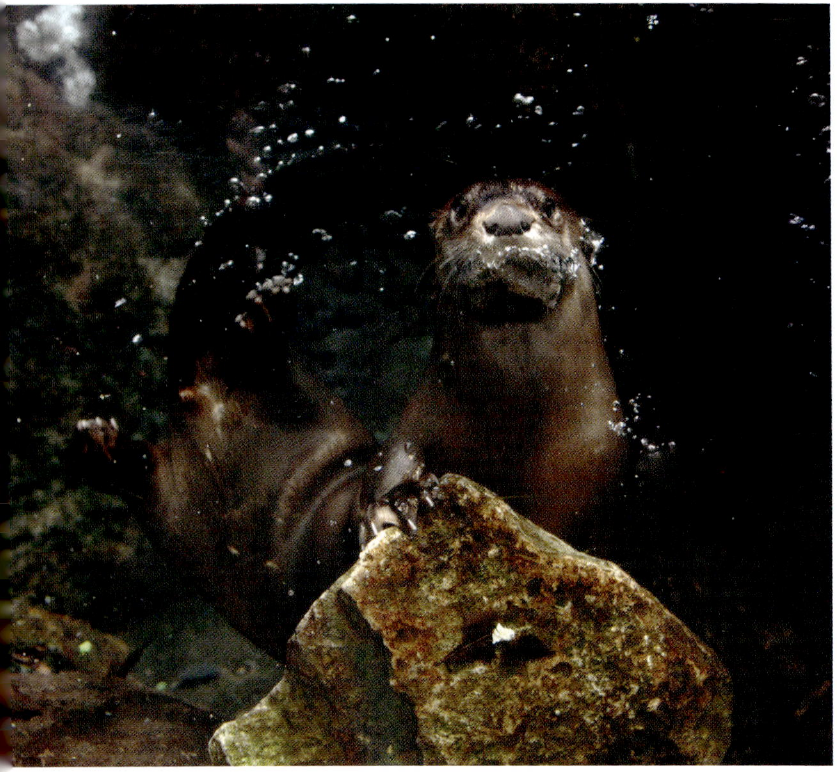

Meet a Florida river otter. These naturally curious and playful animals are often found frolicking in the water of the exhibit located in the Wetlands Gallery at the Florida Aquarium.

By permission of the Florida Aquarium.

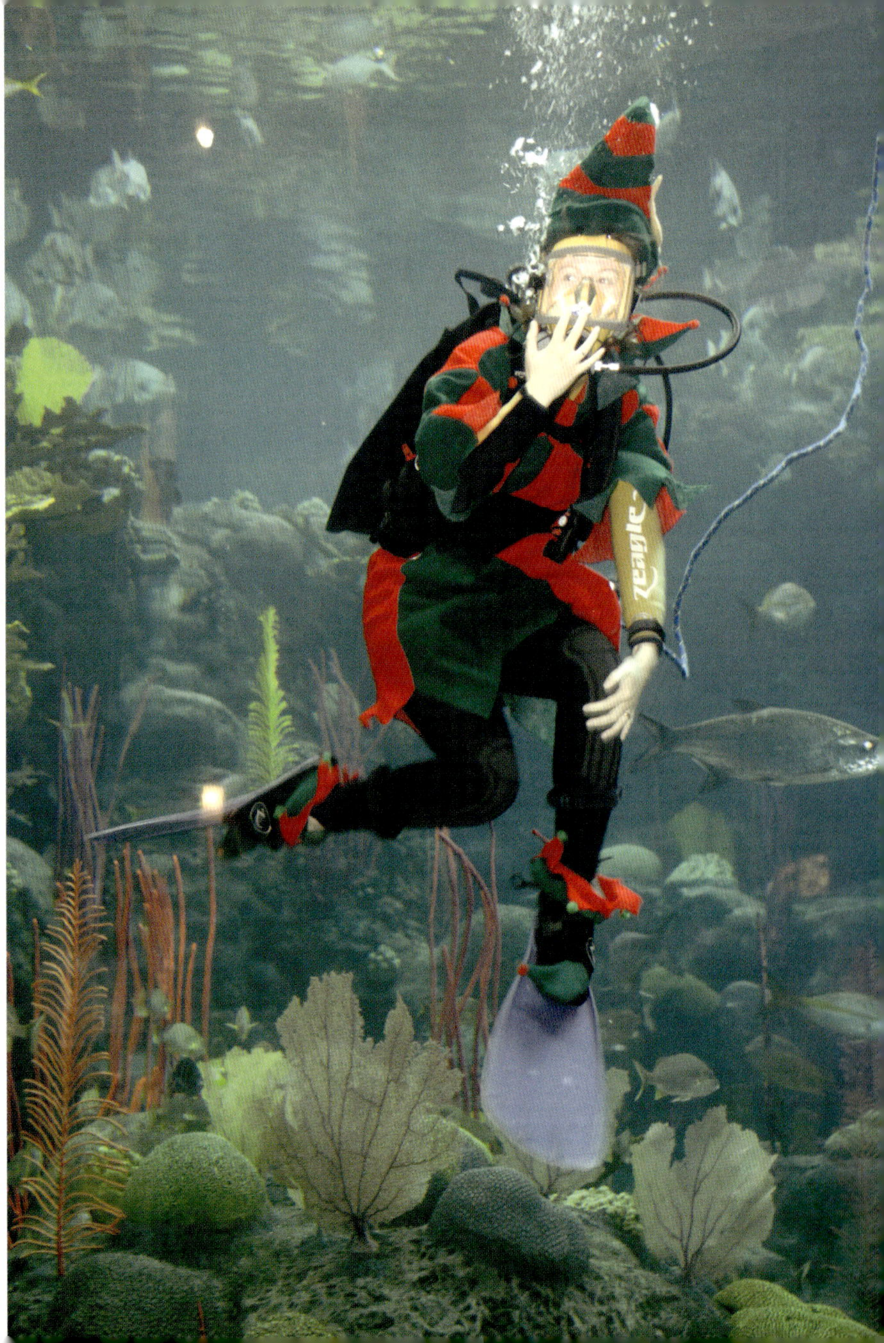

A diver entertains guests in the Coral Reefs Gallery at the Florida Aquarium. A magnificent 42-foot-wide, 14-foot-tall panoramic window offers a spectacular view of the reef. The main tank features 500,000 gallons of natural saltwater with more than 2,300 individual fish representing 55 varieties.

By permission of the Florida Aquarium.

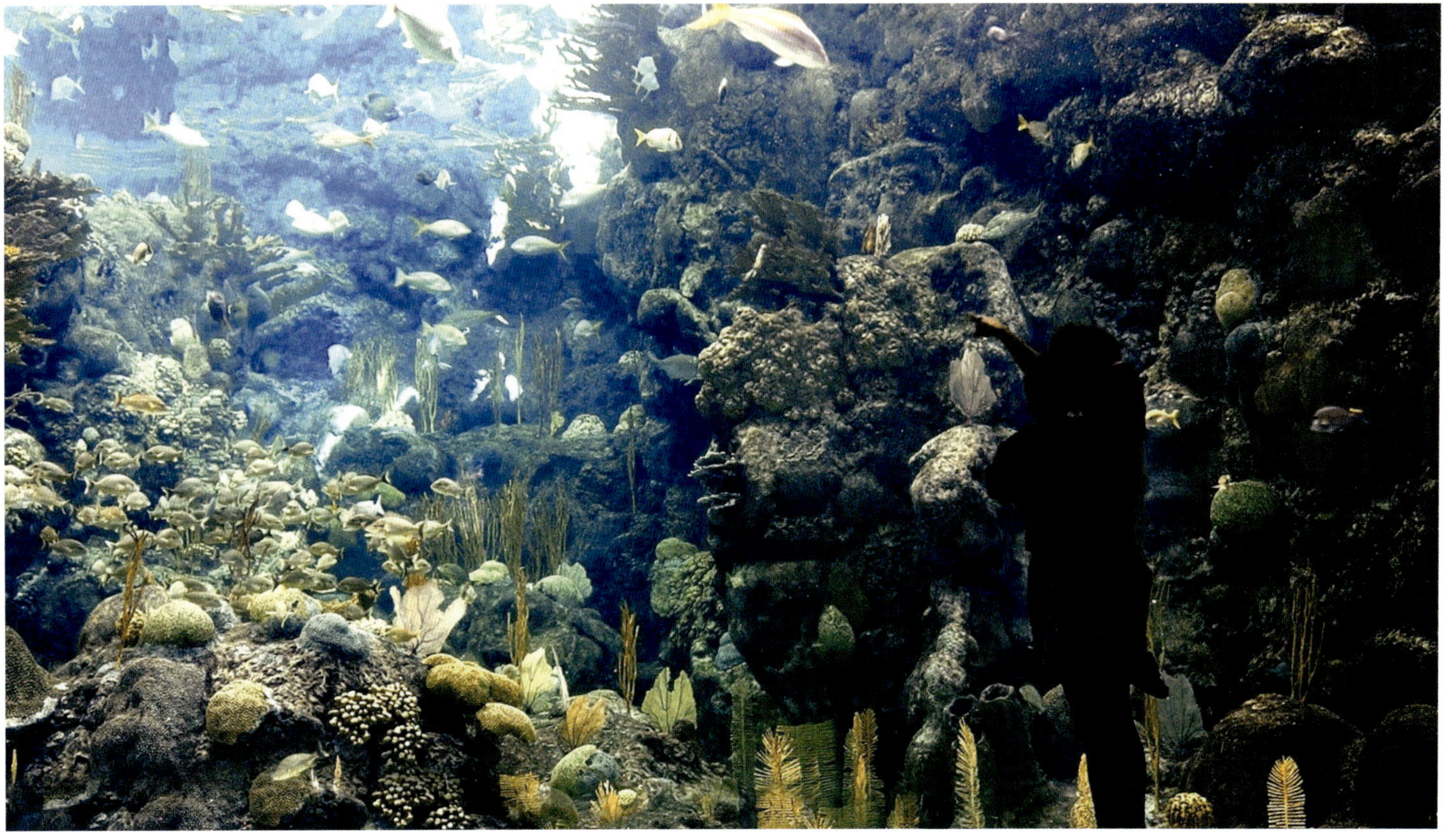

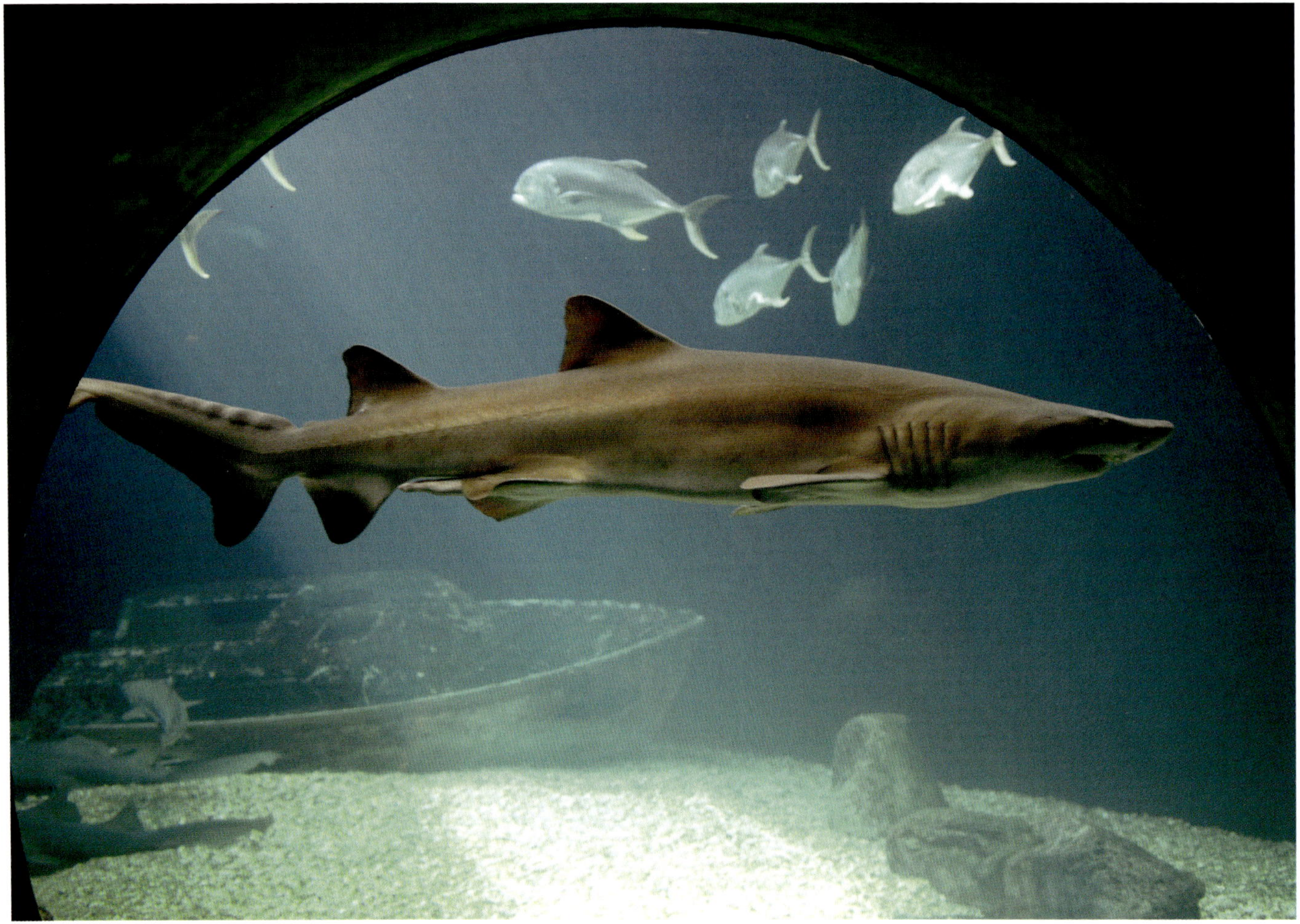

A sand tiger shark swims past a guest diver in Shark Bay, which features five species of shark including Black Tip Reef, Nurse, White Tip Reef, Zebra, and Sand Tiger sharks. Dive with the Sharks is a guest dive experience for certified scuba divers ages fifteen and older and allows guests to come face to face with sharks, a goliath grouper, and a sea turtle.

By permission of the Florida Aquarium.

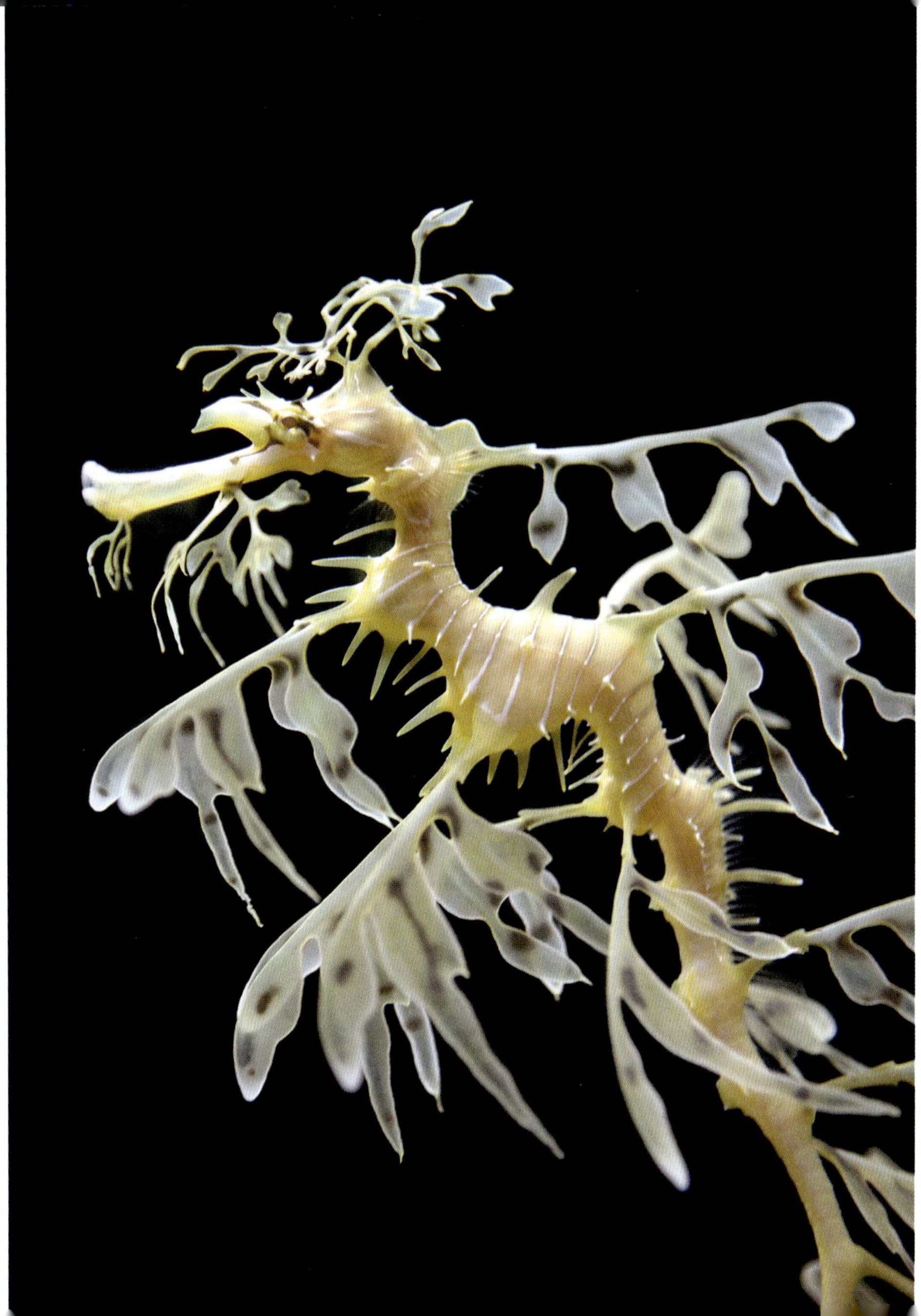

This amazing animal is found in southwest Australia and is very rare in the wild. You can see these creatures in the Florida Aquarium's Dragons Down Under exhibit located in the Coral Reef Gallery.

By permission of the Florida Aquarium.

City in Transition

Tampa is truly a city in transition. The city has experienced an influx of new residents throughout the past four decades and is now home to over 300,000 people.

The city's appeal has encouraged an even more rapid growth rate during recent years. The dramatic population explosion has helped to generate a residential real estate development boom. The expansion has produced a significant number of new homes, townhouses, and condominiums. Tampa has a variety of new residential choices to fit any budget, preference, and lifestyle: Live in a new bungalow, lakeside villa, high rise by the bay, or a home in a gated community. In addition to the wide assortment of new construction of residential properties, the real estate movement has also inspired a wave of renovation efforts among existing homes throughout the city. Both new construction and renovations of existing homes have added a positive jolt to development, investment, and revitalization in the city. The impact is particularly noted in sections that were previously in need of beautification. Areas that were once economically depressed, plagued with neglected homes, or occupied by decaying industrial warehouses and factories are now occupied with stylish and innovative urban condos, lofts, townhouses, and single-family residences.

The real estate development expansion has not been restricted to residential properties. The public sector has also added to the frenzy of new construction, as several new public schools, libraries, administrative buildings, and community resources facilities were built. Commercial real estate development has been strong as well. Scaffolding and construction cranes were permanent features of the Tampa skyline during the past five years as new high-rise buildings, retail centers, office buildings, and entertainment venues took root throughout the city. The city witnessed the development of the Channelside entertainment and retail complex, and new commercial constructions and renovations occurred in Central Ybor City as that historic district was rejuvenated.

The real estate development phenomenon has assisted in producing a renewed interest in downtown Tampa. Like many cities in the United States, Tampa experienced urban flight, as many downtown residents vacated the inner city for the suburbs in the late part of the twentieth century. Consequently, the downtown area virtually became a ghost town following the end of the business day. There is a renewed excitement once again in downtown Tampa with the introduction of new venues such as Channelside, the Florida Museum of Photographic Art, the Tampa History Center, the Florida Aquarium, and many other points of interest. The Tampa Riverwalk project is designed to provide citizens with a 2.4-mile walkway alongside the Hillsborough River. The urban downtown waterfront experience would connect residents and visitors alike to the river and a variety of cultural, educational, recreational, and artistic events. Given all of the changes that are taking place in downtown Tampa, nonprofit organizations such as the Tampa Downtown Partnership have been created to help navigate this period of transition and to encourage continued business development and investment, while also serving as a vital resource of information for Tampa residents.

Construction has been a staple of the Tampa economy, but the city also continues to embrace an economy rooted in tourism, agriculture, finance, health care, government, and technology. It is the key city on Florida's west coast, anchoring Florida's high-tech corridor. The city has the largest deep-water port in the state, thus providing it with the logistical resources required for effective and successful import/export. Tampa Bay is also one of the top growth markets for manufacturing for the medical industry. These facts explain why so many businesses and employees are taking a closer look at Tampa, and why the Tampa Bay region is getting national attention as a relocation destination for many companies. It consistently attracts a healthy variety of businesses, including bioscience, medical technology, international trade, and financial services.

It is apparent that Tampa is indeed a city in transition and that it will continue to experience positive advancements. In recent years Tampa's appeal has lured record-breaking numbers of new residents and companies to the city, and it has become a beacon for financial growth, development, and investment. With all of the dynamic changes that are taking place, one cannot help but to be excited about the city's future. It seems safe to speculate that just like its fantastic weather, Tampa's future will be bright and sunny.

I feel fortunate to be mayor of one of the best cities in America, filled with caring, creative people—enjoy your visit as you explore our city.

Tampa Mayor Pam Iorio

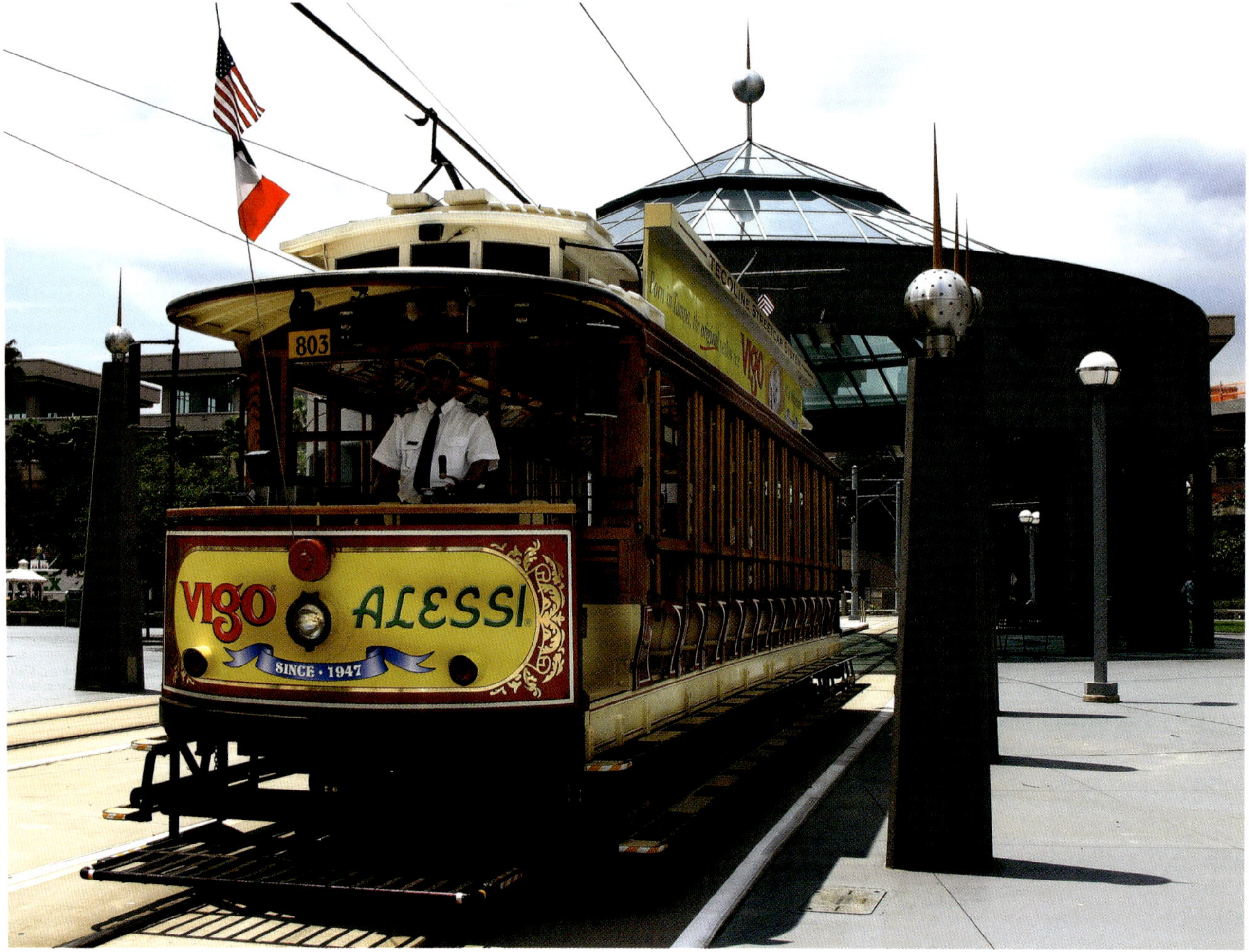

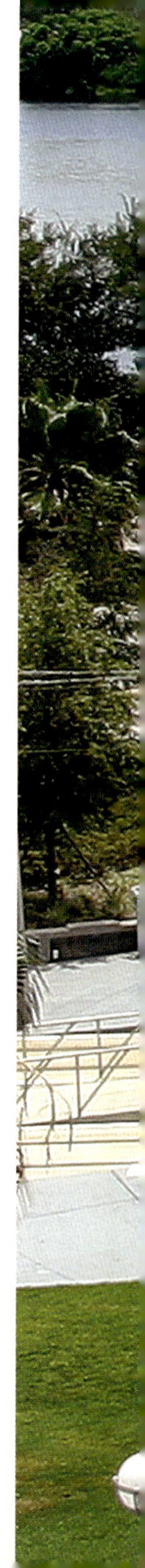

Southern Transportation Plaza is the terminal station for Tampa's streetcars. Since 1892, Tampa's streetcars had carried passengers to and from Ybor City, Ballast Point, Hyde Park, and Sulphur Springs. Carrying almost 24 million passengers in 1926, the streetcar system stopped service in August 1946 following World War II. Once again offering service, today's streetcars connect downtown, Channelside, and Ybor City.
Photos by Ron Williams.

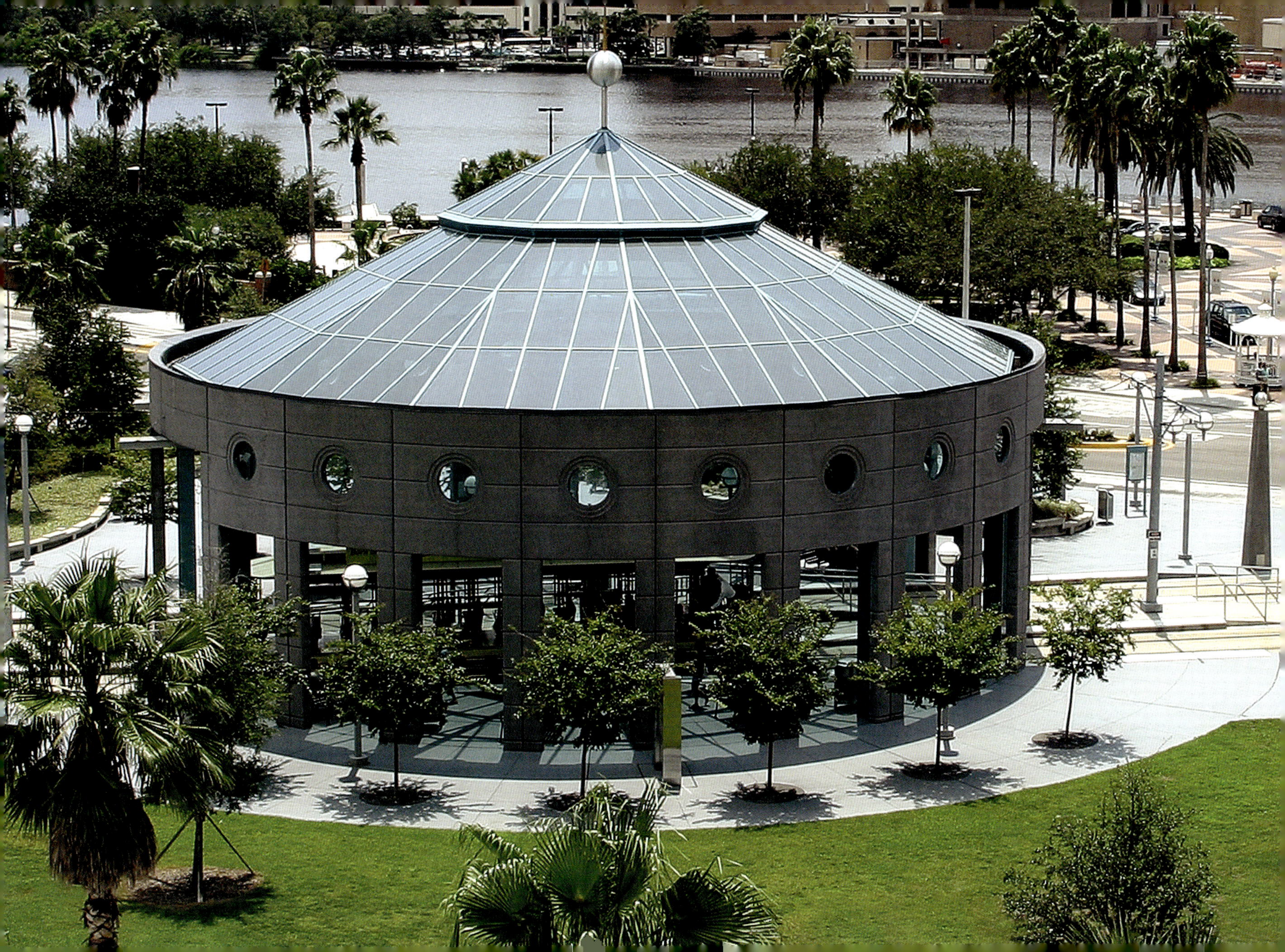

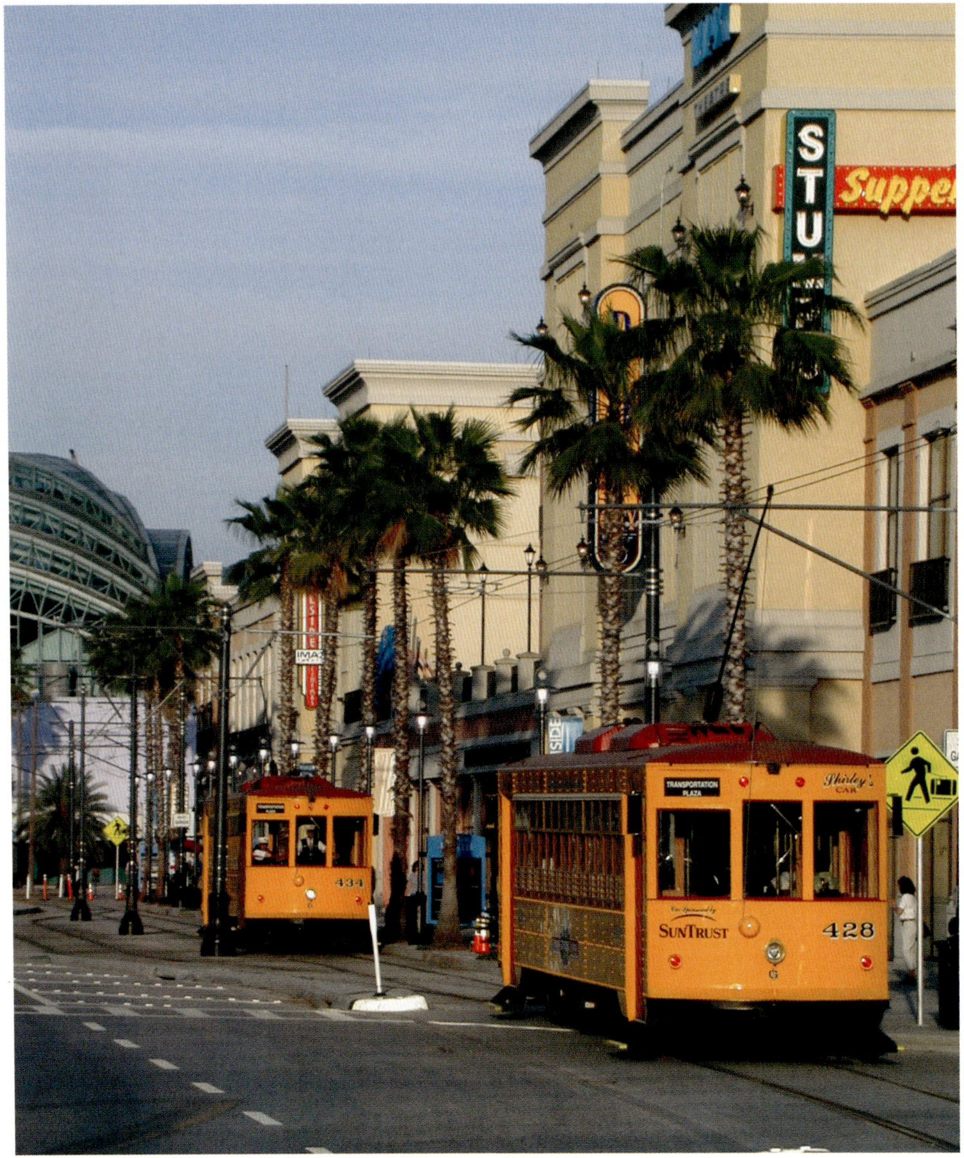

Streetcars depart from Channelside for downtown.
Courtesy of Tampa's Downtown Partnership.

A view of the city reflected in the water.
Photo by Ron Williams.

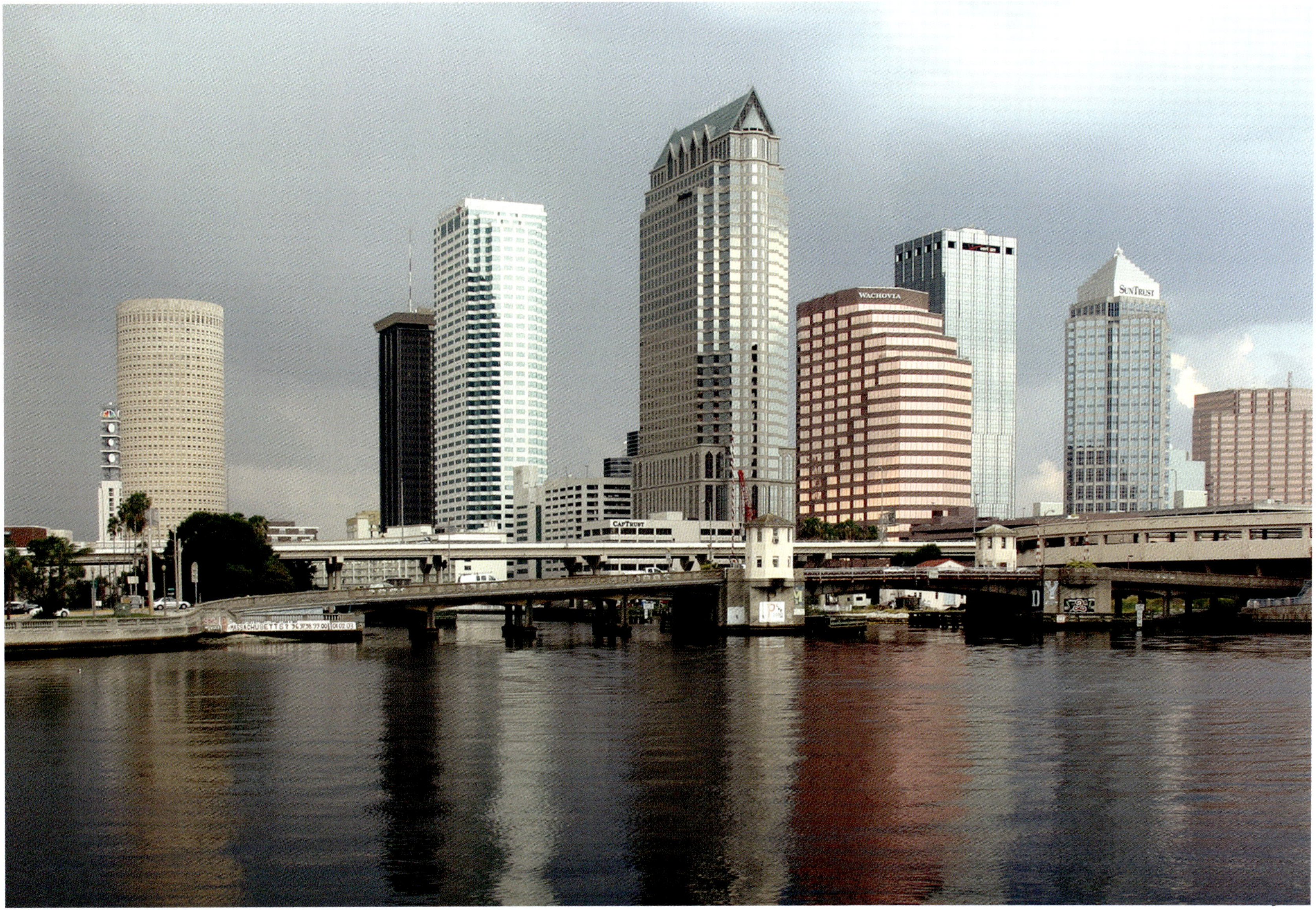
WACHOVIA
SunTrust
CapTrust

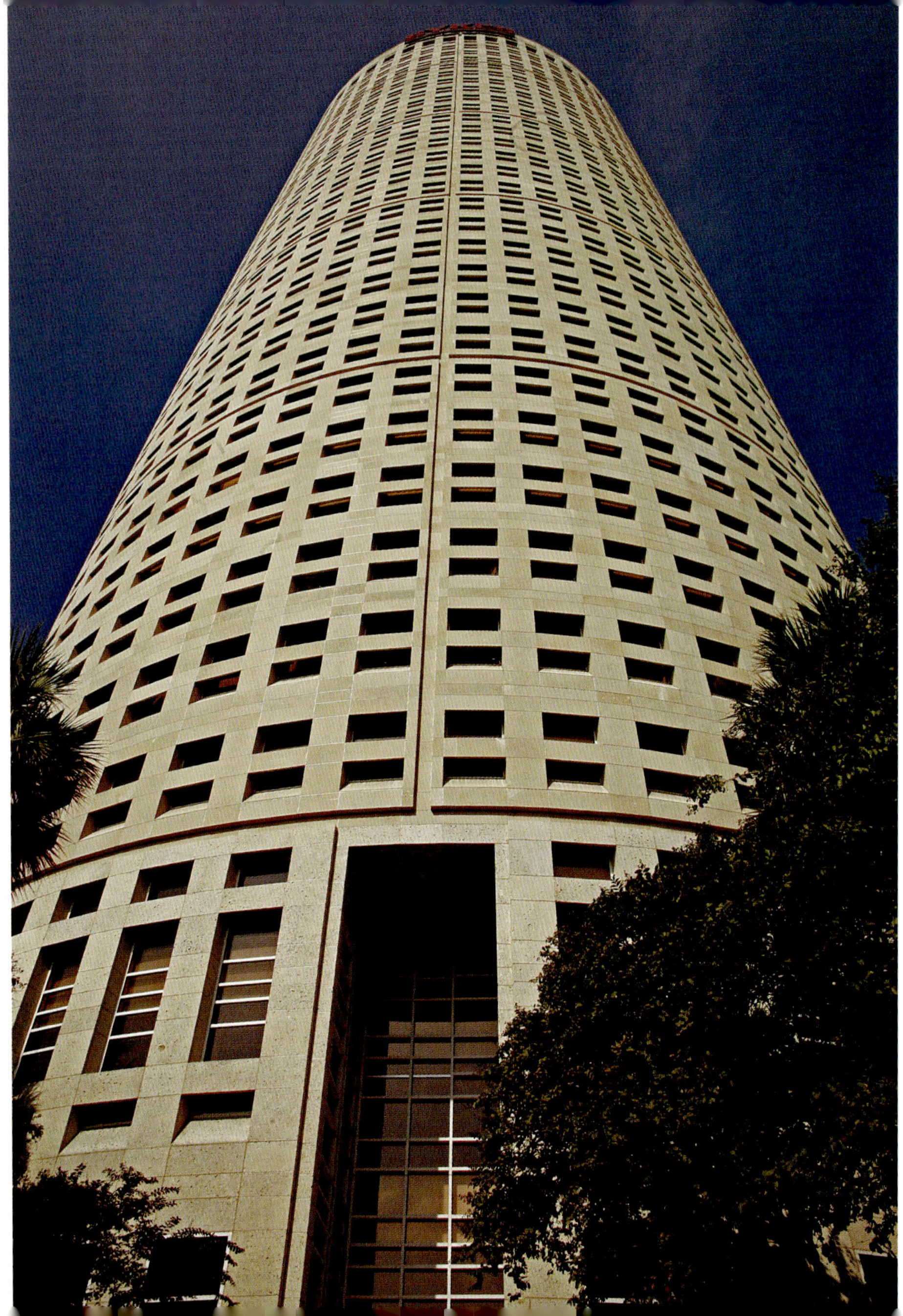

The Sykes Building is a Tampa Bay icon. One of the tallest limestone buildings in the world, the building's cylindrical design was intended to symbolize a lighthouse on the Tampa skyline.
Photo by Ron Williams.

The spiral parking garage of the downtown Regions Building.
Photo by Ron Williams.

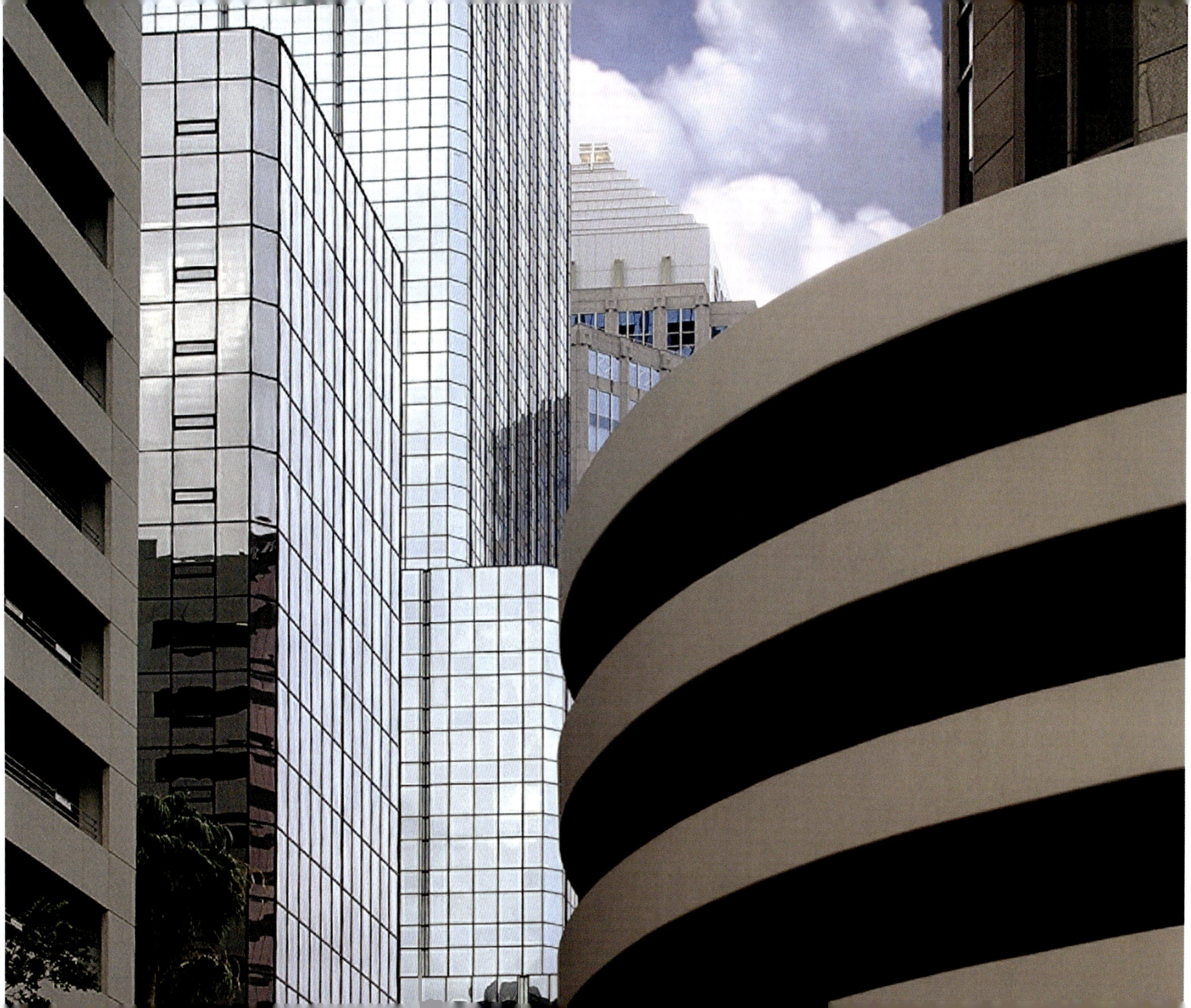

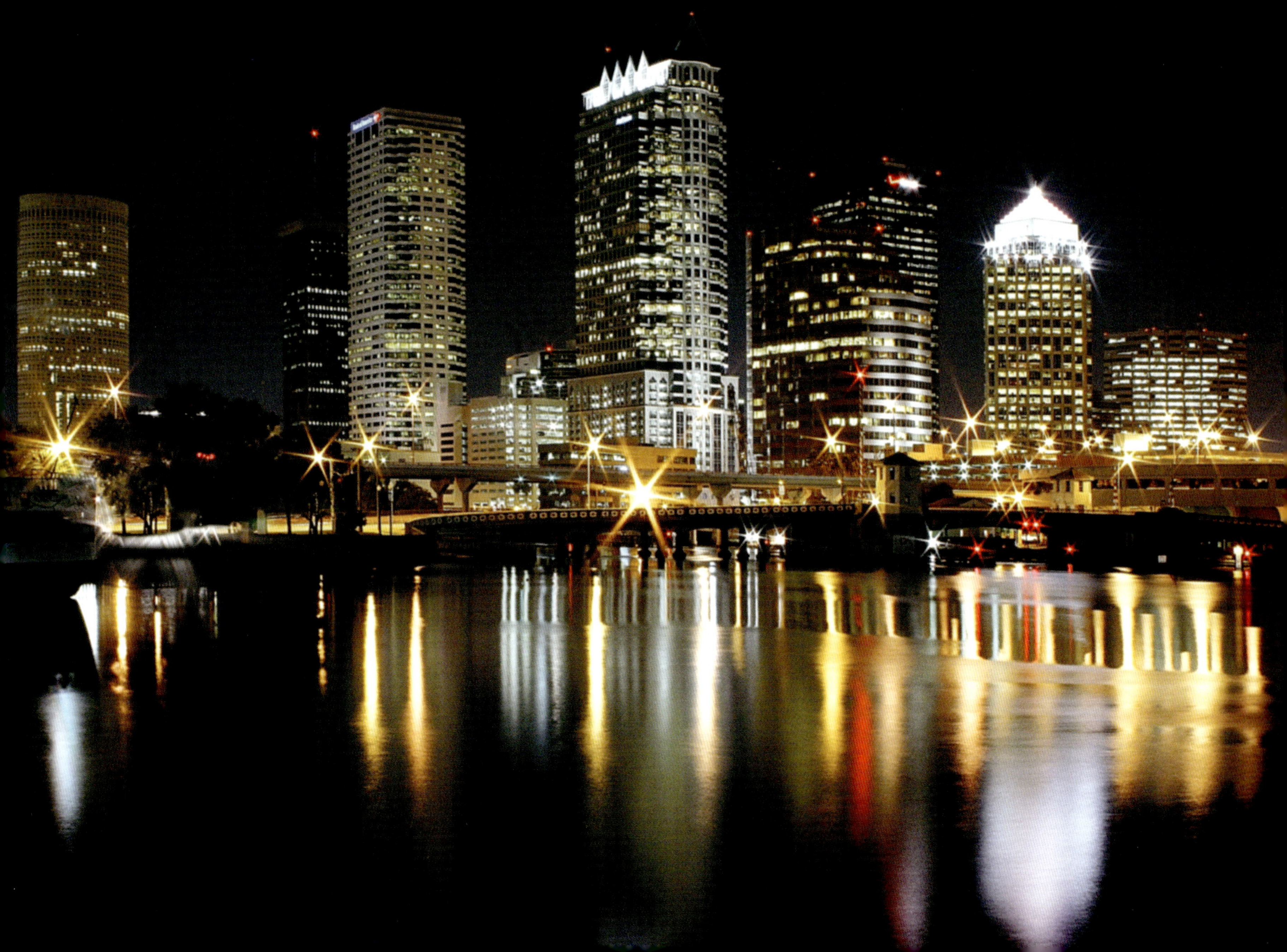

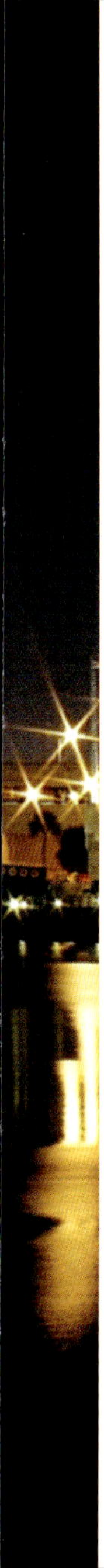

Tampa at night reflected in the Hillsborough River.
Photo by Ron Williams.

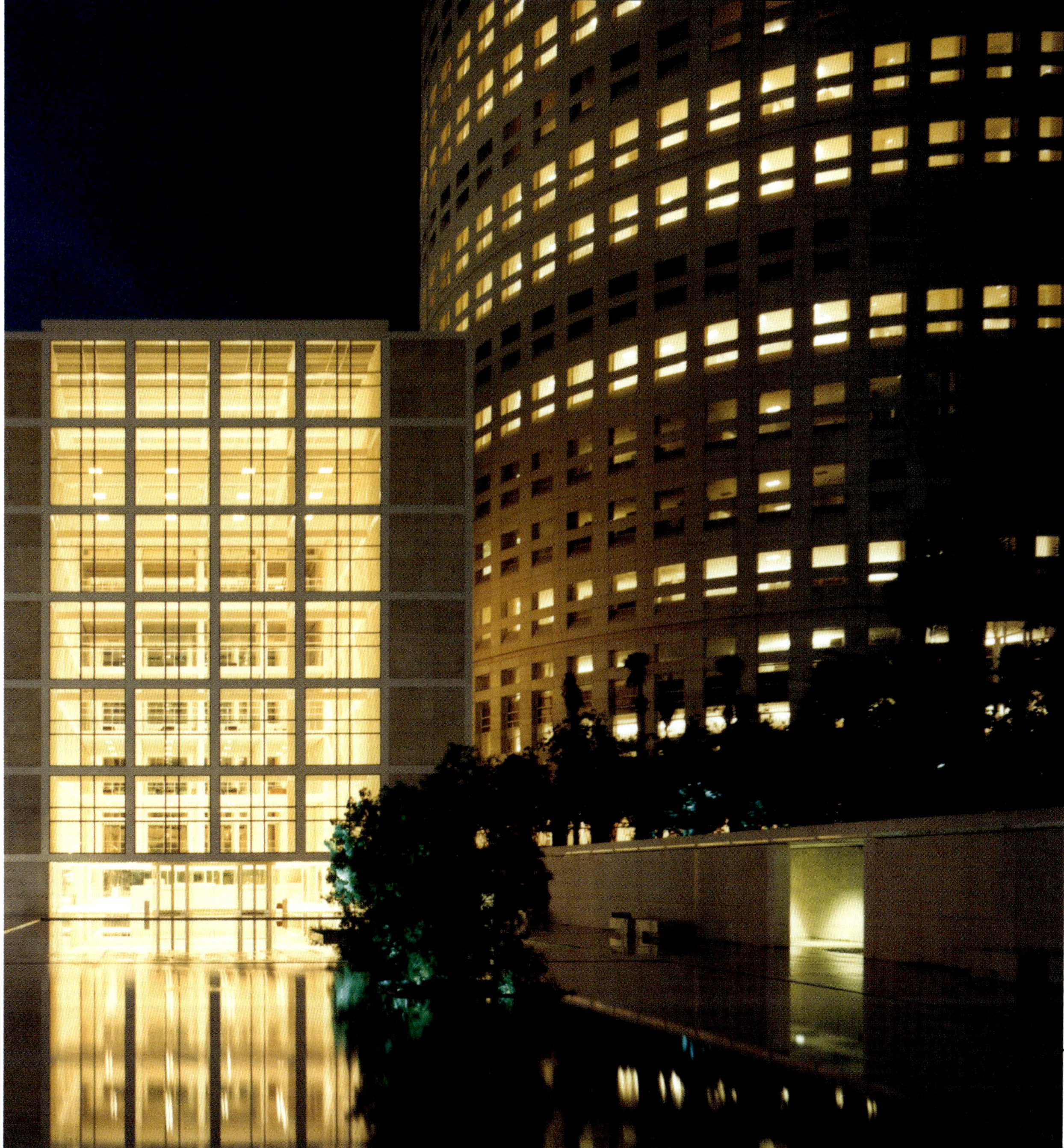

The Sykes Building lit up at night and shimmering in a reflecting pool.
Courtesy of Tampa's Downtown Partnership.

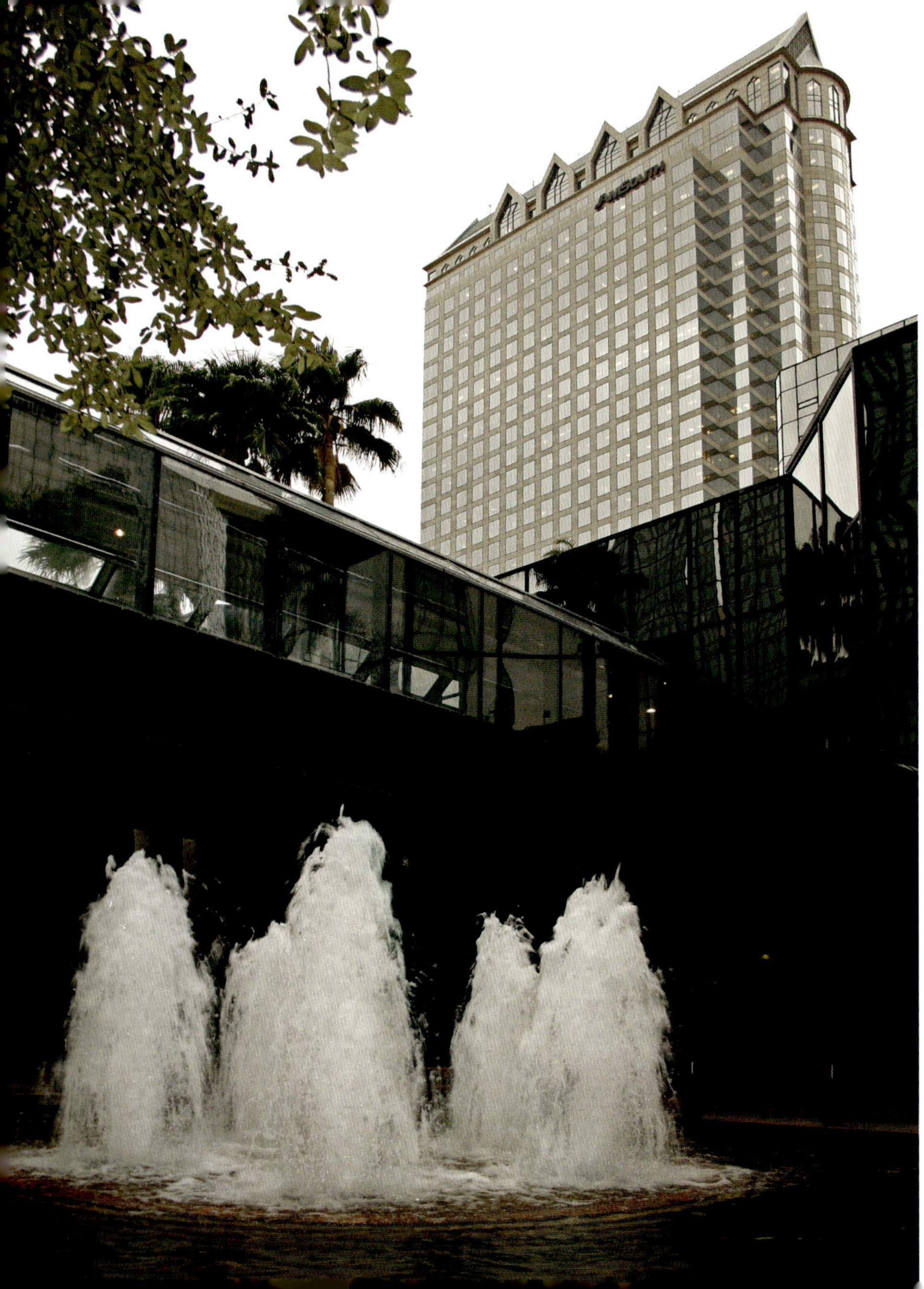

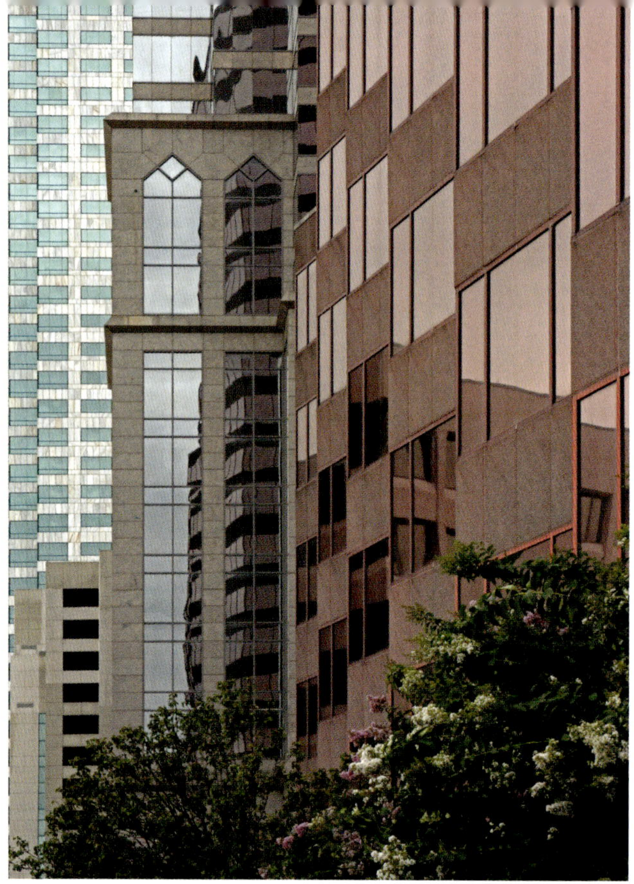

Tampa's downtown buildings are eye-catching marvels. These postmodern structures include the Wachovia Center, the Regions Building, and the Bank of America Building.
Photo by Ron Williams.

Tampa's AmSouth Building, now Regions, is the tallest building in the bay area.
Photo by Ron Williams.

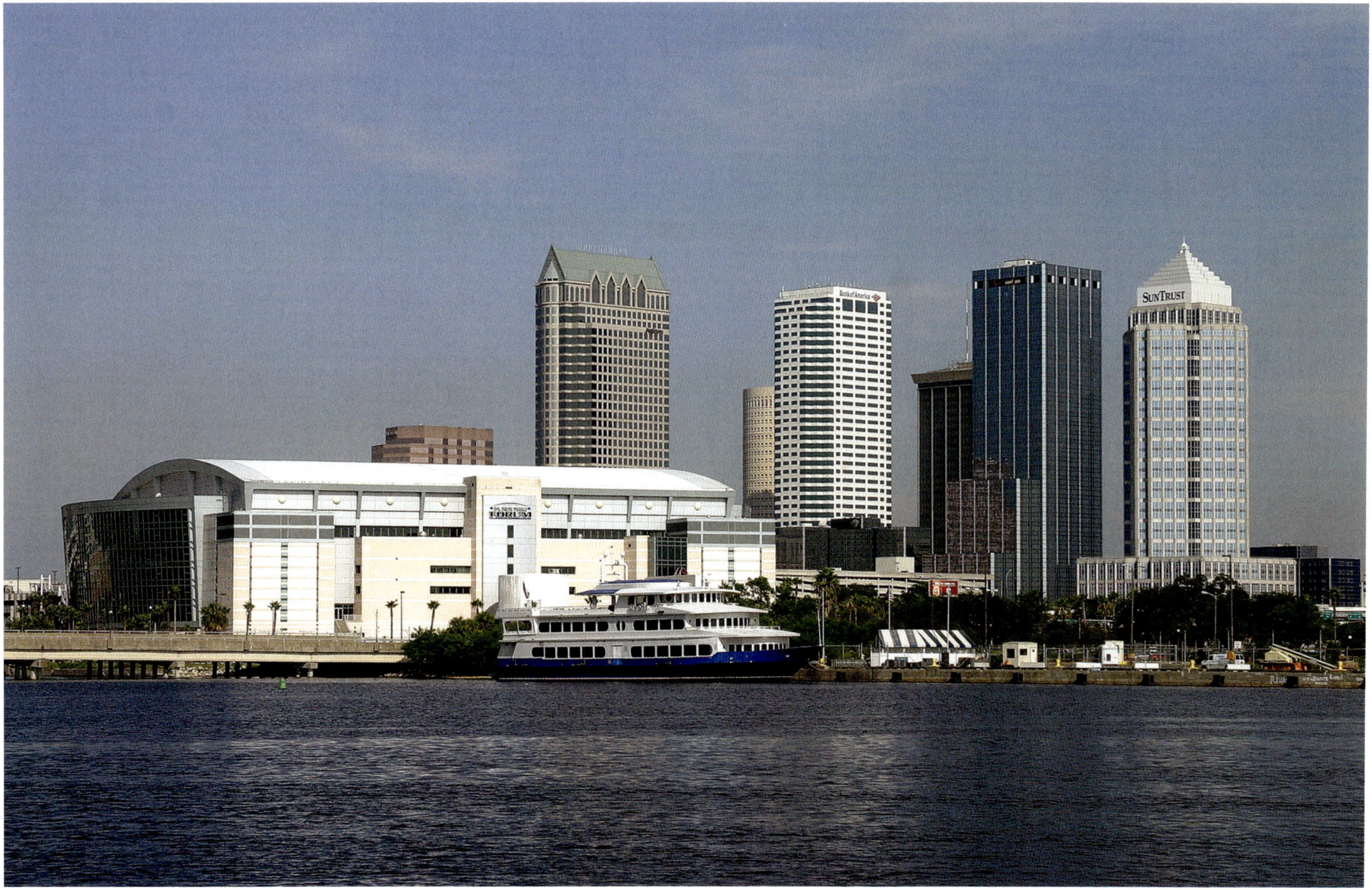

City with the St. Pete Times Forum in the foreground.
Photo by Ron Williams.

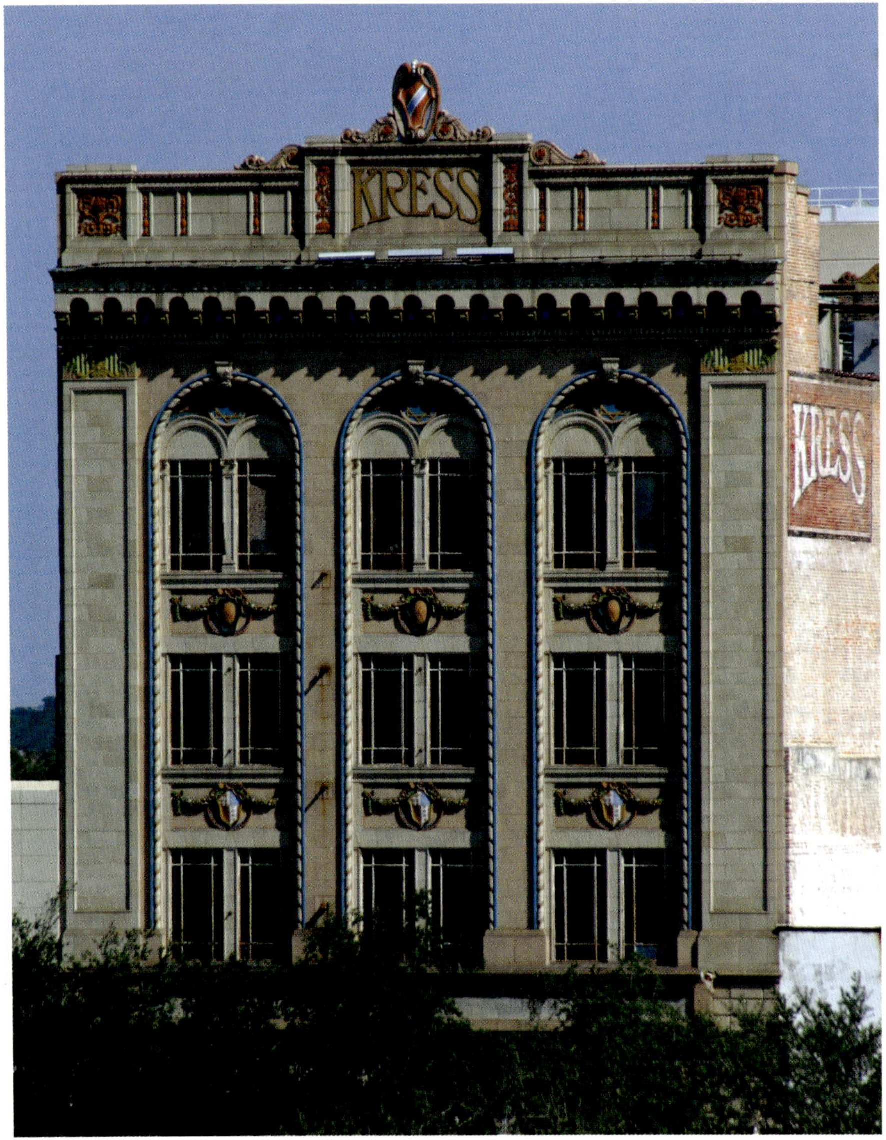

The historic Kress building still occupies a place in Tampa's heart.
Photo by Ron Williams.

Tampa's Regions Building, the Bank of America Building, and Park Tower reflect the early morning light.
Photo by Ron Williams.

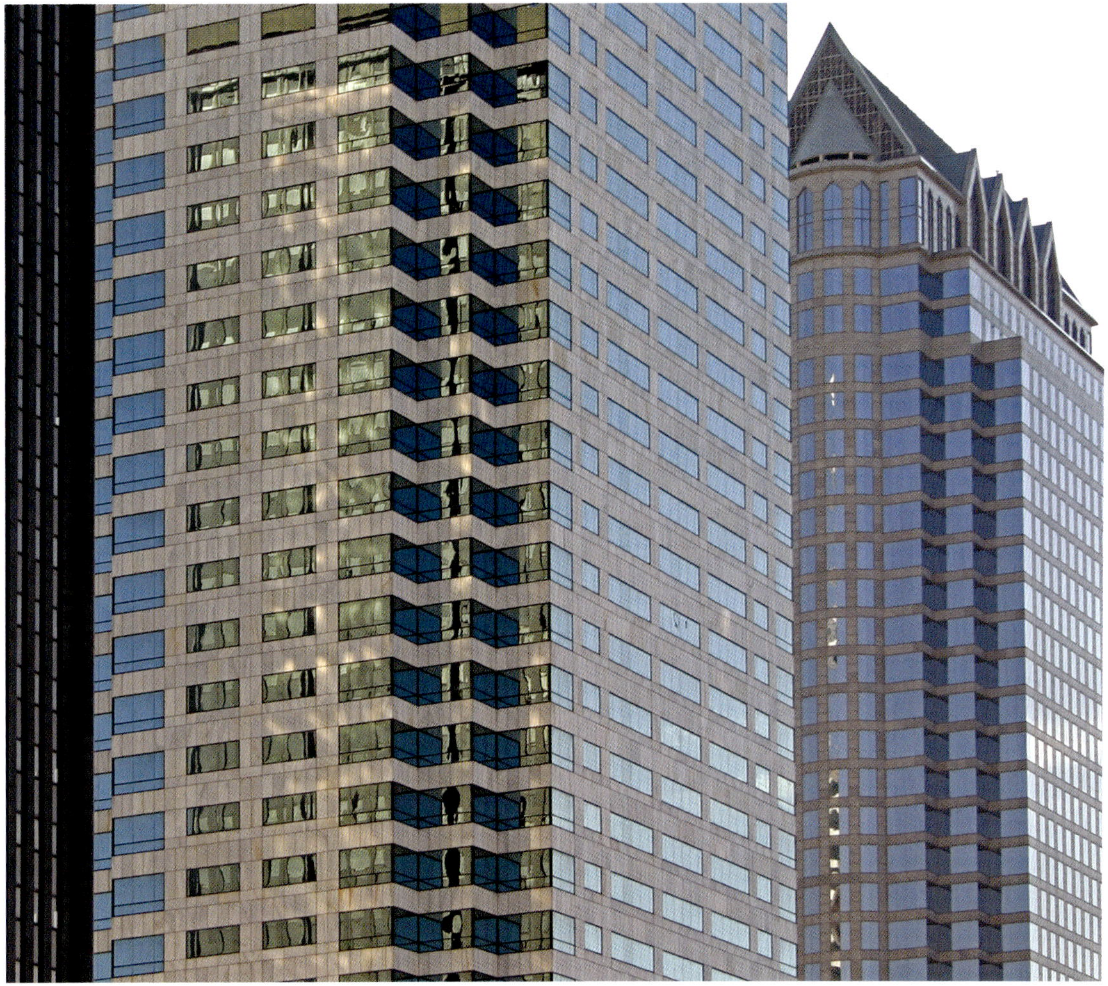

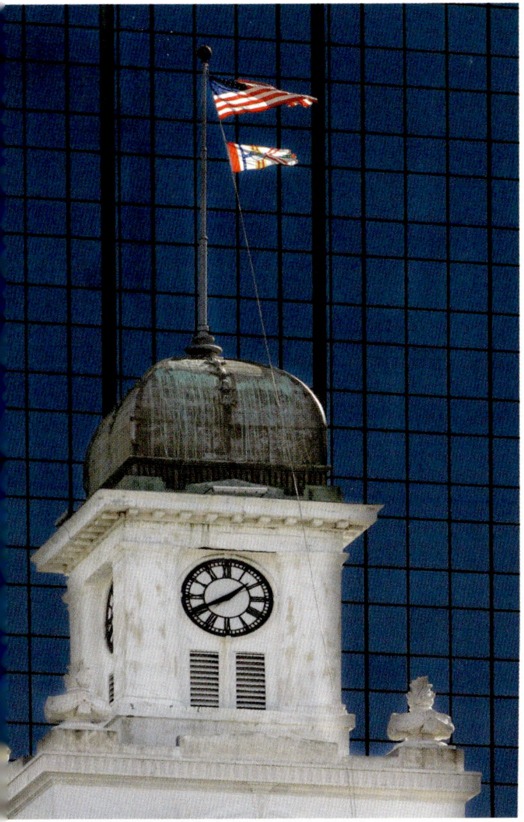

The City Hall clock is named Hortense in honor of Mrs. Hortense Ford, its key donor and the daughter of Tampa's first doctor. City Hall is also home to Tampa's City Council.
Photo by Ron Williams.

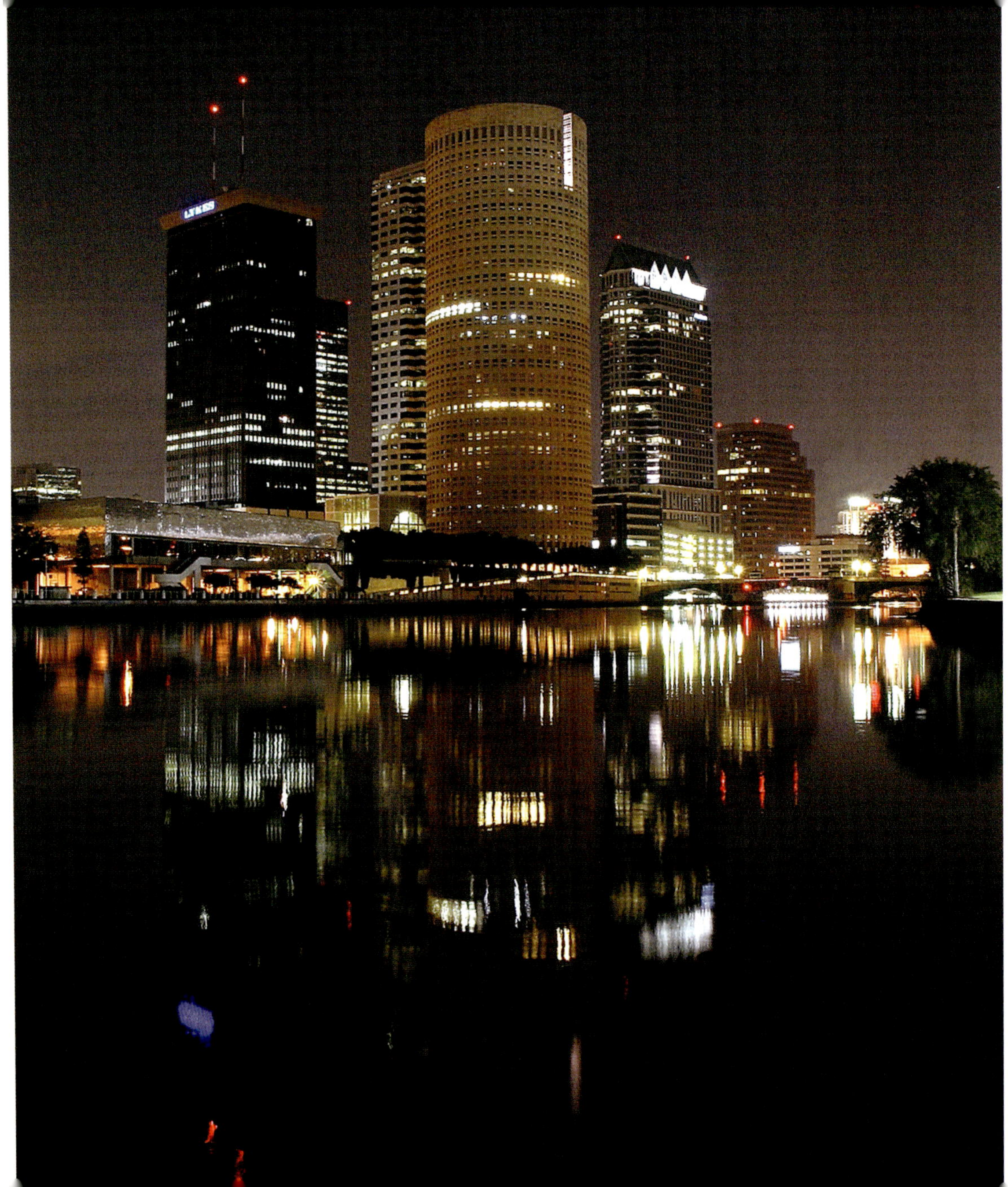

The city at night reflected in the Hillsborough River.
Photo by Ron Williams.

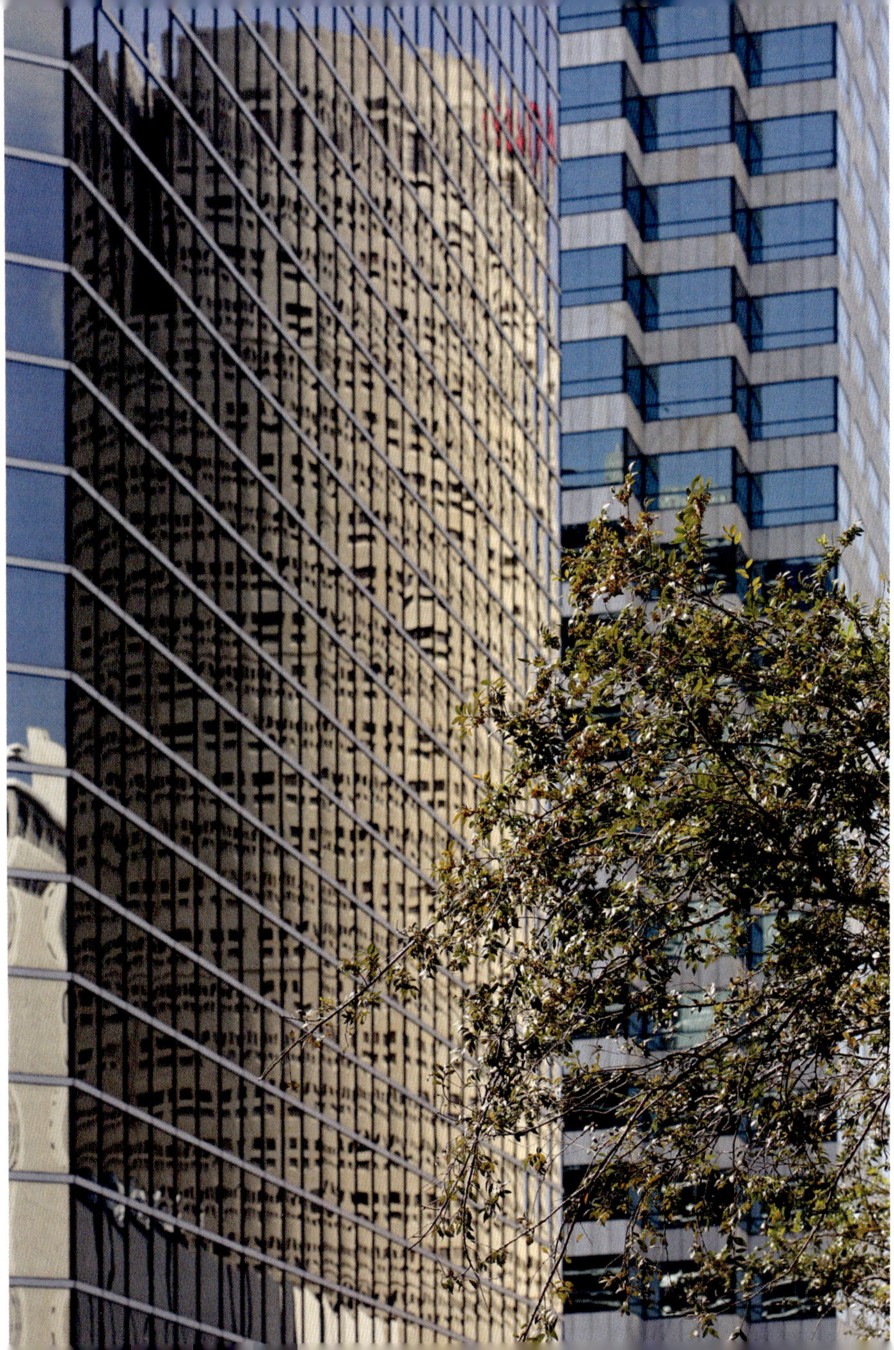

What I love about Tampa is it represents all sections of today's society of America.

Roshanda Bishop, Tampa student

The Sykes Building reflected in glass.
Photo by Ron Williams.

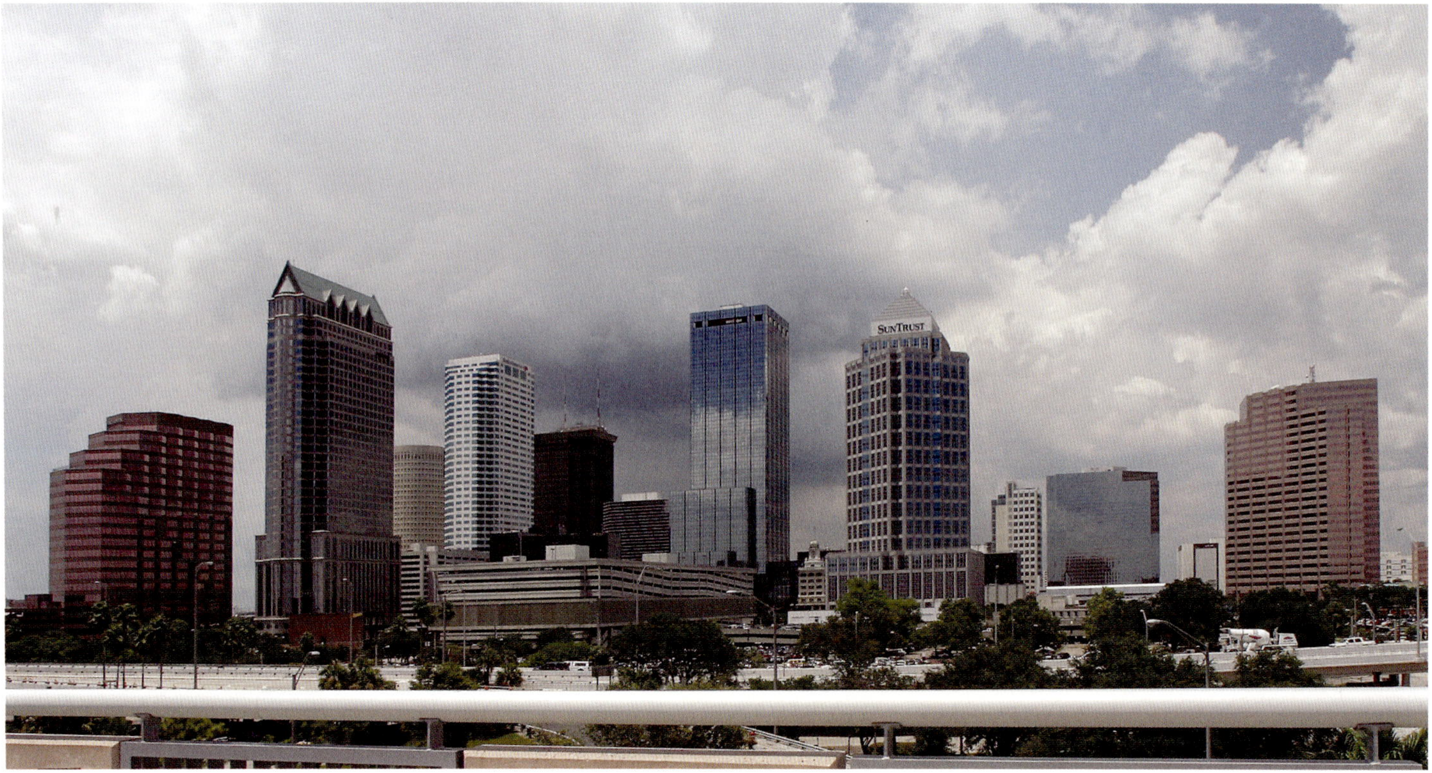

Once the tallest building in Florida, One Tampa City Center (*center*) is home to the Tampa University Club, a private restaurant with panoramic views from the thirty-eighth floor.
Photo by Ron Williams.

The Wachovia Center and the Regions Building framed by palm trees.
Photo by Ron Williams.

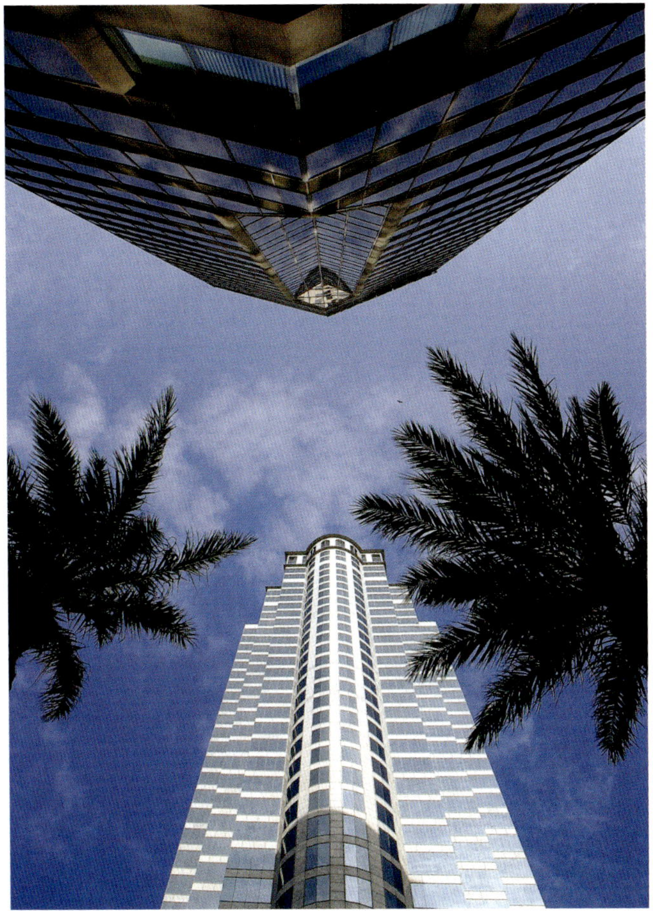

The Hyatt Regency–Tampa.
Photo by Ron Williams.

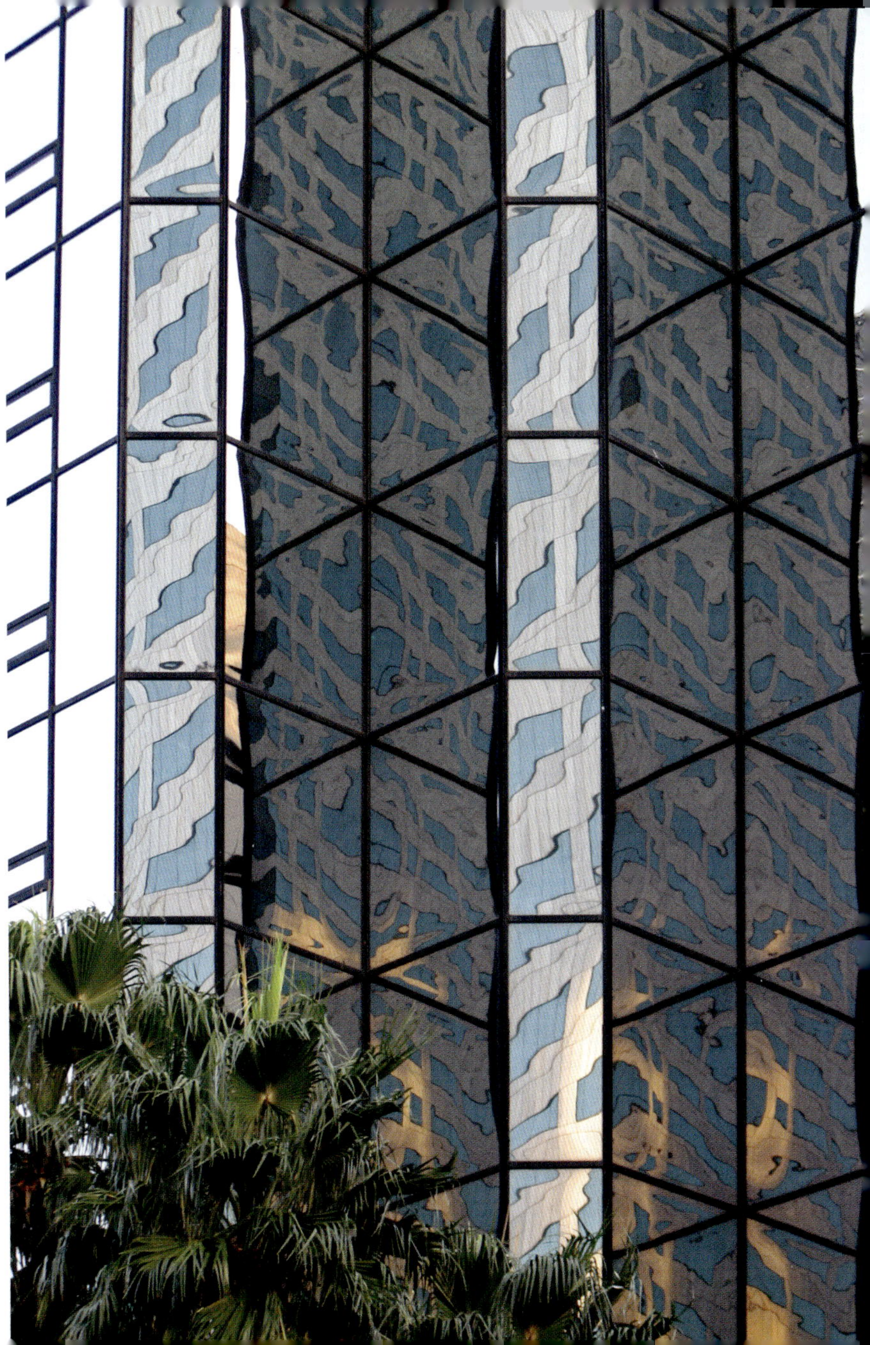

What is the city but the people?
William Shakespeare

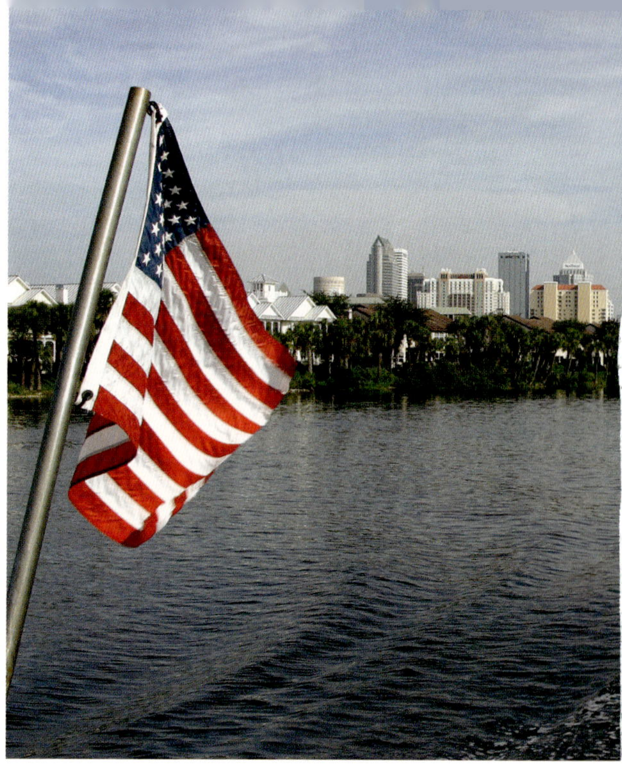

Kimberly Williams is professor of history at Hillsborough Community College and author of *Alexandria and the Sea: Maritime Origins and Underwater Explorations*.

Gregory Thomas is president of Bay Press, LLC. He has served in several academic administrative positions, including executive director of enrollment management at the City University of New York and as dean of student services at Hillsborough Community College's Ybor City campus.

Award-winning photographer Ronald Williams is a regional services and technology manager for the Associated Press in Atlanta, Georgia. During his forty-year AP career, he has had a wide variety of special documentary assignments, including the Olympic Games, the Augusta Masters, and the aftermath of Hurricane Katrina.

Born and raised in Tampa, Cheryl Borman is professor of English at Hillsborough Community College's Ybor City campus.